Heart
of a
Wife

To Doug, Diane & Katie —
I hope you enjoy my grandmother!

Marie

Nov 23, 1998

Heart of a Wife

The Diary of a Southern Jewish Woman

by
Helen Jacobus Apte

Edited and with essays
by her grandson
Marcus D. Rosenbaum

A Scholarly Resources Inc.
Imprint
Wilmington, Delaware

Scholarly Resources Inc.
104 Greenhill Avenue
Wilmington, DE 19805-1897

Library of Congress Cataloging-in-Publication Data

Apte, Helen Jacobus, 1886–1946.
  Heart of a wife : the diary of a Southern Jewish woman /
by Helen Jacobus Apte : edited and with essays by Marcus D.
Rosenbaum.
       p.   cm.
    Includes bibliographical references (p.   ).
    ISBN 0-8420-2745-9 (cloth : alk. paper). — ISBN 0-8420-
2746-7 (paper)
    1. Apte, Helen Jacobus, 1886–1946—Diaries. 2. Jewish women—
Southern States—Diaries. 3. Jews—Southern States—Diaries.
I. Rosenbaum, Marcus D. II. Title.
F220.J5A68   1998
975.9'65061'092—dc21 98-21416
  [B]   CIP

To Nana

❧ About the Authors ❧

Helen Jacobus was born in Hawkinsville, Georgia, in 1886. She spent her early childhood in Hawkinsville and Richmond, Virginia, and her adolescence in Atlanta. She married Day Apte, a Florida native, in 1909. They spent most of their married life in Florida and Atlanta. Helen Apte died in Miami in 1946.

Marcus D. Rosenbaum is Helen Jacobus Apte's grandson. His mother, Alice, was her only child. He was born in Tampa, Florida, in 1949 and is a broadcast and print journalist, an independent editor, and a consultant. He spent much of his professional life at National Public Radio, where he is now consulting. His many assignments included foreign editor, national editor, editor of *All Things Considered*, and senior producer of *Talk of the Nation*.

Rosenbaum's wife, Lyn Ingersoll, is a librarian. They live in Washington, DC, with their two teenage children, Emily and Robert.

❧ Acknowledgments ❧

Because my grandmother did the bulk of the work on this book, I clearly owe her the first acknowledgment. But many others helped in a more timely way. My wife, Lyn, was invaluable in editing the text and researching Helen's many literary allusions. My daughter, Emily, had the artistic instinct for a design that eventually became the cover. And my son, Robert, gave me encouragement when I needed it.

I also am indebted to my brother, David, for his generosity in offering me the opportunity to carry out this project and for his pointed comments and lucid editing. The eagle eye of my sister-in-law Ginny caught many glaring errors. My nephew Daniel, my niece Dottie, and her husband, Toby Halliday—all gave me enormous help in editing and designing this book. Many others also contributed time and ideas. Among them: Janice Rothschild Blumberg, Sean Collins, Bob Kahn, Suzanne Karr, Kee Malesky, Elaine Tyler May, Tom O'Brien, Dale Rosengarten, Louis Schmier, Ellen Silva, Sandra Stencel, Tracy Wahl, and Michael Wegner. To all of them, thank you.

—M.D.R.

❧ Contents ❧

 # Introduction

Marcus D. Rosenbaum

I first met my grandmother nearly fifty years after she died. It was on a balmy Florida afternoon in October 1995. We were at our family's house in Tampa, sitting on the front porch—my brother, my sister-in-law, my wife, and I. My brother and I had grown up in this house, and we were taking a break from sorting through the drawers and closets and kitchen cabinets. Our father had passed away only a few days earlier, and since our mother had died ten years before, his death presented us with the bittersweet task of cleaning out the family home. My niece, Dottie, who had been working on the closet in the front bedroom, walked onto the porch with a small plastic bag.

"I found the diary," she said.

"What diary?" My brother and I looked at each other quizzically.

"Nana's mother's diary."

When Dottie was a teenager, she told us, our mother had shown her the diary, which her mother—our grandmother, Dottie's great-grandmother—had kept for nearly forty years. For some reason we still do not understand, our mother had never shown it to us. I took the diary—diaries, really; there was more than one book—and started with the first one. The leather cover was cracking. And although the stitching in the binding was coming undone, the pages had scarcely yellowed; the paper quality was good.

It actually was a 1910 daybook, *The Excelsior Diary*. On the inside cover was printed a calendar, and the first few pages were filled with useful information for the times: "Principal Cities of States" (New York, population 3,437,202, was followed by Chicago, Philadelphia, and St. Louis); "Values of Foreign Coins" (Country, German Empire; Standard, Gold; Monetary Unit, Mark; Value, $0.23.8); postal rates (first class domestic, 2¢ per ounce; foreign first class, 5¢ per ounce); and so on. The book listed four eclipses, two of the sun and two of the moon; it did not mention the arrival of Halley's Comet.

On what had been the first open page, marked Saturday, January 1, 1910, the manuscript began with a title:

The Heart of a Wife
by
Helene Jacobus Apte
Tallahassee, Fla.
June 24, 1909

I thumbed through the pages. The handwriting was small but legible, and my grandmother had ignored the dates (after all, it was *next* year's daybook) and filled each page to capacity. Sometimes she even wrote in the narrow top margin.

My young children were climbing a neighbor's tree. But my nephew soon joined us, and we started reading random selections. The more we read, the more interesting I found this woman I knew only from a photograph. When we got home to Washington, I read the whole diary for the first time. It was not a difficult task. Helen Jacobus Apte (it is Helen, not Helene; the "e" was a youthful affectation) had an informal style that is modern and conversational, making it easy for a late twentieth-century reader to understand her early twentieth-century life.

My grandmother was born in Hawkinsville, Georgia, in 1886. Her mother's brothers were well-known factory owners in Atlanta, and her father was a prominent local businessman. Even though the family was doing well in Hawkinsville, in 1892 Helen's parents decided to move to a city, where, as Helen put it, "we could have more advantages and be thrown more with Jewish people." They first went to Atlanta, Helen's mother's hometown, and then settled in Richmond, Virginia, where her father had bought a clothing business. The family stayed in Richmond until 1898, when Helen's father died—perhaps a suicide. Her mother sold the business, packed up the six children, and moved back to Atlanta.* It was here that

---

*For Helen's description of these events, see the July 22, 1924, entry on p. 89.

my grandmother spent her formative years, in a large Victorian house on Washington Street, near the new state capitol. It was here that she was schooled until age sixteen, when she had to quit, she wrote, because of her ill health.* And it was here that she married Day Apte (pronounced APT).

The diary begins in 1909 with the wedding and ends the year she died. And although she wrote in it only sporadically, especially as she got older—indeed, there are large gaps in the entries, some as long as several years—her lucid, thoughtful prose offers a compelling glimpse into her life, her times, and her mind. If I had known my grandmother, I might, in fact, have been uncomfortable reading her innermost thoughts. After all, what grandchild thinks of his grandmother as someone with human passions and yearnings like his own? But, of course, I did not know her, and even though I had personal knowledge of some of the diary's characters (especially my mother), piecing together my grandmother's life was much the same for me as for any reader. My research led to many revelations, and, as a result, I have interspersed several short essays throughout the diary to provide personal and historical context. Some of them deal with specific events, such as the 1910 cigar strike in Tampa, which put my grandfather out of business, and some concern broader topics, such as what it was like for Helen to grow up and live as a Jew in the South.

Although I believe that all of the essays are important for an understanding of my grandmother and the times in which she lived, I realize that they break up the diary's narrative flow. So readers should not feel compelled to stop when they first encounter them but may return to them later. Likewise, readers should feel free to draw their own conclusions about my grandmother—there is so much tantalizing material to consider. For me, as I studied her diary and tried to understand her life, several themes emerged. The first and most important was Helen's ongoing struggle between duty and desire—her struggle between her duty to her husband and her desire to be around other men. Whether she ever consummated any of these other relationships is a matter of some speculation. There are strong indications that she did not; for instance, in her July 14, 1929, entry, when she compares her beliefs on infidelity to her husband's not eating ham, she writes, "I was brought up not to and I just

---

*Helen's health caused her problems throughout her life. See Appendix C, pp. 209–15, for a discussion of her illnesses.

couldn't!" But later hints are more ambiguous. On February 25, 1931, for example, Helen writes of "two 'strange interludes' . . . just to break the monotony and make life a little more interesting." Although she then declares that "it is far best to walk the straight and narrow path and never to stray," she concedes that if you do, "you miss a lot of fun." Whatever ultimately happened, she clearly enjoyed the company of other men. And she enjoyed being *desired* by men. Or, as my cousin Joan* once told me, "I do remember Mama telling me that Auntie was a flirt."

As she aged, Helen seemed to resolve her conflict. She continued to delight in spending time with other men, but, like the heroine of a Victorian novel, she chose duty over desire. She actually became a doting grandmother after my brother, David, was born in 1942. In some ways it seems a little out of character, but perhaps she was making up for what she sensed were failures in her own attempt at mothering. She had only one child, Alice, and certainly she was not a *bad* mother. But neither was she heroic, as she thought her own mother had been. David was an opportunity to do better. In 1943, in a piece called "The Truth about Grandma," which she wrote for *Baby Talk* magazine, Helen offered a small insight into her own style of mothering: "There was an Orphan's Home near us, so every year, on your Mommy's birthday, we'd take her there and she'd sit like a little queen while we gave ice cream and cake to the children. . . . Everyone thought that was so cute and so unselfish to give a treat to the orphans instead of a party. I've often wondered tho' if it seemed a tiny bit smug and patronizing."†

Naturally, Helen's resolution of her conflict between duty and desire was based on more than a grandchild. It had a great deal to do with the way her love for her husband grew over the years. And this is a second theme I found in the diary: the dynamic nature of love. Helen married reluctantly. In fact, Day Apte spent three or four years talking her into marrying him by mail. He was living in Tallahassee, she still in Atlanta, and he pursued her intensely. "My beloved Helene," an eighteen-year-old Day wrote her in one of his almost daily letters, "First, last, and for all times— I love you. Though you marry, and I marry, I will still love you with the same purity that I do now." To which Helen would reply: "Do you think it right for you to write in such a manner as your last two letters? You said

---

*Joan (pronounced JO-an) is the only child of Helen's older sister, Sarah, or "Sister."
†The article is reprinted in Appendix D, pp. 217–22.

you would try and not ever be personal. And your letters are not exactly what my conscience requires."

Slowly, with intermittent meetings and his unrelenting letters, however, Day brought her around. Ultimately, when Helen weighed her options, Day seemed to be the best choice. Still, on her wedding day, when she was twenty-two years old, it's not clear how much she really was in love with him. In her first entry, writing about the wedding, she revealed her "fears" and "doubts"; the most she could say was that she was "almost happy." Twenty-odd years later, though, she had a better understanding of herself—and of her husband. Her love matured as she realized what kind of a man Day was and how important his attributes were to her: He was a community leader and a good businessman who provided well, and his unwavering love for her was consistent with his upright character and honesty. In 1930, as she began to resolve her duty-desire conflict, Helen declared that Day is "much too good for me." Four years later, as she filled in the final pages of the first book of her diary, she called him "a marvelous husband" and said that she loved him "a thousand times" more than when she married him. "He is so good, so much better than I deserve," she wrote, "that . . . it makes me humble."

Helen was a complex woman who lived in times of great social change, and this complexity pours out of the pages of her writing. It is the third theme of her diary: changing times and mores. Helen was brought up to understand life with a Victorian mindset, but she found herself squarely in the midst of a post-Victorian world that affected her attitudes toward sex, having children, rearing them, and toward the world around her. So, although she wrote that she longed for a baby, her ambivalence is apparent. And when it came to sex—just look at her description of D. H. Lawrence's *Women in Love*: "vile, obscene, nauseating, but interesting anyway."

Underlying these themes was a central fact of Helen's life: She was Jewish, and Southern, too. My grandmother belonged to Atlanta's established Jewish community, which stressed being part of mainstream society. That attitude allowed Helen to feel very much a part of America—and the South—but it also allowed her to maintain her attachment to her religion. As for Day, he had lived as a child in a small town in northern Florida, an area with few Jews. But he, too, kept his connections with Judaism, both because of his parents' efforts and because his family lived in Atlanta during his teenage years. As their lives unfolded, Helen and Day simultaneously saw themselves as two Southern Americans who happened to be Jews, not just as Jews who happened to be living in the South. It is for this reason that Helen, when they lived in Tampa in 1909 and 1910, cheered parading schoolboys who were singing "Dixie" and also why she started a Sunday School for Jewish children. And it is why Day helped found a synagogue in Miami in the 1920s; why he became president of the Dade County Boy Scouts in the 1930s; and why, much earlier, as a high-school senior, he could proudly deliver a speech on Robert E. Lee before the Atlanta chapter of the Daughters of the Confederacy, a speech as over-written as it was heartfelt.*

One other element to this diary should be mentioned, and that is Helen's brushes with history. Although this clearly is a personal diary, she participated in the world around her. Early in her marriage, in the year of Halley's Comet, she witnessed labor strife close up in the devastating cigar strike in Tampa. Later she sent her brothers off to World War I, and she saw women doing "real" work in men's places. She was in Miami during the Boom years, and she rode out one of the biggest hurricanes of the century. She was present at an attempted assassination of President-elect Franklin D. Roosevelt, and she was in New York for both V-E and V-J Days.

Had Helen been born in the 1940s instead of the 1880s, she certainly would have continued her education and most likely would have taken a job and written for the public. But she could not see that possibility. This story of Helen Jacobus Apte is the story of a woman coming of age with the world around her, a world moving from Victorian times into the twentieth century. It is the story of a woman growing through adulthood not only with war and the Great Depression but also with hope, a sense of justice, and a penchant for adventure. Her story is a fascinating one, written from the heart as well as from the head. I wish she could have told it to me in person, but her legacy is her writing, and this is fitting. Her protests to the contrary notwithstanding, my grandmother *was* a writer.

---

*You can almost see him—young, skinny, perhaps nervous—standing on the platform before the lectern: "The din of musketry, the clash of swords, and the roar of cannon is hushed," he began. "The smoke of battle has cleared away. The memories of carnage and destruction wrought by the war are forgotten, and the animosity once borne by us to our fellow countrymen of the North has forever vanished from our memories; but the names of the brave men who fought for the South and their valiant deeds will be forever kept sacred by us. All these men were brave, all were great, but in the grandeur of his life and character, one, Robert Edward Lee, towers above them all."

Who's Who

Helen Jacobus was the second child born to Joseph Jacobus and Alice Selig Jacobus, both of whom had immigrated to the United States from Germany. Helen's older sister, born in 1883, was named Sarah but was known to the family as Sister or Sis. Then came Helen, born in 1886; Maurice (also known in the family as Bubba) in 1888; Pearle in 1890; Leonard in 1893; and Henry in 1896.

Day Apte was the son of Austrian-born Charles Apte and American-born Zipporah Williams Apte, who was called Sippie. Day, also born in 1886, had a younger brother, Robert Williams Apte, known as Bill, born in 1892.

Family trees are on the next page. Except for this writer, the trees include only individuals who were alive in Helen's lifetime.

Apte

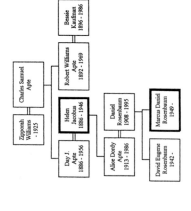

Jacobus

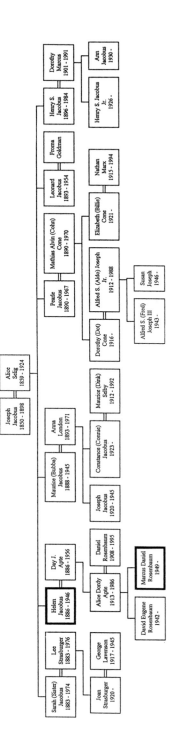

❧ Note on Editing ❧

Helen Jacobus Apte wrote her diaries in longhand, filling every page into the margins. She wrote in a small, cramped handwriting, often abbreviating long words. She crossed out few words and wrote nearly everything in one draft. The diaries have been edited to make them more readable, but in doing so I have made every effort to remain true to their content.

Helen was well read and wrote in a lucid style, but occasionally she misplaced commas, allowed run-on sentences, and misspelled words, so I have corrected grammar, punctuation, and spelling. The use of italics reflects her underlinings. I have spelled out her abbreviations; for example, "afternoon" for "aft." and "though" for "tho." Generally, Helen gave only the date, but I have added the location and full date to each entry's heading to provide context to the entries. When she was more specific, such as noting the New York hotel in which she was writing, I have kept her notation. Because this is a diary, from time to time Helen dropped articles, wrote in choppy sentences without subjects, or connected thoughts without conjunctions. Therefore, I have added a few words here and there to improve the flow of the prose. Finally, I have deleted several mundane passages, which mentioned minor acquaintances or events that added little to the overall understanding of the author or her times.

In addition, I have divided the diary into chapters and written short introductory comments for them. The chapters correspond to the significant periods of Helen's life. I have used footnotes to explain important historical and personal references and to source the many literary passages, which stem from Helen's voracious reading. I presume that she quoted from memory, because at times her citations were incorrect. The footnotes point out these errors and give a full background for her references. Except for these few minor changes the words are Helen Jacobus Apte's.

One final note: This is a diary, so its pages are filled with the names of many characters. Some are members of Helen's or Day's immediate families; their relationships are explained in the family trees on page xviii. A few others I could clearly identify, and I have done so in footnotes. But most of them were friends and acquaintances of the sort who appear and reappear throughout anyone's life, as they did Helen's—first names with immediate recognition to the diarist, but a mystery to succeeding generations.

M.D.R.
Washington, DC, July 1998

—⊛ Chapter 1 ⊛—

Newlywed Bliss,
Newlywed Optimism (1909-1911)

⊛ Married in Atlanta, Georgia, in March 1909,
Helen Jacobus and her husband, Day Apte, start their married life in Tallahassee, Florida, where Day is a manager at the El Provedo Cigar Company.
One of the owners of El Provedo, Julius Hirschberg, is Day's uncle. By fall
the company moves to Tampa in search of skilled labor, and Day and Helen
move with it. They live in a boardinghouse near the Tampa Bay Hotel, the
center of Tampa's social life. Helen and Day are twenty-two years old.

Tallahassee—Thursday, June 24, 1909

It has been said that "the happiest countries have no histories,"* and I
believe the same thing is true of individuals. It is a strange thing that the
greatest pictures are of sad or solemn subjects. Great composers pour out
their anguish in music; "the sweetest songs are those which tell of saddest
thoughts."† Happy people seldom paint great pictures, compose great music, or write great books. How rarely the story of a great joy, a legend of
pure happiness echoes through the ages. And it seems a shame that this is
so. The world is so in need of records of joy. Yet I can well understand how
a happy person cannot write of his happiness. It is such an illusive, inef-
fable theme, and that is why I haven't started a new diary before now.

These days since my marriage have been as a string of pearls to me—
my rosary! I count them over, every one apart. Each is a perfect gem

*Originally from Montesquieu but repeated in George Eliot's *The Mill on the Floss*:
"The happiest women, like the happiest nations, have no histories." It is interesting
that the first quotation in this diary is from *The Mill on the Floss*, which a teenage
Helen declared her favorite book. See p. 197.
†From Percy Bysshe Shelley's "To a Skylark."

1

—here the clear stone of duty, here is fidelity, and here the great flaming gem of passion. How sorely I longed for my jewels and through what travail, what anguish I went to get them; each was attained through long struggle, but now they are mine—mine—and I exult, not with the gloating of a miser, but with meekness and unutterable thanks in my heart to the One who helped me in my search. Verily, "without Him the search is futile and the searcher searches in vain"!

My first diary is a long wail from beginning to end, and I'm no more the same woman who wrote it than if the writer were a stranger to me, and yet how vividly I remember that poor little girl, struggling against the whole world.* How she fought against changing ideals, how her dreams clashed with the stern realities of life, how hard they died, those poor little dreams. Truly, I never knew the meaning of peace, the feeling of rest, until of late. I used to think my nervousness was caused by my health. I believe now my ill health was caused by the state of my mind. I had nothing to think of but myself, and how bitterly I once resented the hint that such was the case. Nothing to think of but myself. Why, hadn't I the burden of the world on my shoulders, the troubles of all my friends, the problems of life to solve? I was never consciously selfish, for my friends' affairs came before my own, but I see now wherein the difference lies. Now *I love*, and in those two words is summed up all. Because I love, my beloved one is the center of all my care, my thoughts, my desires, and the world scope of my life is broadened, because for his dear sake, petty cares and thoughts of self fade away. The world seems a better, brighter place because such love can exist. The loving heart embraces all the universe, and thus I am writing as one who loves her fellow man in a broader, better sense than my maiden heart could dream of, with all its wild ideas of the uplifting of humankind.

Do I love as much as I am capable of loving—"to the height and breadth and width my soul could reach, when searching for the ends of beauty and of ideal grace"?† The very fact that I have never asked that question is the answer. And therein lies the greatest change in me—*I do not analyze.* O, the eternal why and how, which used to torture me night and day. "Out of

---

*Helen later destroyed her teenage diary. See p. 74.
†From Elizabeth Barrett Browning, *Sonnets from the Portuguese*, No. XLIII:
    How do I love thee? Let me count the ways.
    I love thee to the depth and breadth and height
    My soul can reach, when feeling out of sight
    For the ends of Being and ideal Grace.

the night, which covered me, black as a pit from pole to pole,"* I have emerged the mistress of my fate, the captain of my soul. I have evolved a very satisfactory philosophy, and a faith deep and strong summed up in a pagan and a Jewish shibboleth—"Oh take the goods the gods bestow thee."† And, humbly I write it, "I thank Thee that Thou hast afflicted me, and now that my visitation is past, Thou comfortest me and I draw waters of joy from the wells of salvation."‡

I wish I had kept this diary on my honeymoon. Those five days are too beautiful to be lost. My daughter, when you read this book, when you remember the care and sorrow life is sure to bring your mother, remember also the joy, which is worth it all and which I will give some record of here. The last words in my other diary were written by a girl, dazed, overcome with excitement, physically and mentally exhausted!

The days before my wedding, Wednesday, March 10, 1909, are still vague shadows. There was a constant round of entertaining. Never will I forget the thoughtfulness, the sincerity of my friends. I left some true ones, I'm sure. Card parties, theatre parties galore were given in my honor— and some very elaborate ones. Day came on Sunday. I haven't any idea of our conversations. I can't remember feeling one thrill of love for him, nor did I feel sorrow at leaving home. I was like an automaton.

Only the night before the wedding did my calm break down. Our ushers gave us a theatre party to see [Russian actress Alla] Nazimova in *A Doll's House*. The morbid theme and the realistic acting began to wear me down. My heart grew like lead in my breast; may I never again feel such dull hopeless anguish. Afterwards there was a beautiful supper at the Piedmont. The lovely things said to me, the toasts, the thought that I was leaving all this dear familiar world—well, I had to keep up, and I did until

---

*From W. E. Henley's "Invictus":
    Out of the night that covers me,
    Black as the pit from pole to pole
    I thank whatever gods may be
    For my unconquerable soul.
See also p. 25.

†From John Dryden's "Alexander's Feast":
    If all the world be worth the winning,
    Think, oh think it worth enjoying:
    Lovely Thais sits beside thee,
    Take the good the gods provide thee.

‡From the first edition of *The Union Prayer-Book* (1895), in the Evening Service for the Sabbath, p. 32: "I thank Thee that Thou has tried me; for now that Thy visitation is past, Thou comfortest me, and I draw waters of joy from the wells of salvation." This is a condensation of Isaiah 12:1–3.

we reached home, and then the deluge. Day drew me into the parlor, pulled me down on his knee, and on his shoulder I cried out my heart in deep soul- and body-shaking sobs. How sweet he was to me that night, in tacit sympathy with all I was going through. I went upstairs exhausted, as only sobbing can make me. Mama was asleep and I was glad. I fell into bed and felt it shake with Sister's sobs. I shall always regret I didn't even reach out and touch her. I had about as much emotion as I could stand for one night, and after a while we kissed each other and I fell into a deep, dreamless sleep.

My wedding day—it was ideal, and I told myself it was a good omen. Spring was in the air, my dearly loved spring. I felt almost happy! Viola came early, as did lots of neighbors. I watched the decorators, went out on the porch, talked through the phone, absolutely calm. Day was there for a while, contrary to old customs. Dinner was eaten in the kitchen, and afterwards, for the first time in my history, I went into my room and locked the door, and I was allowed to stay there without interruption. Dear old home with its lack of privacy, its doors standing always open. How I used to rave against the lack of individuality its inmates could exert. I see now with what loving unselfish care we surrounded each other. All that afternoon I lay on the bed. I have no idea what I thought of. I had my manicure at 5, then took my bath, and had for my supper a cup of black coffee.

Mrs. Ablert came, and it was time to dress—dress for my wedding. I shall always be glad I had such loving hands to help me. I was perfectly passive and remember my start of surprise when I saw how well I looked in my handsome white satin gown, made in the Directoire style and with a long train, my first. I looked very tiny in it, but I think and was told that my face looked better than ever in my life. I wore Viola's veil. My bridesmaids and ushers came in and raved over me, said I looked like a little doll, etc. The girls all looked so sweet in their yellow satin Directoire dresses, and I succeeded in getting them odd bouquets—Easter lilies tied with palest green tulle, and a shower effect of yellow rosebuds. I asked everyone to go out a moment. All the boys and girls kissed me. Then I looked around the dear old room, started to cry, and laughed instead. A queer little laugh, 'tis true. I was amused at this unexpected calmness of manner.

Suddenly, the orchestra began to play the stately notes of the *Lohengrin* Wedding March, striking me wed. My heart gave a mighty leap and then came calm. I took Maurice's arm, and he trembled more than I. O, my father, how proud and happy and a little sad, too, you would have been to give your little girl away! I shall always regret that I kept my eyes downcast and didn't see my bridal party as I came down the steps, as everyone says it was an exquisite picture. The boys held the ribbons and the girls formed a semicircle around us. Day was standing in the bay window, which was banked with palms; he came forward a step to meet me, and as he drew my arm through his, all the stupor, the fears, the doubts fell from me, and there came to my tired heart such a beautiful and holy peace that my whole being was alight with the glory of it. I looked Dr. Marx* straight in the face and heard every word of the impressive ceremony. Day looked down on me the whole time, and when the rabbi said, "Kiss your wife," he didn't give me the usual perfunctory kiss, but took me in his arms and kissed me with his soul on his lips. Everyone laughed a little breathlessly, and then came kisses and congratulations. Mama was so brave; how terribly she must have missed Father.

The evening passed quickly, and thank goodness no one got drunk, though there was plenty of champagne. At 10, Mort told me good-bye. He drew me into the sitting room—the scene of most of our memories—and for a long time we stood, his arms around me, my head in its bridal veil resting on his breast. I said, "I'm going to be happy, Mort," and he answered, "Of course you are, little girl. God bless you." "And God bless you," I returned. That was all—and I went upstairs to put on my traveling dress.

I shall skim the rest quickly. I still felt calm, though my heart nearly broke when Mama gave way. I don't remember what happened when I was in the carriage alone with my husband. I think I cried just a little. The boys and girls followed us to the depot, and O, the send-off we got! How much trouble and expense they went to, but they got their fun out of it! I slept on the train that night for the first time, and I didn't cry and I was calm. I kept saying, "The reaction will set in," but it never has to this day. *How* sweet he was to me that night, what a *gentleman* he was, and O how he loved me.

The next day in Jacksonville passed like a dream, and then St. Augustine—dear quaint old city and dear old Hotel Ponce De Leon. What memories you will always hold for me, for that was where my wifehood began. And now a veil must be drawn, as all the vital things are too sacred to breathe; they couldn't be written. I need no record of those five days of my

---

*Rabbi David Marx.

honeymoon. I know I loved him when I gave myself to him, and I gave freely and bravely.

The beautiful East Coast Ormond or the Halifax, Sea-breeze, and Daytona, which I've heard is the prettiest town in Florida—what a glorious time we had, like two children. And how carefree I was, living in an enchanted land. The day we spent in Palatka and then home to Tallahassee. The two weeks at the hotel, then to our beautiful house. How I love it and how I work to keep it perfectly, for this is my sphere, and I will excel in it.

How can anyone call the housekeeper's task a sordid one? Does not the office exalt all the menial tasks? "The maker of a home"—could anything be more sublime, more alive with great possibilities? A woman is the center, the core of her home, and all sound is about her. She sounds the key note, and her influence can make discord or harmony, and I shall strive for perfect harmony and beauty and to make this house a home for my husband in the best sense of the word. I am purged of all selfishness. I feel glorified, for all thoughts of myself have vanished—every thought is for him, his comfort, his happiness, his food, and I'd just as soon eat rocks if I knew he was satisfied. And my health has been perfect—I am made to live again!

The first Friday night in our home we lit the candles and read the Sabbath eve prayers, an institution which we shall always continue. And when I lit the candles, my heart surged in prayer. I am a woman in Israel, and Thy words, O Lord, "I shall write upon the doorposts of my house and upon my heart, and bind them as a sign upon my eyes, and I swear I shall teach them diligently unto my children"*—my little unborn dream children, you are near to realization now. O God, I pray I may be worthy, and I feel that a home so dedicated with such a foundation of love and a cornerstone of trust will be blessed.

---

*A translation of the *v'ahavta* prayer in the first edition of *The Union Prayer-Book for Jewish Worship*, published by the Central Conference of American Rabbis. Helen owned a copy of this first Reform prayerbook.

> Thou shalt love the Lord, Thy God, with all thy heart, with all thy soul, and with all thy might. And these words, which I command thee this day, shall be in thy heart. Thou shalt teach them diligently to thy children, and shalt speak of them when thou sittest in thy house, when thou walkest by the way, when thou liest down, and when thou risest up. Bind them as a sign upon thy hand, and let them be as frontlets between thine eyes. Write them upon the doorposts of thy house and upon thy gates. To the end that ye may remember and do all my commandments and be holy unto your God. I am the Lord your God.

Thank heaven I am fortunately possessed of a disposition that can adapt itself and with plenty of interests, or I'd never be satisfied with Tallahassee. It's a beautiful old Southern town—an antebellum town—and folks still talk about "before the war." They are narrow and prejudiced and uninteresting, but I'll be happy. I'll make my own happiness, and it is an ideal place to raise children, far better than a city. Our house faces a park, which is all in bloom overflowing with springtime, and I never tire of watching the myriad birds. I am happy, thank God, and my husband is a man of such beautiful character, such beautiful nature, and such a perfect love for me.

Day Apte

Day Apte (as far as is known, Day was his real name) was born in Madison, Florida, in 1886. His mother also was born in Florida. Her father, Robert Williams, was an immigrant and a true Florida pioneer, who came to the United States from Germany in 1849. According to family lore, shortly after his arrival he was shanghaied to California, where he tried his luck in the Gold Rush but was not particularly successful and returned East with only a single gold nugget. In 1850, Williams made his way to Florida to help build the first railroad across the panhandle to Jacksonville, and he settled in the central part of northern Florida not far from Tallahassee. He married Helena Dzialynski, a Prussian immigrant, whose brother later became mayor of Jacksonville, and tried his hand at a number of occupations. Robert and Helena bore five children. Day's mother, Zipporah, known as Sippie, was the third. The youngest, Wilhelmina—"Aunt Mena" to Day—was a local beauty. She was crowned Miss Florida in the 1850s and later married Julius Hirschberg, one of the owners of the El Provedo Cigar Company, for whom Day went to work after graduating from Boys High School in Atlanta in 1904.

Day's father, Charles Apte, was a native of Vienna, Austria. He apparently immigrated alone, and there is no mention in the diary or other family records of his parents or any siblings.

Tallahassee—Wednesday, July 14, 1909

My birthday, and for almost the first time since I'm married I feel miserable, weak, faint, and nauseated. I wonder if it can be—O, no, how foolish! I wanted Day's "little birthday girl" to feel so bright. Before daybreak this morning he had me in his arms and kissed me, many times, saying such lovely things, and then I went back to sleep still in his arms, my husband's arms. God bless him. It is for him I live and strive. He will buy my present in St. Louis. The folks all love me, and they gave me nice things.

My dear ones and the girls wrote me beautiful letters. I missed them and was homesick, but it is the happiest birthday I ever spent, because I have a heart and mind at rest. Viola wrote she is to be a mother. Can't realize it—it was only yesterday we were children together. May God keep her safe and well.

I leave here July 19 with Henry. How I hate to leave my darling. He will join me in two weeks, and I may never see Tallahassee again, as it's almost decided we will move to Tampa. Of course, I'm glad we will move to a city. It doesn't matter much where I live, but I'm glad I don't have to spend the rest of my life in Tallahassee. Still, there were beautiful days passed here—long, busy days, which I hadn't time to record but were well worthy of record, these first few months of my married life! Now for home and my dear ones.

St. Louis, Missouri—Tuesday, August 10, 1909

Have no time for diaries these days. Have been here a week [visiting Day's parents] and on the go constantly. Mother and Father are crazy about me and do all to make our visit pleasant, and so does everyone, but the fact remains that I don't like St. Louis. It's intensely hot, and the people aren't refined and the shops are disappointing. I wish I was back in Atlanta, and I know I ought to be ashamed to abuse hospitality so.

Atlanta—Friday, September 17, 1909

New Year's Day* was most unhappy. Maurice has scarlet fever, and though it is a light case, of course we are much worried. Had intended leaving Saturday, but don't know if I will, though Day insists, and I do want to see my sweetheart. I long for him terribly, but I hate to leave the folks in their trouble. How grand everyone has been to me. I didn't know I had so many friends, and the days have flown. But my husband, you have been in my thoughts every minute, and I love you and yearn for you, and O, how I want you, my sweetheart.

*Rosh Hashanah.

I'm sorry I haven't kept this diary properly, for never will I have sweeter days to record. We have been free from all trouble, and I have learned to love my husband more every day. I know how fortunate we are to have no financial troubles and to be able to enjoy our lives, and as long as we all keep well, I have nothing more to ask.

I know I shall like Tampa—I go thus decided that I *will* like it, and I'm sure I can be happy there if I was in Tallahassee. "Home, dear, is where the heart is, where e'er its shrine may be."* I'm sure I can make friends, and Day is confident he will do well. He is always so confident and optimistic, though I believe he worries more than he lets me know at times. How I hate to leave my dear ones. They have been so sweet, and I know I shall be worried about Maurice, but I go to my husband ecstatically—yes, for the first time since I'm married, with desire and passionate longing for him, the desire of a woman for her mate, of a *wife* for her *husband*—and I can scarcely wait to be held fast in his arms, to feel his body against mine. Hitherto, I have never wanted him *that* way. I have always had to be won, to submit myself, and *try* to become aroused; he has always been the aggressor, but now *I* want *him*, and I'm glad, glad!

Tampa—Saturday, November 6, 1909

Shall I keep this date unrecorded? It is the most eventful one in my married life, because I've just caught my husband in a lie for the first time. After a while it ceases to be eventful, I suppose. For if Day, *Day* of all people in the world, can lie, what liars men must be. I hate a lie, I always have, and I hate deceit, and the thing I have most admired in him always was his utter sincerity, his almost stern truthfulness. I have searched my heart faithfully and asked myself, "Could I be to blame?" It would be terrible to think I had driven him to lying. Some women do that just as some drive men to drink, some to despair, some to ruin. I have driven my husband to subterfuge, and he was a man so far above it. Was he? Have I been like other women since time immemorial—set him upon a pedestal and thought myself only fit to grovel at his feet when it came to character, to beauty of soul?

Today I feel immeasurably above him, for I have never lied to him, never deceived him. I have kept myself faithful to him in my every thought.

*Attributed to Pliny the Elder. Claimed by Elbert Hubbard in *Thousand and One Epigrams*.

I have been true to him in my heart. It wasn't easy at first, when little doubts would creep in. If the merest thought of *someone else* would come to me, I pushed it away in horror, for a wife must be pure not only in deed, but she must guard every beat of her heart. She must be pure. She must keep her body and her heart and her mind and her soul spotless for her husband. I suppose men don't feel this way—a man of perfect integrity and honorable in business doesn't consider it wrong to lie to his wife. Indeed it isn't a lie at all to them, just a harmless little fib "for her own good," and that in a relationship which should be the most sacred in *life* to him. Still they talk about the inconsistency of women! Well, we are also, of course, for even in my anger, I am finding excuses for him, and I know that my faith in him is still strong, though he has lied and persisted in the lie, for if he had confessed last Sunday when it happened, it would be over and forgiven now. He must have had *good* reason.

My heart is full of tenderness for him and I try to lay the blame on myself. Yet I can't really do so, for I feel I am right in not wanting him to play cards at the club on Sunday afternoon. I feel that it is a bad habit for him to get into, that it doesn't bring us closer, and so I have nagged him, I guess, with my objections, and I swore I'd never nag. It is recreation for him, and he loves it, and that is what *hurts*. He is bored with the Sundays he has to spend with me. I want to be quite fair. Sunday is a hard day for a man, and do I try to make the day attractive to him? I've never felt I had to exert myself for him. Maybe that is a mistake.

I have said I despised a woman who'd try to hold a man. That was before I was married. I *do* want to hold him, most desperately I want to hold onto his love and his worship and his joy in my companionship. It isn't a question of pride—if she is a good wife, if he is the only man in the world to her, his love is the very breath of life to her and she *cannot* let it go.

Of course I was hurt when he left me all afternoon in this big house alone, but I never dreamed of doubting him when he pleaded business. I thought his excuse that night when I sent for him didn't ring true, but I pushed the thought away as unworthy. *Doubt* him? But I couldn't help feeling injured, though I chided myself, and after a day of estrangement, I cried it out in his arms. I told myself I must give him more freedom. The next Thursday night at the club when someone said he'd been there Sunday, I thought it was a mistake, but the guilty look on his face haunted me. This morning I told him I *must* have the truth and he had to swear on his honor he was there at work before I'd believe him. Even now, I can't realize it. Well, it seems I'm the sort of woman who must be lied to, to be pacified. He says he'd rather for me to rave than settle into my icy calm. To avert the "tantrum of silence" I must be lied to—"what difference will it make, if she never finds out?" My usual sense of humor came to me when I saw my tragic face in the glass just now. This isn't the end of the world because he told a fib; he doesn't consider it dishonorable to fib to me. Why, it's for my own good!

It's amusing to think how I used to fear I'd become bored with Day's attentions. When he used to look at me with that fatuous idolizing gaze, I wanted to scream. I didn't love him then, and the thought that it would be that way all my life—well, I needn't have feared. A man seldom looks at his wife fatuously, and we've been married eight months!

Make light of it as I try, down in my heart I feel that it is no light matter. It is an issue, a crisis, and I must meet it. Something is wrong. I must do all I can to set it right, but *how*? Shall I appear satisfied when he plays cards? Shall I make it easy and pleasant for him to go? Or shall I appeal to him, by the consideration he owes me? No, my pride rebels against that, and he would be held chafing in the bonds. How shall I act when he comes home to dinner? I can't keep up this icy silence forever, but the part of sweet, forgiving wife is beyond me, and to rave and storm is beneath me! Indeed, I'm too hurt to storm, and I'd die today rather than cry!

I can't afford to let this go by, though. No, it must be settled. I guess I'll cry in his arms again. What poor weak fools we women are! But we soon find that our idols have feet of clay, and we are so sorry for them, so full of tender pity. I suppose it is our maternal love for them which so often makes us love them all the more for their weakness, as a mother does her deformed or erring son. But, O, I am deeply, deeply hurt. My heart is aching. My pride is hurt, of course, but it has gone deeper than that. I feel as if my heart is breaking, and most of all I don't want to lose my faith in him. Some day I suppose I will laugh at this silly little wife, but that will be after I am used to lies and deceit. It is new to me now, and so I take it hard.

Tampa—Friday, November 26, 1909

Thanksgiving—how many thanks I have to give. The day was ideal, and it was my husband's birthday. God bless him. We had a fine dinner, then went to the races, where we lost $7.00. It's so foolish to throw money away like that. At night, we walked to the P.O., then played bridge at Gertie's. How close we were to each other, for after two weeks of estrangement, we are reconciled, and my heart sings for gladness, for he did have some excuse—but such a sad one, that my heart aches also. He has been terribly worried about Father's business, and he, himself is involved. So we have our financial troubles after all. But that can't touch our happiness much, because it is a joy for me to sacrifice anything for him, and every sorrow becomes lighter when we share them together.

He left me because he was so worried and tried to keep it from me, to spare me, but I never want him to do that again. If I'm to be a true helpmate, I must bear my share of the burden, and I will bear it bravely. Of course, I agreed with him that we must help Father all we can, no matter how we have to stint ourselves. Day is a born optimist and is sure it will all come out right. It will be some time before his own business can be worked up here, but I have caught some of his optimism, and look to the future confidently. I look on the bright side of things now. What a changed woman I am!

Tampa agrees with me well, and I'm in good health, but have had headaches and just had my glasses changed. We like Tampa so much and are enjoying our lives, taking in every amusement, and there is always someone in town we know. Moe Selig was here a long time and is so devoted to us. He said I had the sweetest face and the sweetest smile he ever saw.

We go out every night and have been rejoicing that we have no ties, but I have begun to long for a baby. That sounds hypocritical, when I do all in my power to prevent it, but this month we relaxed our vigilance, and I await developments eagerly. What a problem that conjugal one is. A woman *can't* have a baby every year, but it is surely wrong, physically and morally, to prevent it, so what's to be done? That is decidedly the chief phase of married life, for if the sexual relationship is satisfactory, a couple are bound to be happy, as everything else appears secondary—especially so to a man. I believe that is their chief thought in life, and Day surprises me often. After a very tender scene, in which I feel only deep tender affection and our love seems very sacred, he becomes wild with passion, which seems to spoil it all for me—gives me a little shock. But he calls it the crown of our love and the seal, and that's the difference in a man's point of view and a woman's. It is hard for a woman to become accustomed to it and look upon it as something right and natural. I suppose, though, I'll change when I'm married longer. The novelty and excitement hasn't worn off yet.

A still stranger thing is that a woman is ashamed to show passion. She is afraid she will fall in her husband's estimation or in her own, that it makes her less pure. Of course that's absurd, but I guess it's because of long years of training and of the ideas that are instilled into girls' minds— a maidenly austerity, which is hard to overcome. Really, though, I have often noticed that when the woman is very passionate, the man becomes less so; she becomes the aggressor and the man is often bored and indifferent. Indeed, he appears just a little disgusted. Now, I have known that to be a fact, and I think the wife should never be the aggressor, should take some time to respond, but when she does, to give in fully and freely. Those are the tactics I adopt, except I find it hard to give in and act as I feel, for fear Day will misunderstand—no, that's hardly it, but for some reason, some maidenly shrinking, which I surely should have gotten over by this time. Day says my ideas of a man not desiring great passion in his wife are absurd, but I know I'm right. Man is the pursuer and he likes the chase exciting. I would actually feel humiliated if I made the first advances, yet I know many women do. Lena was here when she was only married two days, and she started out wrong and I told her. How close we four got that day. I will never forget the things that happened. That [here, three lines are scratched out and are unreadable].

Instead of diminishing with nearly a year of married life, Day's ardor grows and grows. I tell him it bores me, but I dread to think the time will come when my touch no longer thrills him, when the mere sight of me will not brook desire as it does now. A woman can never cease to fight, and a wife must be continually winning battles, and it's up to me to always make him think that I am the noblest, the sweetest, the most irresistible woman who ever lived. I owe a great deal to Dr. Malchow, whose book, *The Sexual Life*, has helped us both to almost ideal conditions.* Of course, it will never be perfect until the question of children is settled, but I don't know what I should have done without *"The Book."* He says that women are divided into three classes—first, those who are the aggressors and whose passions can always be aroused; second, those who can help themselves to desire and can be made to respond; and third, those who are sexually frigid. Day

*For excerpts of Charles W. Malchow's book, *The Sexual Life*, see Appendix A, pp. 185–91.

says I belong to the second class, and as Dr. M. says, they are the happiest
and make ideal mothers and adorable helpmates. I'm very glad.

Tampa—Monday, December 13, 1909

I feel as I usually do when the weather is unsettled, only more so! I am
loaded down with neuralgia, shaky, and so nervous I could scream. I wish
I could get over this susceptibility to weather, as I have over other things.
A storm is predicted here. I'm not much worried. Have I changed!!! How
philosophical I have grown—things could always be worse! I had my picture taken, and as I look at it, I see more plainly what a different person I
am. I see a sweet, pleasant face, unlined and not wistful or interesting
anymore. I have entirely lost that drawn look. No one has told me that I
have an interesting face; indeed, I'm not at all interesting anymore. I've
been told I am so "sweet," but the adjectives that used to be applied to me
I believe I'll never hear again.

I don't know what to think of myself. I hardly ever read. I am absent-
minded. When men are here at the house who are great travelers and
provide brilliant talk, I don't join in discussions. I'm just a "sweet, pleasant little woman." I wonder if I'll remain this way, or is this just kind
Nature giving me a rest? She seems to have made me relax mind and body.

Sis will go North. I'm so glad and just *pray* she will fall in love. I sent
her $25, and I don't know when I ever got such pleasure out of anything.
Gertie Abrams and I are quite intimate. She isn't Viola, but she'll do, though
I don't intend to get too thick.

I think I must be waking up a little, as I've started a Sunday School
class. It seemed a crying shame that the children of the few Reform Jewish
families should grow up like heathens, with absolutely no knowledge of
their religion, so I have undertaken to instill the spirit of Judaism in them.
I have twelve children, and they are all enthusiastic. So am I. May the God
of Israel help us! I never saw such stagnation as there is among the Jews
here.

Tampa—Sunday, December 19, 1909

What a difference a mere man makes! And what a difference his absence
makes. Day went to Tallahassee last night and will be back Wednesday. In
the meantime I'll be miserable. Nothing seems complete without him; it is

like part of me that is away. Today passed quickly, though! Heard Dr. Jacobs preach at temple and took dinner with Gertie. Will play cards there tonight. I am getting a lot of help in my Sunday School work. Dr. Jacobs, who came down for Jessie's wedding, has stirred things up some, and I think it likely he will preach here twice a month. It is certainly true that I was the first one to start anything in Tampa, and I hope the movement will grow and grow until we have an influential congregation here and win the respect of others and of ourselves.

It is *so* hot today, and all week it was cold, but I think I'd rather have the warm weather in Florida; it is more fitting.

Tampa—Friday, December 24, 1909

'Tis the day before Christmas and a beautiful bright one, though quite cold—50°. I am getting excited over my Cuba trip. Ruby* will be here tonight, and we leave Sunday afternoon. I do hope we won't be very seasick. I don't suppose I can write on the boat, so the next time I write in here, I will be in the tropics—God willing and the elements being propitious.

Tampa—Saturday, Christmas Day, 1909

Day has been sick all day and I'm so worried, though the doctor assures me he will be well tomorrow. It is very disagreeable, windy and cold, and most of the day have been lying on the bed by my sweetheart who, like most men when ill, has been acting like a cross baby. God bless him. The only fun I got out of the day was watching the kids [in the boardinghouse] with their toys.

Steamer on the Gulf of Mexico—Saturday, New Year's Day, 1910

How I wish I could describe my five days in Cuba. Havana, the picturesque, the cosmopolitan, the place rich in memories, and O the voluble, excited, childlike people. Everyone seemed carefree, and the noise—why it was terrific from the Pasage. All the vehicles have bells on them, and the cabs dash wildly around corners, the fiery coachmen pulling the little horses up on their haunches. It is quite bewildering, as I thought the natives were

*Ruby is Ruby Diamond, Day's first cousin. She is the daughter of Julius Diamond, Day's uncle.

lazy, languid people, but everyone seemed in a hurry. I am told it was due
to the cold weather we had, and that all the rush and bustle meant nothing. I watched a crowd of men scrubbing, rushing so wildly it made one
dizzy, and on close inspection they were accomplishing nothing, just splash-
ing water around. One American could have done the work. Dear old
U.S.A.—fascinating as other countries are, there's no place like home. There
are twenty-three states represented on the boat, and this morning we an-
chored by the wreck of the *Maine*. How my heart thrilled and every man's
hat came off as we sang "America," "Dixie," etc.

I think I loved the Malecon* best of all in Cuba. I could stand for hours,
looking over the seawall, and watch the breakers come surging in. It made
Ruby angry, as she thought we were wasting time and said we could see
water anywhere and was astounded at the tears in my eyes, which she
couldn't explain. Nor could I for that matter, but a sight like that thrills me
to my soul and fills me with the divinest sorrow. And Morro Castle and
Cabañas—well, I was speechless! Poor "Cuba Libre," they are dissatisfied
with American protection and would rather have Spanish rule again than
have "the overbearing Yankees monopolizing everything." They would have
the loveliest little rebellions. I wonder if it wouldn't have been better to let
them work out their own salvation.

On the boat is a diver who was employed by the government to investigate the *Maine*. He says they were sworn to secrecy, but he insinuated
there wasn't a mine under it and it was only an explosion. My country, my
country, I can't help thinking you went beyond your rights and that the
Spanish-American War was brought on by politicians. "If this be treason,
make the most of it."†

I wasn't sick a minute on either trip, though the channel was very
rough. Day and Ruby got on not quite so well, but did fine. We were a few
hours at Key West, and it is horrible, dirty, and fishy—the jumping off
place of Florida. And so we go sailing along to Tampa. Neptune be kind to
us. I love, love, love the swell of the waves, the blue waters of the Gulf.
"Felicia Annu Nueva,"‡—may the New Year bring us peace in our hearts,
in our homes, in this glorious country of ours.

---

*A beautiful road that runs along the coast, connecting downtown Havana with the
city's western residential areas.
†Patrick Henry, speech at the Virginia Convention, 1765.
‡Since Helen was on her way home from Cuba, she probably meant to say *Feliz Año
Nuevo*, which is Happy New Year in Spanish.

Tampa—Thursday, January 6, 1910

I'm so blue today and have been lying down all afternoon thinking while Ruby has gone to the arts reception. Day has just taken stock, and it is terrible. The last two years he has worked practically for nothing, and he gives the best of himself to his work. Dear, dear boy, it is for him I grieve, not for myself. I have everything I want; but to see him worry nearly breaks my heart. I feel as if I'd like to put my arms around him and, holding him close, protect him against all the world. He says we shouldn't worry as one good year will wipe out all his indebtedness, and we don't owe a cent in the world, except to the factory. God has been good to us, and we've had no doctor's bills, no heavy expenses. I am as economical as it's possible for a woman to be and keep up with her friends. I don't spend a cent unnecessarily, so I can't reproach myself for the $3,000 spent this last year.* Day says he has the grandest, noblest helpmate in the world, and as long as we have each other, we are rich beyond a miser's dream.

Money, money, money. I used to say it didn't count, but that was before I knew its value and its great power for weal or woe. Whatever happens, we can only grow closer, though. In adversity my heart goes out to him in vast tenderness, in faithful love, and my one desire is to please and cheer him, which I can so easily do, thank God. When good luck comes to us, I shall love him exultantly, rejoicing in the fruit of his labor. I love him more every day of my life—my husband!

Tampa—Tuesday night, January 11, 1910

Day is out playing pinochle, and though I know he needs the recreation and even beg him to go, it makes me furious when he does, and I know by the time he gets home I will be in a terrible state of icy indignation and imagine myself the most ill-treated wife in the world. I wonder why I'm that way. He insists that my true self is gentle and noble and sweet and that my other self isn't a part of me, that I force myself into it. I wonder. Sometimes I say horrible things to him and just see how much I can hurt him, when down in my heart I'm ashamed of it. But I can't seem to help

---

*They were living well; $3,000 in 1910 is roughly equivalent to $50,000 in 1998. Figures, which are estimates, are based on data from *Historical Statistics of the United States* (Washington, DC: USGPO, 1975) and recent Consumer Price Index information (CPI-U, a broad measure for all urban consumers).

acting ugly at times, and now he needs all my tenderness. I just get spells sometimes and act like a female cad.

Still, while I'm writing thusly, I'm getting angry that he let me persuade him to go. I know how it will end, though. He will come in sweet and affectionate, and I will lie in bed like a statue and let him talk and caress me, and he will say, "My darling, my queen, *don't* get angry with me, it breaks my heart when you are cold to me. *Please* put your arms around me. O, I love you so, I worship you, the noblest little woman in the world, my own darling little wife." And my heart will go out to him while he is talking, and then I will melt into his arms, and I will feel so mean and self-contemptuous. I can tease and play with him and he's an easy victim, but sometimes I wonder if he hasn't his tactics also, and if I fall into his traps.

Yesterday we were married ten months. How our love has grown and broadened. Ten months of happiness, whatever comes. I am thinking of that "whatever comes." It seems too good to last.

Got a letter from Victor. He wrote he thinks of me often, and lots of other stuff I can't understand. Formerly it would have been so easy to translate, but I seem to have lost the key. Living with a man who is open as the day has made me lose my love of winding paths.

Tampa—Thursday, January 13, 1910

Again I hear the "Hep Hep" of the Gentile resounding through the ages. Yes, Jerusalem "est perdita," lost to us in every way, but not lost is the ancient pride of race that makes a Jew raise his head nobly and feel that he is a fit associate for princes. After years of persecution and even while he cringed, the Jew still feels that, but alas, in this year of 1910, *Christian* Era, it is still considered a term of opprobrium to be called a *Jew*.

I had thought this house singularly free from prejudice, but might have known it would come sooner or later, this clash. I just heard that Mrs. Davis tried to make Mrs. G. turn us out when she found we were Jews. Said she didn't want any "stinking Jews" around. O, if I had only known it! After I was here, I hear she said I was grand and she liked me, but Mr. Apte was so common! I'd like to wring her neck! At first I laughed, because it seemed so funny. She has been so nice to me, has told me her troubles, confided in me, and accepted any help I would give to the babies, which was considerable, but as usual I get more furious the more I think of it. And she says my husband is *common*! I am bound to secrecy now, but O, I shall tell her a thing or two someday—that little cat.

Tampa—Monday, January 24, 1910

Ruby has gone to town with Gertie, as I am sick today. Thank goodness the worst is over, as I acted absurdly all week. Sometimes I wonder if I am quite sane at these times. I am surely much better than I used to be, as far as pains are concerned, but O, the terrible nervousness and irritability; that seems to be worse, and I'm going to get a strong hold on the reins and pull up, as I know what a woman can become by giving away to that morbid hysteria, and I must be careful. Day is so sweet to me, and he ought to be stern. Whatever I do, he says, "It is just your condition; my little girl couldn't say that if she were herself." And then I feel so ashamed, but keep on saying horrid things, and I get so blue and homesick and am sure Day is ceasing to love me, etc., even while I know in my heart I'm making a fool of myself.

My cold seems to have left me pulled down. I thought I was getting so strong, but I still can stand nothing. If I go out in the afternoon, by night I am exhausted, the same old nausea and overpowering weakness. I can't account for it. Perhaps I'm anemic again. I can hardly wait until I'm in bed at night and seem to be in a daze all evening. I wonder if I don't overtax my strength, or rather overrate, and if it is just willpower which keeps me going at all. Or can it be that I haven't enough to do, and would be better off if I had responsibilities and had to work.

If I had a baby or two, maybe I wouldn't have time to get tired. I believe it is time I was assuming my lifework, yet I keep putting it off. The circumstances don't seem propitious. My little dream children, I wonder if it is only in theory I want you! No, no, my mother-heart cries out for you, but O the fatal tendency of putting it off in this twentieth century. Next year, please God, I will assume my responsibilities and the rest of my life will be devoted to my children. I am merely existing now, as I don't even give the best that is in me to my husband. It would be better for us both if he were sterner, harsher to me, and it isn't very conducive to effort to have your husband tell you you are the most beautiful creature in the world and look perfect in anything you wear. Still, it's very pleasant to hear "O, my little queen how beautiful you are" when you first awake in the morning, feeling at your worst.

Tampa—Wednesday, February 9, 1910

Maurice left this morning, having been here since Saturday. How glad I was to see him, and what a fine fellow he is, and good to look at. Thank God Mama can be proud of all her sons. I surely hated for him to leave, as he helped the homesickness greatly. Viola's baby was born Saturday, February 5, four weeks sooner than expected. They are well, I'm so thankful to say. How my heart thrills for joy in her safety! Viola, a mother, and only yesterday we were children together!

Dr. Granthan gave me some iron pills. He says I am run down and must make up my mind that I constantly have to be built up. I've heard that so often before! I weigh 101 pounds and look fine, sleep like a log, and eat well, but can stand absolutely nothing. If I go out in the afternoon, I am exhausted by night and don't see how I've been able to make a good impression on so many of the men who have been down. There is always someone we know here, and they seem to regard us as a sort of haven, phone us as soon as they get to town, and devote themselves to us exclusively. They spread the news of how happy we are and how kind, and broadcast and write us how they look forward to being with us again.

Jerry and I quarrel faithfully, and Sol Gans and I flirt outrageously. Thank goodness Day is far from jealous (right here, let me say I wish he was sometimes!!). Sol is a nice, clean boy, and he says it makes him "feel so funny" to dance with me, or touch my hand. How I have changed. I don't accept challenges anymore. I'm simply a woman satisfied with her husband. How uninteresting! I wonder if the little devil in me is dead, or only sleeping. Sometimes, I think I feel the slightest stir of life, but love and loyalty quickly stifle it.

Tampa—Wednesday, February 16, 1910

The Panama Canal celebration is going on, and Tampa is very lively. I have shaken hands with a real sure-enough count from sunny Italy, and with Right Honorable James T. Bryce, ambassador from Great Britain. He is a dear, venerable old gentleman, and I was proud to touch the hand of such a great scholar and statesman. Yesterday, I visited the U.S. gunboat *Dubuque* and the Italian battleship *Etruenia*. Our hearts swelled with pride as we compared our bright-faced, clean young sailors with the villainous looking "dagos" on the adjacent ship.

I was walking down Franklin Street Monday when I heard a great commotion and noticed everyone looking up. There was a great dirigible balloon, flying right above my head. What a wonderful age we live in, but I wager we will be telling our children how we remember the first air ships and how everyone gathered in the street to watch "what is now so common a sight, my dears. My, my what will be invented next? Have you heard about the new thought wave? Why, last week I talked to a cousin in San Francisco and heard as plainly or far more so than over the old-fashioned long distance phone, and merely by concentrating my mind!"

Tampa—Tuesday, February 22, 1910

And he was "first in peace, first in war, and first in the hearts of his countrymen."* What an ideal day to celebrate his birthday. The thermometer stands at 74°, a light balmy breeze is blowing, and a glow of expectancy is over Tampa, for not only is it Washington's birthday, but the day of the great Gasparilla Parade and Ball.† We will attend, and I'll wear my wedding dress. The German Saengerfest is also convening here, and last night we went to the concert at the club.

A group of school children just passed. Singing with great spirit, they carried American flags, and the tune they sang was "Dixie." I wonder if they felt true patriotism, or were only so happy that school was out. At any rate my heart thrilled to their fresh young voices and the ever new song. And "I'm glad I live in Dixie, I am, I am. In Dixie Land I take my stand to live and die in Dixie"—I hope!

Tampa—Monday, February 28, 1910

My beloved spring comes early here in the Land of Flowers, but it comes quietly, gradually, and I miss the ecstatic, sudden thrill of it I felt at home. The trees are never bare here, but they are taking on fresh foliage. The air is nearly all winter-sweet and balmy, so it isn't more noticeable now, and how I miss the sight of little flowers peeping up from the pulsating earth. It is pitifully true that Tampa is woefully lacking in flowers. Sweet little growing

---

*The actual quotation is "first in war, first in peace, and first in the hearts of his countrymen," attributed to Henry Lee's eulogy of George Washington in December 1799.
†Tampans still consider Gasparilla—which celebrates the alleged exploits of the pirate José Gaspar, who once landed on the shores of Tampa Bay—to be the Florida city's equivalent of New Orleans's Mardi Gras.

things don't thrive very well in sand, and one can't feel Mother Earth's bosom throbbing here. The only thing that reconciles me to this Southern spring is the scent of the orange blossoms. Faint, delicious, fraught with the languor and beauty of the tropics, it is wafted on the gentle breeze, evoking thoughts of love and passion and stirring the breast with sweet unrest.

Tampa—Friday, March 11, 1910

Yesterday we were married a year. The flight of time is unbelievable, but it was a year of good things, of peace and love and devotion. And I thank God for the happiest year of my life, and the gift of a good man's heart. Verily his price is far above rubies. As usual on my anniversaries, the day wasn't what I had expected. I fought against grippe all this week and yesterday was sick and faint, but struggled up, and even went to a card party at Mrs. Brown's. Last night, as I had fever, Day sent for the doctor. We retired at 9, missing all the celebrations we had planned, but how happy I was when my husband's arms went round me and I felt his deep, his infinite tenderness and responded to it. Such beautiful, beautiful things he said to me, and how I love him. He said, "How grateful I am to God for giving me you, my wife, my sweetheart, my little gift of God." What a sacred thing to be called. God make me worthy.

How surprised I was to get letters from all the girls and boys. So many wrote that I didn't expect to. And such lovely presents. Whatever comes, O Lord, I thank Thee for a perfect page from the book of years. Whatever comes!—Whatever comes? Grace has a daughter, born on the 9th, and had me informed at once.

Tampa—Sunday, March 20, 1910

Home, home, home—I'm going home. But as always there is little rift within the lute, for my husband will be on a long Western trip, and this trip really means the *future*. It is practically a crisis in his business, and I pray with all my soul it will be a success. We have both been worried over business, but I have caught his bright outlook. We are blessed with youth and health, and the world is before us. I am so busy and so excited, as I will surprise the folks. God keep my dearest one safe. We leave tomorrow night.

Atlanta—Saturday, April 9, 1910

I think Day is coming tonight, and I am so excited. By evening I will be worn out, as I can't keep still a minute. How I have wanted him! Happy as I am to be home, and as grand as everyone is to me, there is no denying the fact that I am happiest when I am alone with him—I seem more contented, more at peace.

Somehow the ghosts of other days seem vaguely to haunt me here—the days of my indecision and fear and countless little worries. I never go into the sitting room without a slight shudder. I see Jim's white, intense face. I feel again the half-fascinating, half-repulsive influence of Samson. I see Mort, his beautiful head against the pillars, his dear wistful eyes following me wherever I move. I miss Mort when I'm here. I saw him in Jacksonville, and walking home together I slipped my hand through his arm as of yore and felt his muscles stiffen at my light touch as of yore. Poor, poor boy, the wanderlust is on him again. I sadly fear that what in the boy was merely instability may make a derelict of the man. I asked, "Do you ever think of me, boy?" and he said, "God, Helene, don't ask," and then went on to tell me how much I meant to him and that he wouldn't live in the same town with me for all the riches of the world. He said he was glad I am happy, but was brute enough not to want to watch my happiness. I said, "Mort, find some nice girl, love her," and he answered that he measured them all by me, and all were found wanting. "When I find another Helene, when some girl means as much to me and stands for what you do, then maybe I can love, but that time will never come! For there is no one in the world like you." Poor, poor lonesome boy.

Tampa—Wednesday, May 11, 1910

And so it goes—my visit was like a dream, and now I feel as if I've never been away. I got back Saturday, and O, my husband's rapture when he held me in his arms, the golden hours we've had together since I'm here. By every sign I know he loves me more tenderly, more reverently, more passionately than ever before, and I am content. But how I miss the folks! How much more dear Mama means to me than ever, as I realize more and more her nobility, her mother love. Everyone said that never a girl visited home and had the attentions showered upon her I did. O, it is sweet to feel I have so many friends, and I miss it here in Tampa.

I had engagements every day for the whole six weeks I was home and enjoyed every minute. The opera was divine—no other word will describe it. I think I liked *Lohengrin* better than *Aida*, even though Caruso sang in the latter, but *Lohengrin* entered into my very soul, and every bar of its stately music is dear to me. Yet the magnificent chords of *Aida*, the sensuous, Eastern setting of it, thrilled me too deeply for words. Atlanta is a wonderful city to attain Grand Opera. No less wonderful was the weather while I was there—in March warm as July, and the last of April freezing cold, with the deepest snow of the season. I know it will be very dull here this summer, but I shall be very comfortable, well stocked up on reading and sewing, and I must become better acquainted with my diary.

Tampa—Monday, May 16, 1910

This morning, at 3, we got up to see the comet—Halley's Comet, the Great Celestial Wanderer. There it was, blazing across the eastern sky, one of those phenomena that go to make us feel our pitiful insignificance in the great scheme of things. Considerable uneasiness is felt concerning what will happen to us when we pass through its tail Wednesday. It is the one topic of conversation, and everyone is wishing for the day to be over. It is a debated subject if it can be true that weather conditions are due to it. One thing sure, it is most unusual to have such a cool May, and snow is falling in Georgia.

Yesterday was one of the happiest of my married life. Day and I were together every minute. In the morning he read aloud, and in the afternoon I slept in his arms. That night we didn't want to spoil the sweet communion of our souls by contact with others, so we rode out to Ballast Point and had the whole place to ourselves. A strong breeze was blowing, making the baby waves almost like ocean swells breaking on the shore. The moon shone, not brilliantly, but with a gentle soft blue light, and my heart fairly ached with the beauty of it all, until my husband's arms around me, his dear understanding of my mood swept away the ecstatic pain with which such nights fill me and left only peace and contentment in its place.

Tampa—Sunday, June 5, 1910

With all the worries and fears I had for my married life, the one thing that never occurred to me was financial troubles, and strange to say that is the only cloud on our horizon. I had thought the future so bright for Day, and it was bright, but the Panic hit him hard; he is losing money every day. I don't see how they will ever make good here, and if after stocktaking in July they find they can't go on, actual poverty stares us in the face. Day seldom loses his indomitable courage, his marvelous optimism, yet once in a while he loses faith, and then I see everything crumbling around me, for not only has he lost all he had, but thousands more besides, and I don't know which way he will turn. But it is for him I grieve. As for myself, I don't feel the gravity of it. He is so young, the whole world is before him— it is ours to conquer.

And O, I thank God for our youth and health, our faith and our courage. With those four things, life is bound to yield us of her store of wealth and happiness; we will wrest it from her, and joy is in the struggle. O, there are so many things to thank God for, and with all my soul I thank Him: for my newborn optimism, for the fact that life can never be stale or flat for me, that impending trouble has made me love my husband more, that sorrow can never embitter me, that I have changed from a neurotic girl to a cheerful woman, that nature speaks to me, that books are my friends in weal and woe, that my husband adores me and thinks me an ideal helpmate, that it is so easy for me to do without material things, that the greatest thing in life still awaits—the crown and the glory of motherhood. Whatever comes, I will look back to these words. They shall be my litany. I *will* be thankful for these blessings which nothing can take from me and I will remember that:

> No matter how dark the night,
> How fraught with punishment the scroll,
> I am the master of my fate
> I am the captain of my soul.*

Tampa—Thursday, June 23, 1910

Day is at a manufacturers' meeting and no telling what time he will come home, as this is a most important meeting. A great strike is impending,

---

*A slight misquote of W. E. Henley's poem "Invictus":
  It matters not how strait the gate,
  How changed with punishments the scroll,
  I am the master of my fate:
  I am the captain of my soul.

and tonight will decide whether labor or capital will be master of the Havana tobacco business. The same old struggle, the same great question. I have always thought organized labor a good thing, but it becomes a menace when the demands are as insolent and puerile as in this case. I hope, though, it will be adjusted, as a strike will paralyze business, and the El Provedo, at least, has enough to contend with.

I have been to the picture shows with Mr. and Mrs. Luyser and Mr. Strasser. Am not feeling so well, as I've been on such a nervous strain. First, Day had ptomaine poisoning, and I was nearly wild. Then, for the first time, I saw death snatch a victim. Mrs. Beatly committed suicide, taking strychnine, just as she sat down to the supper table. Strange to say, I was the only woman who didn't lose my head and was with her to the last, when she died in horrible convulsions. I kept my remarkable coolness until late in the night, when even Day had gone to sleep at my side. Then I had a nervous chill and hysteria. Dr. G. says he knew I was going to break down, and it would have been so much better not to hold back, but it is hard for me to relax. And I discovered one thing, both in Day's illness and in that: that I can be calm in time of emergency, and I am very thankful. Of course, my mind dwells constantly on the poor, unhappy woman who couldn't face life, and there is just a little remorse, too, that I shared the feeling against her, for it has taught me to be more charitable and less quick to judge in the future.

Pearle is in Montgomery. Dear girl, how I love her, and how I want her to enjoy her young life, for she was meant for joy and luxury. She is so sweet and wholesome and sincere. I think so much of my dear ones, and what an interesting family it is. Every one of them would make food for an author's pen! Mama, so independent, self-reliant, so practical, and so wise. What wonderful influence she has had over us all. And there's Sister. What a wife she would make a good man—absolutely dependable, and trustworthy and capable, too, though she lacks self-reliance. Whenever there is anything to be attended to, "Sister will do it," and it will be done well. Yet how little we have appreciated her. She has so little tact, and sometimes I believe she is utterly lacking in sex-consciousness, or in the little ways, call them what you will, that attract men. She has had more "beaus" than the average girl, but—there it stops. They will rush her for a while, then seem to tire. I'd give anything to see her happily married.

Then Maurice, the man of our house, simple as a child, innocently vain, loving ostentation a little too much, yet with a heart of gold. The highest integrity and a fine businessman, too—what a help and comfort he is to Mama, and how she adores him! Sometimes I wish he was more manly and cared less for clothes and what people think, but he is only a boy and steady as a rock.

Pearle, my darling—she thinks there is no one on Earth like me, and we are much more congenial than Sister and I. We have such good times together.

Sometimes, I fear a bit for Leonard. He is so handsome, with his great green eyes and his perfect physique, and he is just the sort women go wild about. And he is somewhat inclined to be a sport, too. Like Maurice, he loves to "show off," and he has the pride of Lucifer. Very sensitive he is, too, and I fear Mama often makes the mistake of scolding him when she should appeal. His heart is as tender as a girl's, and though he is inclined to like girls too much, as young as he is, he is decidedly chivalrous and respects all womankind. He is at the dangerous age now, and I'm so afraid of the pitfalls that beset boys' feet, but I'm sure his innate refinement, his respect for his mother and sisters, and his sweet young heart will carry him through.

Henry, our baby—I think he has more character than all of us put together. Though only thirteen, he has a will of iron, a perseverance and energy that is astounding, business ability and initiative that many a businessman might envy. And when Henry sets out to do a thing, you bet on Henry's doing it! And nerve—he is the only one of us who has that very necessary adjunct these days. Leonard and Maurice would die before they'd do some things Henry does as a matter of course. When other little boys are walking, Henry is getting a free ride; when the other kids want to see a ball game, but haven't got the coin, Henry has thought of some way to make the money, and if he can't get in the grandstand, why the bleachers are good enough! Public opinion means nothing to him—he is the sort to hew his own way. Sometimes I fear he will ride roughshod over other people; he lacks Leonard's and Maurice's tender heart—it is straight ahead with him and "get out of my way." I feel that he will make good. If I'm not mistaken, he'll be a rich man someday, for he has those attributes of ambition, energy, and initiative that make successful men, and he is a successful man in embryo.

Of the six of us, not one of us could do a mean, low thing. We couldn't lie, and we couldn't steal, and we are well-bred and refined—mature and mannered. So there is the beauty of our inheritance. Our parents have given us some beautiful things, and now it is up to us to make the most of them and pass them on to our children.

Tampa—Monday, July 4, 1910

The Glorious Fourth, but my heart is very heavy today. Day is taking stock, and things are even worse than we thought. I don't know how it all will end, but even he—I have thought so for a long time—doesn't see how he can keep on here. Then what? In debt for $10,000 and no one to turn to for help. We will be worse than penniless, but I do not despair. I do not forget my watchword. We consulted over our assets last night: They are health, youth, courage, hope, ambition, energy, and ability. Doesn't that far outweigh the paltry $10,000 liabilities? Yet, alas, the cash might help us more right now. My heart aches for my boy, so brave and yet so tormented that his aching brain will not let him sleep. We merely doze at night, and every little while I awake to find his arms around me, his aching head on my breast, and I strain him to me close, with a *fierce*, tigerish sense of protection.

Once he suggested that the best thing would be to go to St. Louis. My heart stood still, all my brave defenses seemed crumbling round me. Would fate be so cruel as to send me there, the place that I most dislike, and have often said I'd die if I had to live there? Well, I won't think of that, yet. But I feel that's where we'll end! St. Louis, the sordid, the repellent, the commonplace second-rate people I met, the life with—O, well, I *won't* think of it yet.

I am so grateful that I am to my husband a source of comfort and help. All during the night and many times in the day he tells me how sweet and true and noble he thinks me and how my happiness is the greatest thing in the world for him. I am on the threshold of life's struggle, a woman's struggle, and I realize now what a sheltered, protected life I've led, far from the strife. Now I step out on the firing line. O God of battles, help me to be brave when the bullets fall around me; heal me if I am struck!

Tampa—Tuesday, July 5, 1910

The Fourth turned out so much better than it promised. A crowd of us went out to Ballast Point for supper, and I felt myself relax, grow rested under the blessed influence of the fresh air and the bay.

The much discussed prizefight is over, and a Negro stands heavyweight champion of the world. What difference does it make? And yet there have been race riots all over the country, and many are dead or wounded. It's a brutal custom and should be abolished.

Race and Responsibility

America has never been particularly hospitable toward people of African descent, but some times have been worse than others. By 1910 life clearly was better than it had been during slavery. And perhaps it was even a bit better than it had been fifteen or twenty years earlier when the number of African Americans lynched in the United States peaked at more than 150 per year. Still, these were dangerous times. Sixty-seven blacks were lynched in 1910,[1] and the lynchings were regularly reported in the newspapers. Thus, African Americans lived with understandable fear, not knowing when a mob might turn on them for indiscretions real or perceived.

Into this ring stepped John Arthur "Jack" Johnson, who had had few opportunities to exercise his boxing skill in America. The prizefight—at least where it was legal—was a whites-only sport. Nevertheless, Johnson had made a name for himself, fighting abroad and beating everyone he met, including white men. In Reno, Nevada, on July 4, 1910, boxing's color barrier came down in America. A title bout, amid great hoopla and hype, matched Johnson and former heavyweight champion James L. "Jeff" Jeffries. Jeffries was the Great White Hope, pulled out of recent retirement to "remove the golden smile from Jack Johnson's face," as Jack London put it in a newspaper dispatch.[2] The nation's attention was riveted to the fight, not only because of the racially charged nature of the event and the intense advance publicity but also because of the $101,000 purse, easily the largest business deal ever consummated by an African-American to that time.

More than twenty thousand fans looked on as Johnson kept his "golden smile," easily beating Jeffries, fair and square. As the Great White Hope went down in ignominious defeat, white America reacted swiftly and violently. The next day's headlines told the story: "HALF A DOZEN DEAD AS CROWDS ATTACK NEGROES; REIGN OF TERROR HERE," proclaimed the *New York Herald.* "AFRICANS DRAGGED FROM NEW YORK STREET CARS AND ATTACKED IN STREETS IN FURY OF WHITES OVER JEFFRIES' DEFEAT. NEGROES ALSO ATTACKED AND LYNCHINGS THREATENED IN PHILADELPHIA, WASHINGTON, PITTSBURG[H], CHATTANOOGA, ATLANTA, ST. LOUIS AND MANY OTHER POINTS."[3] In all, thirteen blacks were killed and hundreds injured.[4]

Reading the news, Helen certainly must have recalled the time that she had seen violent racial hatred firsthand—in Atlanta in 1906. She was twenty years old. For weeks, sensational reporting in the city's newspapers had told of a "crime wave" of rape and murder committed by blacks against whites. Finally, tensions erupted into what was probably the most violent race riot of Atlanta's history. Twelve people were killed—ten blacks and two whites—and seventy were injured.[5] Helen wrote about the riot in a letter to Day dated October 2, 1906:

> If you ever hear anyone say Atlanta is dull, you have my authority to deny it, as even the most exaggerated craving for excitement must have been satisfied last week. Of course you read about the riots in the paper, but as they weren't allowed to print half that happened, you can't know how bad it really was. All day Saturday excitement was rising, as one extra after another told in flaming headlines about five different attacks on women in one day. Felix was out here that night and remarked that there was sure to be trouble soon, and he left here just in time to run into the mob at its worst. We knew nothing about it, though, until the next morning, but the Loebs had been up all night, as Helen, coming home from theater, was in the midst of it. The poor child saw three people killed.
>
> Sunday things were pretty bad, the wildest sort of rumors going the rounds, and by that night we were all scared half to death, but Monday was the climax. Not a woman ventured out, and every citizen was armed. Imagine the novel sight of men passing the house in broad daylight with Winchesters over their shoulders or pistols in their hands. Factories were closed, not a cab to be had, and all business practically at a standstill; 18 companies of infantry and one light artillery were ordered out, 200 policemen and 400 deputies on duty, but that didn't prevent the awful riots of Monday night, which broke out all over the city, but especially in South Atlanta and Pittsburg, which you know are out this way. About 7 o'clock, Major Woodward phoned out to the citizens on Washington Heights that a mob of Negroes was marching on the city from that direction, and he told the men to get all their womenfolk together and then patrol the streets, all night, to be in readiness. Of course, the news spread, and every man was on the streets. Every time we heard a pistol shot, we were sure the mob was upon us, and none of us retired that night. I undressed at 5:30 the next morning, after a night such as I never hope to spend again. The Gatling gun they were obliged to take to South Atlanta made these sylvan dales re-echo; and the tramp of soldiers and bands of organized citizens passing the house at all hours wasn't very conducive to slumber.

Tuesday matters were little better, as rumors grew more wild every moment, and no one knows what really happened and what didn't. Every hardware store was entirely out of ammunition, and hundreds were being armed in front of the courthouse by the city. Not a Negro could be seen on the streets. We had a regular house party here, our cook's whole family and several ex-cooks taking refuge with us. If it wasn't pitiful, their fright would be laughable; the cook's little boy wouldn't move from behind the stove all day, and such a chattering of teeth and rolling eyes I never saw outside of a drama. Tuesday night was quiet in comparison to Monday, but it was bad enough, and very few people in Atlanta slept, I believe.

Wednesday the Negroes left town in droves. The factories began to run somehow, as labor is entirely disorganized—cooks, waiters, cab-men, and wash-women making a wild dash for the depot, trying "to git out of this yer town, 'fore we all gits murdered," as I heard one Negro remark. I really feel sorry for them. Of course we had a great provocation for the riots, but it is a blot all the same in the South that the innocent should die for the guilty, and lawlessness is always to be deplored, no matter what the cause. Matters are getting normal now, but we'll always feel the effects of our week of terror.

Overall, Helen's attitudes toward blacks were not atypical of white, liberal-minded Southerners of her time: paternalistic and a bit condescending, never overtly racist. As she matured over the years, so did her views on race. Although she never lost those paternalistic attitudes, she may have gained a bit more understanding. In 1945 she wrote about learning of Franklin D. Roosevelt's death this way: "The colored waitress said, with tears in her eyes, 'I just heard on the radio our president is dead.' 'Our' president—from a Negro. What greater eulogy?"

Tampa—Thursday, July 14, 1910

My twenty-fourth birthday. The weight of the past few weeks has lifted today, and in spite of the unsettled state of affairs I am happy. How can I help it when I feel my husband's adoration, the love and thoughtfulness of my friends, and O my youth, my dear, dear youth. I want so desperately to hold on to you. I have felt miserable all week. I never know, when I'm worried, if it is that or illness, as worry affects me physically, weighing down my limbs like lead, making my back ache, my head and heart throb too fast, and a deadly nausea almost overcome me. That is my chief drawback in all struggles—I lack the physical stamina.

We are waiting to hear definitely from Uncle Julius if we shall remain
here. Day gave me $24 and Aunt Dordy sent $12, and I am waiting eagerly
for the expressman now. A lovely breeze is blowing. The weather is most
pleasant.

Last night we went to town to hear the cigarmakers' side of the con-
troversy. Both sides are right according "as they are given to see the right"!*
I wish it was settled one way or the other, and from a personal standpoint
I wish there'd be a strike, so Day would have an excuse to shut down. At
daybreak he had me in his arms. It was very sweet to awake on my birthday morn with my husband's lips on mine. God bless him—I love him.

Waynesville, North Carolina—Friday, September 9, 1910

In the "Land of the Sky"—my beloved mountains and my husband together. What more could I want? And I have enjoyed our little trip; we
lead the "Simple Life," in which bridge is included. I am not able to walk
much, as I'm here for my health. I have malaria and the same anemic
trouble, and that is why Day brought me here. Somehow I can't feel the
mountains as I used to. I have relaxed and feel peaceful and happy, but the
old ecstasy doesn't come. I wonder if I'm not going to have it again—all
the poignant joy of "the mountain, the cataract, the deep, mysterious for-
est."† Perhaps it is my physical condition—my old enemy! I don't suppose
I will ever be strong. Dr. Huguley says I won't, and he says I ought to move
away from Florida, that the climate is too enervating for me.

Who knows where we will be next year this time. Business conditions
look far from good to me. The strike is on full force at last. All factories are
closed, and goodness knows what we will do. Day is drawing what used to

---

*An allusion to Lincoln's March 4, 1865, inaugural address: "With malice toward none;
with charity for all; with firmness in the right, as God gives us to see the right, let us
strive on to finish the work we are in; to bind up the nation's wounds; to care for him
who shall have borne the battle, and for his widow, and his orphan—to do all which
may achieve and cherish a just and lasting peace among ourselves, and with all
nations."
†Perhaps from William Wordsworth's "Lines Composed a Few Miles above Tintern
Abbey":
  The sounding cataract
  Haunted me like a passion; the tall rock,
  The mountain, and the deep gloomy wood
  Their colors and their forms, were then to me
  An appetite; a feeling and a love,
  That had no need of a remoter charm,
  By thoughts supplied, nor any interest
  Unborrowed from the eye.

be considered enough to support a large family, but these days it's hardly enough to live on. But I have all I want—all but one thing. And I hate our poverty for that. I want my little baby. O I do, I do. I rebel against my lot because we can't afford it. I so freely expected to have one this year, but things are getting worse instead of better.

Ah well, I am sick now, anyway, so maybe it's best. I must build myself up again. I feel like a dilapidated house that must always be renovated—a rotten tenement that is unsafe. God only knows, my little daughter, how bitterly, horribly it hurts me to give you such a home. If only it could be torn down, even unto the foundations, and a beautiful temple arise in its place—a sacred temple for you, my little one, where light and sunshine and God dwell. But I will have to do my best with the poor materials I have, and my whole future from now on shall be a preparation for motherhood. In thought and in deed I shall try to put my house in order for you, dear.

We leave here Sunday. Day will go back to Tampa, and I shall miss him sorely, but know as usual I shall enjoy my stay at home.

Asheville, North Carolina—Sunday, September 11, 1910

Day was very busy with his salesmen all day, and I've been talking to Arthur Fox, of all people. He told me all his troubles and lots of lies and says he still loves Ara and wants to go back to her. He of course told me how he'd always loved me next to Ara and that I was the only person whose opinion he cared for. Wants me to write him what Ara says. O, no, I've learned better than that, and told him that helping in love affairs was a different thing from meddling between husband and wife. He's a liar, but such a good one. I haven't quite gotten over the habit of believing what a person tells me, if they look me straight in the eye and swear it!

I've been sitting on the porch of the Battery Park watching the sun set. At last the peace of my mountains has entered my soul. It is all very beautiful.

Atlanta—Thursday, October 20, 1910

It is still like summer. The leaves are green, and people are just beginning to wear winter clothes. A suit is very uncomfortable. I thought I'd go home this week, but the strike is still so unsettled. The factories have opened their doors, and only twenty men have so far gone to work. Day thinks it will be settled this week, and if so he will go on his trip soon and I'm to remain here.

I've been nearly crazy as today is the first I've heard since the storm, which the papers grossly exaggerated, and I couldn't reach Tampa by wire. Day wrote that he slept through the worst of it. How like a man, and I here, in agony.

I feel much better again. I think I only needed a steady course of iron and a little cool weather, though we've hardly had that. Still sit outside at nights. Though everyone has been grand to me, I've hardly enjoyed this trip, as I've had to force myself to go out and have felt so terribly weak, sick, and nervous. The doctor says I will probably be cured of anemia when I'm forty, and the best of my life will be over! Had my blood tested for malaria, but no germs were found. Only a lack of iron, which can surely play the deuce!

Tampa—Monday, October 31, 1910

Halloween—what fun we used to have on that day, and will I ever forget the night at Irma's first, and then when I slept with Beulah! How good it is to be back with Day, and how much better I feel. My nerves always feel quiet and soothed when I get back to my room!—

> And so I find it well to come
> For deeper rest to this still room,
> For here the habit of the soul
> Feels less the outer world's control;
> And from the silence multiplied
> By these still forms on every side
> The world that time and sense has known
> Falls off and leaves us, God, alone.*

The strike is still on in full force; it seems impossible to get the men back to work. The town is painfully quiet, and things seem strained. Some think it will drag itself out, but I believe a crisis is approaching and that even more violence will be perpetrated. The St. Louis specter looms large again. I fear we will have to go there. I don't see any chance of making

---

*From John Greenleaf Whittier's poem, "The Meeting." The stanza actually is ten lines long. In quoting it, Helen dropped lines five and six, namely:
> The strength of mutual purpose pleads
> More earnestly our common needs;

good here. We got such a pitiful letter from Father begging us to come, and the old man's heart-hunger touched me to the quick. It would be well worth a sacrifice to make his last years peaceful. But ah, what a sacrifice it would be for me to go there! He adores me, and I feel ashamed that I dread to live with them, but sufficient unto the day is the evil thereof.* Perhaps something else will turn up, and if I have to go there, I will do it cheerfully and make the best of it.

Our first cold spell came on the 29th, the earliest known in years, and gee, it was cold—44°, but how the cold here pierces to the bone. It is warmer and in a few days will be like summer. I miss the folks so and don't know what to do with myself in the afternoon. It is sad not to have girl-friends here. Day is more devoted than ever, as tender and as passionate as a bridegroom. Our meetings after a trip are always very sweet. Truly, I love him better every day and never do I cease to thank God for it.

Tampa—Thanksgiving Day, November 24, 1910

Can it be a year since I sat at this same desk, writing my thanks? How little I accomplished, but how much I have to be thankful for. O, that next year will find us happy and with more of good and useful things to write down. It is quite warm today. I'm going to town in a white waist and skirt. Hope is going with me to help me select something for Day's birthday tomorrow. Don't know how we will spend this afternoon. There is nothing to do here, and I long for a good show.

Tampa—Wednesday, December 7, 1910

Touching wood and holding my breath, I hasten to write down how well I look. I didn't want to put it off, as no telling how long it will last. I couldn't believe it was I who just looked in the glass. My skin is clear, and my cheeks are *rosy*, my eyes are bright and I'm *too* fat. That's the joke of it— none of my clothes fit, and my figure looks too funny. I've finished my second 100 iron pills, and that and living more in the air is what has cured, or rather benefited me so greatly, as I'm *not well* yet. I still have indigestion, though not as constantly. I have lots of headaches, but I'm sure they are from my eyes; still get nauseated if I overtire myself, but I can stand so much more, feel so much brighter and stronger. So God be praised, and O,

*A New Testament reference: Matthew 6:34 (King James version).

if He will only let me stay this way—give me a respite from my terrible
languor and pain. Day says I'm so different when I'm well that I am the
most irresistibly sweet thing in the world, and that I make him so happy,
shed such sunshine. And it is true I am never irritable or cross when I'm
well. O, la joie de vivre, my beautiful, beautiful youth—how much more
you'd mean to me if I were well and strong.

Tampa—Monday, December 26, 1910

Christmas Day was clear and cold (50°) and passed very pleasantly. We
arose at 6:30 to see the kids with the tree, then all went downstairs in our
kimonos and bathrobes to get our stockings, which were full of ridiculous
things—yet not so ridiculous, as I got a doll with a verse saying they knew
above all else I wanted a bouncing baby. Now how did they know? Is my
heart-hunger so apparent?

Christmas Eve, Day played pinochle, and Mr. Coatis took Hope and
me bumming. Never saw Tampa so lively. We filled the stockings when we
got home and didn't get to sleep until 2. Mr. Rosenberg and Uncle Julius
were here last week; but don't know any more now than we did before.
Day is sorely puzzled. So am I. Had belladonna put in my eyes Thursday,
and they are not normal yet. Didn't read a line for three days. Changed my
glasses.

Tampa—Tuesday, January 3, 1911

The New Year is with us. God grant us health and peace. Our hearts and
brains are sorely tried, but I feel I *know* that whether we decide to go to
St. Louis or stay here, it will be for the best. God is with us. Mr. Rosenberg
is still here. I have been so sick since Sunday, whether from the dissipation of New Year or the worry I don't know.

We ushered in the New Year at the German Club amidst noise and
revelry. Why are people so glad to see the old year die? It is solemn and
awful to think that another page of the book of life is turned and we are
that much nearer the grave, but it is the hope that springs eternal in the
human breast that makes us greet the New Year so joyously—it is "another chance" for a failure, the vague promise that draws us on through
life. Sometimes, it is true, providing but a mirage, but we never cease to

hope it may be an oasis. And so ring out the old, ring in the new, and let us on with our journey. I will keep my face toward the sunshine, and the shadows will fall behind me. That shall be my resolution for the New Year. We danced until almost dawn and had a great time, in spite of the fact that we both felt blue before we went out.

I had a few little experiences that would have seemed exciting before I was married but don't seem to matter much now. I had the joy of calling down a man in my old approved style, and I was told that my face was so *restful* and that I was a pleasure to look at, the intellect and refinement of it amongst the drunk, flushed mob. That was early in the evening before the tired lines came.

I was nearly dead Sunday. Got up at dinnertime. Day played pinochle in the afternoon, and I sat on the porch, too utterly exhausted even to come up and lie down. My head was throbbing, and O, the awful prostration. At 5, Hope persuaded me to walk down in the park. Had to come upstairs immediately after supper, could hardly get to bed, had a nervous chill and sobbed until Day wanted to send for the doctor. Thus I spent my New Year's Day. But I fell asleep in my dear one's arms, and that was a happy ending to a bad day. I still feel miserable, weak, and nervous. Just a little warning of Nature that I am still far from strong and mustn't overtax myself.

Tampa—Thursday, January 12, 1911

The die is cast, and probably next week I shall leave here, stopping in Atlanta before I go to my home in St. Louis. *My home*—as I write those words, a flood of rebellious feeling arises in me, and I could sob and wring my hands, or any other futile thing, at the bare thought of it, but what's the use? Go I must, so I will go cheerfully and bravely and make the best of things. At first I felt as if I couldn't bear it, and though I said little to Day when he would mention it, the tears would flow, with the result that he got miserable and I got ashamed. So I took up all my weapons, called my faithful warriors—peace, courage, hope—and on to the fray.

The other night, when neither of us could sleep, I told him to try my plan of saying the three words that meant most to him over and over, and when we compared, I had silently called my henchmen, and he had said to himself, "confidence, love, happiness." After all, they mean about the same. He is so brave in the face of adversity, so glad to go to St. Louis, so enthusiastic that my heart goes out to him, and I pray that his splendid optimism will never fail him.

I shall hate to leave Tampa. There is something fascinating about Florida; I love my beautiful southland. Everyone is so grieved we are going, and it seems genuine. How can I leave my babies? To think I may never see them again.

Last Sunday night Mr. and Mrs. Guerry took us to a Spanish dinner at the Pasaje, and there I got my closest view of the half-world. Two couples had a room next to us, and—the rest is unwritable. We had to have them put out, and as they passed our door one woman said, "I know them, that's Guerry, and he ain't so much," with the result that Mrs. Guerry nearly fainted and he turned very white, but vowed he'd never seen her before. As the poor drunken creature went down the steps, she yelled, "Those women he's with needn't think they're so high up. They're no better than we are. They needn't put on any airs." Poor thing, I wonder if she ever had a chance.

This morning I was called to the phone, and my heart leapt at the sound of Mort's voice. He will be here some time, and to think we're going away. Maybe that also is for the best! I feel somewhat better today but have to take more iron; have been very nervous. Yesterday I entertained my card club.

The 1910 Cigar Strike[6]

Uncle Julius's* El Provedo Cigar Company was moderately successful in Talla-hassee and Philadelphia, but in both locations the company found itself with an insurmountable problem: a shortage of skilled cigarmakers.[7] The only way to solve the problem was to move the factories to Tampa, where there was skilled labor.

Tampa was a booming city in 1909. Its population had doubled since 1900, to nearly 37,000 people. It boasted more than one hundred cigar factories, making it the world's leading supplier of what were known as "clear Havana" cigars—that is, cigars made with 100 percent Cuban tobacco. Moving to Tampa was bound to be profitable for El Provedo, and it was. It also was profitable for Day and Helen. They lived in a rooming house on tree-lined Plant Avenue in the fashionable Hyde Park neighborhood, just across the Hillsborough River

---

*Julius Hirschberg, who married Day's mother's sister.

from downtown. They had an enjoyable life in a city that had a lot more to offer than sleepy Tallahassee. They could walk to the sprawling Tampa Bay Hotel, topped with shiny onion domes, which was then the center of Tampa's social life.* They could take a streetcar several miles along a shore of Tampa Bay to Ballast Point for a romantic evening on the huge pier. And Day could ride another streetcar across downtown to the factory in the Ybor City area, the center of much of the city's cigarmaking and now Tampa's Latin quarter.

But as cigar manufacturers like Day prospered, their skilled workers, mostly Spanish, Cuban, and Italian immigrants, did not. Wages were low, and working conditions were poor. The situation was ripe for organizing, which the Cigar Makers International Union gladly undertook.† The union met with immediate success. Membership tripled in the winter of 1909–10. The workers organized into locals divided along craft lines and formed the Joint Advisory Board to coordinate their activities and to publish a newspaper.

Unionization brought some immediate benefits to members, specifically a general wage increase in early 1910. But after winning higher pay without a strike, the cigar workers then called for a union shop and formal recognition by the manufacturers, who refused even to negotiate the issues. The energized union responded with a general strike of the entire cigar industry. "The primary issue," Robert P. Ingalls explained in *Urban Vigilantes in the New South*, "was power rather than wages." With factory owners saying they would never discuss union recognition "even if it becomes necessary to close every factory . . . indefinitely," and with the cigarmakers equally adamant that they needed recognition to protect themselves from "the encroachments of those who would oppress us and treat us unfairly," the situation was ripe for deadlock—or worse.

To Tampa's establishment, the future of the city was at stake. Not too many years earlier the cigar industry had moved there from Key West because of labor troubles, and the city fathers did not want to see Tampa on the losing end of another migration. Indeed, with the cigar industry responsible for fully 75 percent of the city's entire payroll, they knew that the strike could

---

*The building now houses the University of Tampa.
†The Cigar Makers International Union was a leader in the union movement. Much of this leadership was due to its most famous member, Samuel Gompers, who had joined in 1864, a year after immigrating from England, and had served as its president from 1874 to 1881. By 1910, Gompers was president of the American Federation of Labor, which he had helped found in the 1880s and led until his death in 1924. During the Tampa cigar strike, Gompers was actively involved in complaining publicly about anti-union vigilantes and in attempting, unsuccessfully, to convince state or federal officials to intervene.

destroy the city. On September 3, about a month into the strike, the Cigar Manufacturers' Association officially locked up the factories and temporarily increased production at other cities. The action shook the establishment, and tension increased on both sides. That tension soon led to violence. Shots were fired on September 13, and the next day J. F. Easterling, the bookkeeper at a West Tampa cigar factory, was shot as he got out of his car to go to work. Six days later, as he lay mortally injured in a hospital, police arrested two Italian immigrants, Angelo Albano and Castenge Ficarrotta. Just hours after their arrest, they were seized by a well-organized vigilante gang and hanged, still handcuffed together, from an oak tree. A note, signed "JUSTICE," was pinned to Albano's clothes. It declared: "BEWARE! OTHERS TAKE NOTICE OR GO THE SAME [W]AY. WE KNOW EVEN MORE. WE ARE WATCHING YOU. IF ANY MORE CITIZENS ARE MOLESTED, LOOK OUT."

Although Easterling's shooting may or may not have had anything to do with the strike, the lynching definitely was designed to intimidate strikers. An Italian official sent to investigate the incident (at least one of the men was still an Italian citizen) confirmed the conclusion that many others had reached: "The lynching itself was not the outcome of a temporary outburst of popular anger," he wrote, "but was rather planned, in cold blood, to the most trifling detail, by some citizens of West Tampa with the tacit assent of a few police officers, and all with the intention of teaching an awful lesson to the strikers of the cigar factories."

No one was ever charged with the lynching. Indeed, as the Italian official noted, there were strong indications of official complicity. Three weeks after the lynching, on October 4, Tampa's elite met at the courthouse to organize a Citizens' Committee to reassert control. The mayor, D. B. McKay, called the meeting to order, saying its purpose was no less than to save the city. In no uncertain terms, he meant that its goal was to end the strike.

"The well-organized and well-armed vigilantes wasted no time in attempting to intimidate strikers," Ingalls notes. But the intimidation was unsuccessful. Thirty-six of the largest factories reopened on October 17; however, only a handful of strikers returned to work. The city leaders escalated their pressure, arresting union leaders and holding them in jail on high bail. Vigilantes patrolled the streets to break up gatherings of strikers. The union hall was shut down, as was the union newspaper.

By the end of January, with their union funds depleted, cigar workers called off the strike. It was a clear victory for the manufacturers, but the union could report some success, too. It had stood up to overwhelming opposition from Tampa's official establishment and the vigilante group that the establishment supported. It had kept the backing of other unionized workers in the city, and it had hurt the manufacturers, causing a significant drop in production. The secretary of the Joint Advisory Board was therefore able to declare without irony that "our fight in this long struggle was for the union, and although the manufacturers have not agreed to recognize us, we have won the union, and we are going back to work organized."

Cigar Manufacturing in Tampa, 1901–1913.

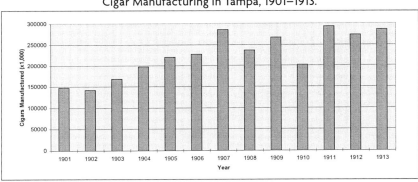

Source: Tampa Historical Society

When the workers returned to work in 1911, Tampa's cigar industry roared back into production, and by 1911 it had set a new production record for the city. But if the industry survived, not all of the producers did. Among the casualties was the El Provedo Cigar Company, and Helen and Day left their pleasant life in Tampa for a far less satisfactory one in St. Louis. It would be thirty years before they returned.

NOTES

1. Tuskegee Institute figures, quoted in the table, "Lynchings, Whites and Negroes, 1882–1962," in *Afro U.S.A.: A Reference Work on the Black Experience*, eds. Harry A. Ploski and Ernest Kaiser (New York: Bellwether Publishing Co., 1971), 267–68.
2. John Durant, *The Heavyweight Champions*, 6th rev. ed. (New York: Hastings House Publishers, 1976), 57.
3. Jack Johnson, *Jack Johnson: In the Ring and Out, The Classic Autobiography by the First Black Champion* (London: Proteus Publishing Ltd., 1977), Appendix IV.
4. Arthur R. Ashe, Jr., *A Hard Road to Glory: The African-American Athlete in Boxing* (New York: Amistad Press, 1993), 22.
5. Franklin M. Garrett, *Atlanta and Environs: A Chronicle of Its People and Events*, Volume II (New York: Lewis Historical Publishing Co., 1954), 504.
6. I am indebted to Robert P. Ingalls for much of my account of the 1910 cigar strike. His chapter titled, " 'The Cossacks of Tampa': The Citizens' Committee of 1910," on pp. 87–115 of his book, *Urban Vigilantes in the New South: Tampa, 1882–*

1936 (Gainesville: University Press of Florida, 1988), offers a thorough explanation of the strike and how it was broken. Except where otherwise noted, the quotations and factual information about the strike are taken from him.

7. Armando Mendez, *Ciudad de Cigars: West Tampa* (Cocoa, FL: Florida Historical Society, 1994), 115.

Chapter 2

Hard Times among the Flat Dwellers (1911–1913)

☙ With *El Provedo* put out of business by the 1910 *strike, Day and Helen, who are twenty-four years old, have no choice but to move to St. Louis, Missouri, and live with Day's parents. Charles Apte, an immigrant from Austria, gives the appearance of a stern man. "Sippie," as Day's mother is known, is more personable. She was born in Madison, Florida; her father, Robert Williams, immigrated from Germany around 1849, arriving in Florida a year later. Day's brother, Robert Williams Apte (Bill), also lives with the family in St. Louis. Both sons work with their father in his wholesale cigar distributorship. These are decidedly unhappy times for Helen.*

St. Louis—Saturday, February 25, 1911

My little friend in need, I have longed for you sorely these last weeks of bitter trial, but I'm never alone long enough to even think. You know what that means to me—that lack of privacy and quiet meditation, which was what I most dreaded in my life here. But once more I've found out that I can struggle and *win* if there is any big issue at stake. In the face of tragedy I can remain, rather become, brave, cheerful, comforting, and I thank God for it!

But I still have to fight the petty things. I almost go wild when I try to read and write and the folks talk to me the whole time. I weep bitter tears when I get up at 6:30 to eat breakfast with my husband alone and my mother-in-law joins us. I almost go into hysterics when at last I am alone with Day at night and we are just beginning sweet confidences, and Father calls in from the next room to find out if Mr. Jones bought any cigars. Oh, well, I came up here prepared for those things and ready to fight them. I

said I will not worry about those things. So long as business and our health
goes alright, that's all that matters, but it seems that no sooner do I fight
out one trouble than Fate joyously swats me one again and down I go. But
I come up smiling every time. After life has dealt me a few more poor
hands, I'll see more and more how little those things matter. I only pray
that I can always meet the large things as I've done here.

Instead of a well-established business here, Day found things in awful
shape, and how proud I am of my boy that even in his terrible disappointment he did not once upbraid or reproach his father. We both realize that
it wasn't deliberate deceit but lack of system and business knowledge that
made the statements sent Day so different from the real thing, but it puts
him in a terrible position. We haven't a penny in the world, and now things
are so tied up here that we don't know where the next dollar is coming
from. I can't realize it—I look around this room at my handsome silver
toilette articles, at my fur coat and the dainty hand-embroidered petticoat
that is hanging over a chair, and yet we are poverty-stricken. O, this gen-
teel poverty, this striving to keep up appearances to move in a circle that
we belong in—honest poverty would be far better. I say *honest* because it
is surely dishonest to live in a manner you can't afford. Of course, we are
very economical, but we *must* keep a servant, we *must* have a new suit,
we *must* entertain our friends, we *must* give engagement and wedding
presents—and there you are!

Of course, Day could get a lucrative position today. There is demand
for men like him. But he has to stick to his father, who has been ill ever
since we're here and hasn't left the house. With quiet strength, courage,
and ability he took hold of the situation, had the books straightened in
one day, consulted the lawyer, and put the thing up to the creditors, with
the result that an involuntary petition for bankruptcy will be entered against
his father, as there seems nothing else to be done.

We had great hopes for El Provedo; we thought, of course, that the
men for whom he had worked hard and faithfully for fifteen years would
help him out, but it seems we have lots to learn of men yet, for so far they
are the only ones to refuse a compromise and are pushing him hard, wanting Day to give his personal notes for the money Dad owes them. I had the
pleasure of meeting one of the big creditors, a man and a gentleman. We
had a long talk while Day was out of the office, and he said, "Your husband
is intelligent beyond his years, and I was never so well impressed with a
young man—truth, honor, and ability show in every act and word, and I

feel so sorry for him with this great responsibility. Of course, it isn't pleasant for me to lose my money, but no one would ever question your husband's honor, and the thing can't be helped now. I will go with him to his lawyer and do anything for his best interest, and he can consider me a friend rather than a man to whom money is due. And after this is all over, he can get all the goods and credit he wants from me."

O, I'm so proud of my boy. The most wonderful thing about him, and something I could well emulate, is the way he never shirks an unpleasant task—whether a duty is pleasant or unpleasant, he gives it the same careful and energetic attention, and he does it cheerfully. I must remember that, and so I must stop now, without a sign, and tell Mother what to order for dinner!

St. Louis—Thursday, March 23, 1911

The business isn't settled yet, and we've all had La Grippe. I took it a week after we got here but didn't stay in or give up, with the consequence that I got back to a terribly run-down condition, and my throat has been seriously inflamed. I kept up until our anniversary and then had to go to the doctor. Isn't it strange how those days always find me sick? He told me the same old story of nervous exhaustion and my high-strung system, etc., and gave the same old advice of never exerting myself, etc., which I never take. We were to celebrate by going to the theatre, but I felt too sick, so we went the next night (Saturday) instead. I lay down in the afternoon, and Nettie came with her work, and that night her mother and father came, and we talked until 11. All this week Day has been in bed, and of course it has been like taking care of a sick baby. He went to town today against the doctor's orders.

Struggle as I do, I can't help from feeling very blue sometimes and just a wee bit discouraged, but I guess it will all come right. I'm not the first girl who has had to live with her mother-in-law, but the little home of my own still seems the most desirable thing in the world, and O, it seems so far off! I go out very little. I much prefer to stay home and make few acquaintances, as I know the set we start to go with will always be our set, and God forbid I shall always have as my friends the people I've met. They are second-rate. There is no *class* in them. I'll have none of 'em! How different the people are here than in the South. I'll never get used to their manners and customs, and how much more refined we are than they.

It seems so strange that I can't aspire to the "best set" here. The people I've met speak of them with awe and are perfectly content to be out of that sphere, but it actually *galls me*. Why shouldn't I go with them—I who by birth, by right, by my social status belong with them? Suppose they are very rich. At home a millionaire belongs to our set, and he isn't held in higher esteem than we are. I've always gone with very wealthy girls, and I've never felt the difference. Our family is in everything, and it seemed only natural it should be so. Here I associate with people I don't speak to at home. I want the best or none at all, and I'll bide my time.

We had intended moving on some nice street among nice Jewish people, but of course we can't afford to now. So I have joined the modern order of Flat Dwellers—I, with my love of open spaces and the sunshine. We have to light the lights in the daytime, and when I lay in bed last week, I thought I should go wild if I could only see a little patch of blue sky. I sighed, and then the blank red walls of the house next door seemed to come up and hit me, to close me in. That is the view I have from my bedroom window.

They take me to walk in the grand residence district, they point out the magnificent homes, but I cannot even feign enthusiasm. The most gorgeous architectural pile leaves me cold, uninterested. The homes here have no individuality, no charm. Ah, the dear little Southern *homes*. The rambling red colonial house, with the roses climbing over the porch, the flowers in the yard—the yard, mind you, not the lawn, the half-drawn curtains, with the glimpse of firelight and moving figures within. It has the charm of a woman's half-revealed figure, of beauties half-concealed, half-revealed. It whets the imagination, it stirs the blood. Here—well, that elegant pile of stone around the corner, which must have cost five times as much, reminds me of nothing so much as a beautiful woman wrapped in her shroud—the beauty is there, but it is cold, unresponsive. It repels instead of attracts. I do not care to look longer. Her soul has flown; it is nothing but the shell.

St. Louis—Wednesday night, March 29, 1911

Call as I might, my henchmen won't come to my assistance tonight. I need them sorely, but I know they have not deserted me. I have overworked them and they are sleeping a little. My cold and my cough is worse, and I'm so weak I can scarcely sit up. Have changed doctors and like the new one, as he is frank, thorough, and sincere. He is coming tomorrow to closely examine my lungs. Good God, how frightened I am. For the first time in my life I am nervous about myself. With all my troubles I've never felt discouraged. I get angry and disgusted but never felt fear, but this time I'm about to give up, for my one horror has been lung trouble. Well, all I can do is pray and hope. In any event, the "building process must begin" again. How I hate myself when I get this way.

Mother is grand to me. My own mother couldn't do more, and I am ashamed of the petty anger I have felt and even shown when she does things I don't like. When I first came, I boiled over with rage—yes, and jealousy too, I guess—every time she advised Day or did things for him. But it only lasted a moment. I'd only have to come in a room alone and reason with myself. She is his mother, and she has the right to exercise her mother-love. But I want to do everything for him. Every little task is a pleasure.

There is also maternal love in me, and I must expend it. We have a little fox terrier called "Kiddo." I have never liked dogs before, but now I love them. I was never so flattered in my life as when Kiddo first came. He was a tiny puppy and a frightened one and would have nothing to do with anyone else. I can't describe my feelings as he rested his little head under my arm, and I can now see how people become so attached to animals that they mourn when the pet dies. I'd always thought it rather silly. I have also made another discovery: I've vowed I'd never spoil a child and didn't see how parents could when they knew it would harm the child, but I fear my theories won't last, as, when Kiddo cries for more milk when I *know* he's had enough, I simply can't refuse him. And when he tries to get on my lap, I put down everything I'm doing, because I *can't* resist the appeal in his eyes.

Another thing that pleases me immensely is the friendship I've formed with the children on this block. They all know me, and as soon as I come out they flock around me. I take many solitary walks, and almost always some child will speak to me even before I speak to them. The other day a little boy asked me to stop and watch him spin his top, and this morning, when I was coming from the doctor, I felt someone touch me and a little girl was patting my coat. I said hello, and she answered me as naturally as if we were lifelong friends. We chatted sociably for a few blocks, and when she left me, my heart was throbbing with pride. Positively I couldn't have felt more complimented and vain if the President of the U.S.A. had asked to be introduced.

Day is playing pinochle. For the last few nights he has been relegated to the lounge, as the doctor thinks it better not to sleep together, but we are in the same room, and often I can just *feel* his arms around me just as he says he is holding me. And last night, I closed my hand on his as tangibly as if he really were beside me, and just at that moment he said, "I am squeezing your hand."

Oh, well, I will stop and go to my lonely bed. The doctor said I was like a little tropical plant that had been transplanted to a northern clime and of course I will find it hard to thrive.

St. Louis—Wednesday, May 3, 1911

For the first time in my life, spring has failed to bring its message to me. I feel no thrill, no joy in the reawakening of the year. In fact, there has been no spring yet; only cold, dreary winter. The leaves are green on the trees, but there is no hint of sweet, growing things, no soft balmy breezes. Today is freezing cold, and not only is the weather bad, but it's been sickness, sickness, sickness. Day and I got one cold right after the other. I never knew where my lungs were before, but I bet I know now. The doctor says we will be alright as soon as the weather settles, but it is terrible. I have been tied to the house until I get fearfully nervous; and it seems to me Day actually gets thinner. The doctor says my chest is far better than Day's!

The funny part is that I'm growing stouter all the time. I have never seen a figure change and develop as mine has since I'm married, and in the last few months especially. I don't look a bit girlish any more, am really becoming matronly looking. I can't get into any of my clothes.

We haven't been out six nights since we've been here, and I've come to regard home as a prison. Sometimes my head hurts so that I can't read, and I wander around like a lost soul, from cell to cell, as the rooms are scarcely more than that. I'm no nearer liking St. Louis. In fact, at times I *hate* it. Father is home sick again. I fear he is worse than we can realize. I wish I had something nice to write—I'm tired of croaking.

St. Louis—Saturday, July 24, 1911

Just time to record my birthday: nothing very exciting but still a pleasant day. It came on a Friday, and that night we went up to the roof garden in my honor. Aunt Dordy is here with us. She gave me a dress and $10. I got

$7 besides and other nice things. Day selected a handbag for me himself. Poor little helpless boy—it was old enough for my grandmother. I returned it as unostentatiously as possible to avoid hurting him. I will leave next week for Atlanta and there will have more time to write. It seems I never get a chance to do anything I want to do up here. Mother and Dad are in Okawville [Illinois] and I am keeping house.

St. Louis—Monday, September 25, 1911

My road to Atlanta is always paved with good intentions, but that's all the further it gets—intentions! I'm always going to do so much there, write often in here, get my clothes, have nice long talks with Mother, etc., but the days fly by, and before I realize it, it is time to leave. My visit was cut to six weeks this time, as I had to come back to help the folks move. Day came down on Sunday, September 7, and we had a glorious week together. As usual everyone was grand to us, and it was never so hard to leave my family and friends. I had the best time I've ever had there, I believe, as I felt so well and all my dear ones looked so well and were O, so sweet to me. God bless them all. There is nothing like "your own."

Day said I could stay until October 1 if I wished, but I thought it my duty to come back here. Everyone told me I was a fool and wouldn't be thanked for it, and they were right, but that's neither here nor there. We have been working like mad to get things in order for the holidays, and of course I overdid myself. I am so nervous that everything grates on me. I work myself into an awful state over nothing, and I know I imagine injuries that never were meant. I've argued and reasoned with myself until I'm more upset than ever. The fact is, I was never meant to live in the house with anybody else. It's really a cruel thing that I must do it.

Mother and Aunt D. are downtown for the whole day, the girl is washing, it is pouring down, but I have relaxed, and am so happy for this day to myself. I won't have to talk when I don't feel like it, I won't have to listen to senseless arguments or foolish details all day; in fact, I can do as I like, which is a very unusual thing for me.

I have written very little about my mother-in-law. She is a good woman, one of the best I know, and there is nothing too much for her to do for those she loves. She is unselfish, she is kind, but she is the sort of woman who has certain fixed expressions, and you always know what she will say next. To give the best keynote to her character, the following may be cited:

"Everything must be put upon its proper place, there is a place for everything and everything must be in that place," and this one, "You have to get
up early in the morning if you want to fool *me*, no one yet has pulled the
wool over my eyes." This is the one though that I hear oftenest—"Nobody
in the world has the bad luck I do; nothing ever goes right for me." Ah,
well, this is a nice way for me to be writing right after New Year, and after
all my resolutions. I took no vows, but I said, "I *will* be patient and cheerful and brave." And with God's help I will be. I guess that sounds hypocritical, though, as I've said the same thing before and I failed miserably.

New Year's Day fell on Saturday, September 23. O, but I was homesick
and wanted to kiss my Mama. We went to temple night and morning and
heard the new rabbi, Dr. Lipkind. He is earnest and sincere, and though he
hasn't reached his zenith, he gives great promise and I enjoyed his ser-
mons. But I got *sick* there Saturday morning and came home and went to
bed. One more disappointment. My little baby, will you *never* come? Day
went out in the afternoon after I persuaded him, as I wanted to be quite
alone.

That night the folks went out, and we had one of our rare, dear eve-
nings alone together. We lay on the bed and he read aloud to me. O, my
sweetheart, my darling, darling husband, you are the whole world to me; I
love you, and that makes up for all my petty anger and disappointments. I
have the greatest gift of all, and I know I should be more worthy of it. He is
so thoughtful and considerate. He understands so well, and he is always
tender and sweet to me through all my tantrums. I vow I will not tell him
of my daily trials, but I always end by sobbing it all out on his breast, and
then I seem purged of all ill thinking. I feel at peace, and I relax. He says it
is all nervousness with me. O, I wonder if it is so, or do I only gladly seize
that as an excuse? Don't deceive yourself, Helen. In fact, you know you
never could. I want to be just, but this much is true: It is only when I am
overworked, overworried, or have had a nervous headache that I give way
to the state I've been in these last few days. It seems I am always on a
strain, and at those times something breaks, and O, it's hard to get a grip
on myself again.

St. Louis—Thursday, November 30, 1911

Thanksgiving Day! Alas, I don't feel very thankful now, as I've just been
through the worst disappointment of my life, and yet, I must be thankful

that for three short weeks I had the joy and the ecstasy of anticipated motherhood. That cannot be taken from me, but of course it made all the worse the bitter end, when I was suddenly taken ill—and it was all over! I had an attack of appendicitis at the same time and high fever, and of course suffered very much, but didn't realize I was threatened with blood poisoning. The doctor said it was caused from inflammation, but I don't believe it. I think I overdid myself as usual.

Sis and I were invited out every day, and I tried to be out all the time and attend to the house, at the same time doing, of course, all sorts of unnecessary things. When I found I was pregnant, I determined to think as little about myself as possible, to go out a great deal and take plenty of exercise, so I would be in a normal wholesome condition, but I reckoned without my miserable constitution, and I should know by this time that I can't do as other women. Now I will have to go through an operation. It seems I must always go through great travail to gain happiness. Well, it will be worth it in the end, I know, just as my life will. Day now repays me for my doubts and fears. I am also thankful Sister was with me. I can never repay her for her loving care of me.

As usual I don't expect to have a very exciting time on this holiday. Was busy all morning with dinner. This afternoon we will lie down and tonight go to a picture show. Sis is out for lunch with Joe Selig and will go to the theatre tonight. It's too bad I haven't been able to show her a good time. Of course am terribly rundown and weak and O so blue, as I did so desperately want my baby. I was taken sick November 6.

St. Louis—Monday, Christmas Day, 1911

Another festive day, and I am lying down and Day is playing pinochle. How many days we've spent this way, and it makes me so unhappy. Of course, we were going out this afternoon; we always are *going* to, and equally, of course, Day says if I have no objections, he'll play until I get ready. Immediately I lose all zest, as I wouldn't ask him to stop playing for a farm. As usual, also, I'm working myself into an awful rage—not that I care about going out. I've been on my feet all day and am tired, but it's the principle of it. O, well, the only rival I've had since I've arrived is cards, and I guess I ought to be very thankful for that. It seems that a woman must be grateful these days if her husband is true to her, and that, I suppose, I can be sure of. Wouldn't it be funny if I were like those women I've heard say, "I could stake my life on my husband's constancy to me," and everyone else begins to talk very fast about something else, as the latest scandal is that that same man is keeping an establishment for another woman? Ah well, another case of "what you don't know won't hurt you."

We also spent a pleasant Christmas Eve. Day and I were *going* to the theatre, but they began to talk business after supper, and when they do that, I subside. They have these talk-fests periodically, not that they ever amount to anything and all end the same. They all talk at one time, and no one listens to anything the other says. Father always gets insulted, Bill nearly tears the walls down, and Day gets so nervous I have to shut my mouth tight on all the things I'm dying to say, carry him off to bed, and soothe him to rest by telling him he's always right and I will always trust him and whatever he does is best—when in reality I don't think it is at all. Ralph came in in the middle of it, and the discussion stopped for a while. But it seems this time they really intend to do something.

The business isn't succeeding; in fact, they're losing money, and I'm crazy for Day to get out of it, but what would we do then? He has nothing to turn to. My heart sinks within me sometimes, though I try so hard to be brave. We are young, I know, but it's time we were up to getting settled in life. Just to be comfortable, that's all, just to feel free from strain and struggles, and to put a little aside—to make some *headway*, that is what I want. Of course Day can't desert his father. He needs us, but if Day only *made* more, I'd gladly give him half, do all I could to help support them, but I want my own home if it's only two rooms. I want my independence. And I want Day to be independent, and I want him to get some thanks for all he has done for them.

Tonight we expect to go out someplace. I guess we'll end by staying home, though. Mother will be home soon. I'm glad she was away, but I shall relinquish my household duties without a pang. They are almost more than I can bear. One man is enough to keep house for, but *four*—well, it's unspeakable. If I have something fried, they want to know why I didn't have it steamed, etc. I don't think a woman minds doing anything in the world for her husband, but when it comes to fathers-in-law, brothers-in-law, and cousins-in-law, I don't think she is quite so willing to sew buttons, to clean clothes, and to pick soiled linen up after them. Amy Linz just phoned. She's coming for supper. I hadn't prepared for any, as we had such a big Christmas dinner, but I'll have to get up and see about something. Of such is the kingdom of housekeeping!

It isn't cold today but dull and dark. I like a white Christmas, but a gray one is the limit.

St. Louis—Friday, January 12, 1912

We've had a regular blizzard all week. It began last Saturday when we were to go to the matinee with Moe and to the theatre at night to see *The Pink Lady*. I had to forgo the matinee, though, and went to bed with my friend, the hot water bag. Felt so bad that I wanted Day to dispose of my ticket, but he couldn't, so I got up and dressed, ate supper alone, and went down to meet them. Never was so cold in my life, and the show was boring. I hate musical comedy anyway. We've been almost snowbound, but though today is 8° below, we go to our sewing club at the Mands'.

Another New Year is here, with its promise and its fear. We don't feel very bright regarding business prospects, but we still have our assets, youth and health and love. Have been almost free from colds this winter, and I think the climate now agrees with us well. Spent New Year's Eve at the Elks Ball. Had a nice time, but not nearly as much fun as last year in Tampa. Got home at 5 A.M., almost frozen; had to ride all the way downtown and back in order to get a seat on the car. Such a rowdy crowd, too. Down South there would have been noise and laughter but none of the rudeness and coarseness. One man offered to knock Day's block off because I was cold and told Day to request him not to open all the transoms.

New Year's Day very tired, of course. Julia was away and I had to get dinner. Made eggnog in the afternoon, and Ruby Mands came out. Then Day and I lay down. Dr. F. came but didn't see him. Don't want to see him anymore after my $37 bill from him came! Think it too much, but of course it could have been worse.

That night Sis went to a dance and we retired early. They all laugh at us or get angry when we go to bed so early, but those few hours are all we have together, and we have so much to talk over. Last night we went to bed at 10 and talked until 1 A.M. To think of how Day's brilliant prospects have come to naught! We know wherein our fault lies, but we cannot change. Much against our will, we've been obliged to admit that it is the ruthless man who succeeds, he who rides roughshod over everyone else to attain his own ends, and we, neither of us, have learned yet to put ourselves first. We always think of our relations to others and to our ideals, and I guess that is a mistake in this age and day.

Well, after all, the greatest blessing we have is sweet, restful sleep. We talk and talk and philosophize, then we hold each other close and say, "Well, we are happy anyway, we love and understand each other, we are secure in our knowledge that we are upright and honest and self-sacrificing, and so goodnight, dear heart, and pleasant dreams." And in a minute we are asleep. We couldn't do that with uneasy conscience. I have found out how very easy it is for a businessman to be dishonest, how *very hard* it is to be strictly honest, and sometimes I think maybe Day is too quixotic, but I love him for it and would not have him swerve for the world. Plenty of opportunities have we had to serve our ends at someone else's expense, but we never even consider it. We do the right as it is given us to see right, and we may get our reward in heaven, but I fear we'll get it in the neck on this planet (not a very elegant expression, but it will suffice).

I'm not cynical or bitter, but it's just common sense talking; it's what I've seen with my own eyes. Take his uncle, for instance. He used Day, body and brain, for his own use, demanded and accepted his very life for ten years, and then when he'd finished with him, dropped him like a sponge he'd squeezed dry, and apparently goes on the even tenor of his ways, earning money and getting all the luxuries of life, who knows—though maybe at nights the spirit of Day's young life rises up before him and banishes sleep. And so I say, Thank God for His blessed gift to us, for our clear conscience and our clean hearts, and with His help we'll keep them always, even though we suffer more disappointments and struggles.

If only I hadn't lost my little baby. Somehow, that seems a bad omen to me; I feel fairly well, but sometimes I mourn as if I'd really lost a beloved child. My little dream child seemed so near to me. I know it would be wise for me to have the operation the doctor so strongly urges, but the truth is, I don't see how we can afford it, so I fool Day and fool the doctor and try to fool myself.

St. Louis—Sunday, September 22, 1912

I look back at my last entry and smile when I see I didn't fool Day and I *didn't* fool the doctor, although I almost succeeded in fooling myself. How much I have left unrecorded. On March 13 I went to the hospital for my operation and was operated on the next day. Thank God nothing else was found wrong, much to the doctor's surprise. It is the same old story of no organic disease but a general weakness, or rather nervous condition of the organs, and that is what caused my trouble last fall. I suffered the tortures of Hell, which sounds exaggerated but isn't, but had no complications and got on fine. Sister was so grand to me, and my darling, of course.

And we are still paying doctor bills. I feel sometimes it was too much of a luxury to indulge in an operation, though the doctor assures me I'd be dead by now if I hadn't, as of course it was one of those "just in time cases." It always is—gee, how bitter I'm getting. I can see myself change, and it isn't a good change, either. It is my greatest wish to keep young in heart, yet how can I when bitter thoughts *will* come? I try hard, and yet I only conquer once to fall again. My ambitions, my dreams, my aspirations; where are they? My beautiful house on the hill, my husband's wealth and position and power, do I still dream of these? Alas, no. All I ask and pray and *covet* in this world now is a little place, be it only one room, which I can call my own, where I can be mistress, where I can have and *make* a home. Wealth? No, only a certain sum, be it ever so small, but *certain*, coming in every month, just enough to live on, to support my child on, my baby! That is one ambition that has not died. I aspire to you, my little one, more passionately, more desperately than ever, yet you are still so far away. O, I do try not to get despondent and bitter, but when I think of some women who would sell their souls for diamonds who accept a child as a punishment, who long for social power, I wonder why I have been denied just a normal, natural woman's lot, just a little home, be it ever so humble, just a little baby. God is so prodigal with His gift of human life. Will He deny me—I, who have the mother-heart and the mother-knowledge even if I haven't the mother-body?

I went to Atlanta in June, and I had as usual such a grand visit with my dear ones. Mama is more wonderful than ever, and how I love them all. I never hated so to leave them, and I came back to St. Louis August 25 with a heavy heart, though I'd never been away from Day so long before. I was quite frightened at my emotions on coming back to my husband: no ecstasy or joy was there, only a great feeling of fear as to how I was to adjust myself again to my life here, a feeling almost of repulsion. I said, "I just can't stand it. O how can I live this way? Why do I have to?" And then common sense came to my aid as usual, and I said, "You are homesick. You are spoiled by your life this summer. You miss your friends and your family, and it will take longer to adjust yourself this time, as you've been away so long. But have patience and courage, give yourself up to your husband's love and let it melt the thin coating of ice around your heart," and he did melt it, God bless him, and I see once more that in his arms is my only real rest and refuge.

St. Louis—Monday, December 16, 1912

A rainy night and somehow, little book, my thoughts turn to you on such an eve as this. Day is away. He is working, as the Christmas rush is great this year. Business is good, he says.

And now comes the most wonderful, the *most* divinest news I've ever put on paper. At last, at last, my wish, my dream, my prayer is about to come true. *About* I say, as I must not hope too much, the doctor says. He is almost sure it is so, but says I am in a very weak condition and all the organs are inflamed. In fact, a miscarriage is threatened, and I'm to remain in bed indefinitely. I can go to my meals, and my friends all come. It is very disgusting, but I have my dreams, my beautiful dreams. God grant that you come to me, my little baby. I went to bed the first week in December. I am happy, but I am fearful. It seems too good that this miracle should happen to me. Alas, I've gotten to be a hopeless sort of person. I just *can't* make my life run in the right grooves, but if this divine thing happens to me, it will mean my redemption.

St. Louis—Monday, January 6, 1913

I've been through torture of mind and body again this past week. I had a desperately narrow escape December 28, but the danger is past for the present, though the doctor doesn't encourage me much, as he says the same trouble can start up at any time. The miserable old story of a weakened and nervous condition, all the harder because there is nothing specific to treat. I got a trained nurse last Saturday and kept her until Tuesday. She was so sweet and jolly, and I was sorry to see her leave, except for the expense. Well, the hope of near motherhood is still with me, though it's precarious and full of suffering as all my pathways seem to be.

And now the question arises: Am I fit to be a mother? Can this poor body give a healthy child to the world, or care for it properly? I can't have trained nurses and several servants as all my friends do. I must tend my little one myself. Am I fit? O, God help—God pity me as a poor fool who prays for a gift and then is afraid of it, but I swear it isn't for myself I fear. My poor life, I'd do better to give it that way than another, but to bring a poor little suffering soul into the world, O God, let me never know the joy of motherhood, rather than that.

Such a night—sleet once and all the menfolks out. They had to stay downtown on business, and O, the day is long when my dear doesn't come home by 7. The hours seem interminable even by then. I can sit up tomorrow. No telling when I can go out. Christmas Day I went out for the first time, as the doctor said I could try walking. Day and I went to the picture show, as usual as happy as two kids because, mirabile dictu, we were allowed to go alone. Christmas Eve, to bed early. New Year's Eve and Day, I lay on a bed of pain, praying God he'd spare my baby to me, and he did.

St. Louis—Monday, March 10, 1913

My fourth anniversary, and as every previous one, I am ill. This time it is a bad cold, which, added to my weak condition, makes me miserable, of course, and the doctor is afraid the cough will prove harmful. It is a rainy, dismal day. I would have gone to a charity bridge if it had been clear, but it's just as well, I guess, that I spend a quiet day at home. I am alone too, which I always welcome. I am left to myself so little, and that is why I write so seldom in here. Mother always stands over me—*stalks*, if I try to write and read. She thinks it very miserable of me to read when she is in the house.

We will celebrate our anniversary by retiring early. Even if I were well, I don't suppose we'd go anyplace. Day sent me a box of candy and a bottle of perfume. He always sends me perfume, dear boy, and I have about four untouched bottles now. Bless his heart, he does his best. He swears that he loves me a thousand times more today than he did four years ago.

Mama was with me five weeks. O, how glorious it was to have her dear, unselfish care and devotion. I was in bed nearly the whole time, but was able to go about a little before she left. I was very ill again the first few days she came, and the doctor decided to examine me under chloroform, to find out the real trouble. What he found I don't know, as he is the most noncommittal man I ever saw. There was a lump on my left side, which worried us all, but he says it's nothing much and gives us no satisfaction.

They say all women in my condition indulge in morbid thoughts and are sure they will die during their ordeal, but I must be an exception, as I have no fear; only sometimes, in the dead of night, I wake in a cold perspiration, full of unformed fears, so it must worry me subconsciously. I get very close to my loved one and say God's will be done, and then go back to sleep, happy in the knowledge that it is my privilege to go down into the valley of the shadow, to give another little life to the world, to fulfill my mission even if I should have to give my own poor life in exchange.

Childbirth: A Matter of Life and Death—and Duty

Almost every couple struggles with it at one time or another: ambivalence about whether to have children. They may long for a baby, but they know it will unalterably limit the freedom of their childless lives. They may want to teach, to nurture, to love, but they are not sure that they will succeed as parents. And when a child is on the way, whether it is by design or otherwise, they know that childbirth brings its own set of concerns—discomfort, pain, fears about the health of the baby. In this regard, bearing children was not so different in Helen's day. What was different was the nature of childbirth—it was much more dangerous—and the quality and quantity of pressure on young women to have children. It was not just the potential grandparents who were nagging; the whole society was demanding that women have babies.

Take first the danger. In 1915, the first year for which statistics are available, there were more than 600 puerperal deaths—that is, maternal deaths related to childbirth—for every 100,000 live births in the United States. Today, fewer than seven women die for every 100,000 live births in this country. It is hard to imagine how high that 600 figure is, because in the 1990s there is *no* cause of death for young American women of childbearing age that comes close to matching it. Today a young American woman is twice as likely to die in an automobile accident as she is to die in childbirth.[1] "Today," says Hani Atrash of the Centers for Disease Control in Atlanta, "many obstetricians spend a lifetime delivering babies and never see a woman die in childbirth."[2] The figure for maternal deaths in Helen's day* was about the same as the figure for deaths from cardiovascular disease for men over sixty years old today.[3] Just as we all know men who died of cardiovascular disease late in life, so did Helen know women who died in childbirth. "It would be impossible for her *not* to have known someone who died of it," says Everett Lee, a demographer at the University of Georgia.

---

*The actual maternal death rate for childbirth was even higher than 600 per 100,000 women because the figure as given is based on 100,000 live births, not on 100,000 women. Women had, on average, several live births in their lifetimes, so their lifetime risk of death from childbirth would be considerably greater than 600 out of 100,000.

For Helen and her contemporaries, then, the danger of childbirth was not just discomfort or pain. Their very lives were at stake. This is why the pregnant Helen wakes up "in a cold perspiration" and why, when her good friend Viola has her first baby, Helen doesn't say she is thrilled about the baby. She says she is thrilled that Viola is safe.

Maternal Deaths in Childbirth, U.S., 1915–1995.

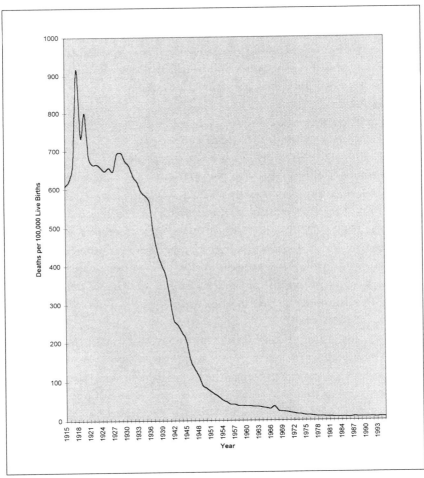

Sources: U.S. Centers for Disease Control, including *Vital Statistics of the United States, 1989*, vol. 2, "Mortality, Part A" (Washington, DC: U.S. Department of Health and Human Services, 1993); and, for 1989–1995, annual *Advanced Reports of Final Mortality Statistics* (Hyattsville, MD: National Center for Health Statistics). (The peak in deaths around 1918 was due to the devastating influenza epidemic.)

The primary causes of puerperal death have always been toxemia (blood poisoning), hemorrhage, and infection. In the nineteenth century virtually all babies were delivered by midwives at home. Starting in the 1920s, pregnant women increasingly turned to physicians for care, and they increasingly chose to give birth to their children in hospitals. Although the medical/hospital regimen was not always soul-satisfying for women—indeed, at times it was downright traumatic[4]—better medical care for pregnant women led directly to the dramatic fall in maternal deaths. Competent care by doctors meant early detection of toxemia, vastly improving the prognosis. Hospitalization— plus the introduction of efficient blood banks—greatly reduced deaths from hemorrhage, as well as providing generally more sterile conditions than those found at home. And the introduction of antibiotics after World War II virtu- ally conquered puerperal infection, allowing death rates to plunge to today's minuscule levels.[*]

If American women were more likely to die from childbirth in the first part of the twentieth century, they also were more likely to have larger fami- lies. In fact, the birth rate in 1909 was twice what it was in 1995—30 per 1,000 people in 1909, and less than 15 in 1995.[5] (The fertility rate, based on births per 1,000 women aged 15–44, shows a similar decline, from 126.6 in 1909 to 65.6 in 1995.) There were many reasons for this, of course, not the least of which was the unreliability and unavailability of contraceptives. They were illegal in many states. Despite those difficulties, however, women like Helen were beginning to limit their families. By 1900 native-born white women av- eraged 3.56 children, half the birth rate a century earlier. But immigrant and black women continued to have more babies, with foreign-born white women averaging 4.54 children.[6]

There emerged a term for the phenomenon: "race suicide." With "Ameri- can" women shirking their duty, wrote obstetrician George B. H. Swayze in 1909, the country was set to be overrun by "the unrestricted progeny of the underfed ignorant toilers, the underrated 'mudsill' grade of population, the encroaching offspring of the prolific Negro, of the stoic foreign representa- tives of recent immigration more and more profusely encumbering our shores."[7]

---

[*]Tragically, throughout sub-Saharan Africa—and in some other parts of the developing world where health care is poor or nonexistent—maternal death rates are still as high as they were in the United States in the early twentieth century.

Even President Theodore Roosevelt took up the cause. "When home ties are loosened; when men and women cease to regard a worthy family life . . . as the life best worth living," he warned in a 1903 message to Congress, "then evil days for the commonwealth are at hand. There are regions in our own land, and classes of our population, where the birth rate has sunk below the death rate. Surely it should need no demonstration to show that willful sterility is, from the standpoint of the nation, from the standpoint of the human race, the one sin for which the penalty is national death, race death; a sin for which there is no atonement. . . . No man, no woman, can shirk the primary duties of life, whether for love of ease and pleasure, or for any other cause, and retain his or her self-respect."[8]

Of course, as American Studies Professor Elaine Tyler May wrote in her book about childlessness in America, "Those who were concerned about the low birthrate offered little tangible help to struggling families."[9] But they did conduct a marvelous public relations campaign under the auspices of what they called the eugenics movement. They offered registries; they sponsored contests. And although their ultimate success is debatable—the birth rate continued to decline; many women continued not to marry—there is no doubt that their campaign convinced the nation that motherhood really was a duty. There was little debate over the principle. Childlessness led to guilt. Even feminists like Charlotte Perkins Gilman called motherhood a woman's "patriotic duty"[10]—if only because, as May put it, motherhood "conferred upon women the moral superiority that was the foundation of their public activism."[11]

So was Charlotte Perkins Gilman speaking to a young, Southern, Jewish woman like Helen? Perhaps. But what about Theodore Roosevelt and other leaders of the eugenics movement? Did they have women like Helen in mind when they issued their exhortations to be fruitful and multiply? Perhaps not. Nevertheless, Helen certainly *thought* they did. She heard their message and took it to heart. She felt it was her duty to have a child; it was, she wrote, "the greatest thing in life." But mixed with that sense of duty is her fear, her concern, and her doubt. She knew the dangers, and her ambivalence is palpable.

"What a problem that conjugal one is," Helen writes eight months into her marriage. "A woman *can't* have a baby every year, but it is surely wrong, physically and morally, to prevent it, so what's to be done?" The answer for Helen was to do her duty, have the baby, and suppress the fear—to risk her life.

St. Louis—Monday, March 10, 1913 (continued)

I've thought often what great world events I've neglected to record. The *Titanic* disaster last spring, which shocked and thrilled the universe—the loss of life was appalling, but how beautiful were the acts of self-sacrifice, the women and children first and the men standing bravely, calmly, even gaily back and going down to their watery grave with the ship's band still playing. It is said the men in the steerage fought like animals. It was men like Major Butt* and John Jacob Astor† who helped the women into the lifeboats and waved them a gay good-bye. There is food for thought in that. All had the same instincts. Beyond a doubt they all wanted life, but the first primitive instinct of self-preservation was conquered by these men of culture. Their life of ease may have softened their muscles, but "noblesse oblige"! And then to the story of Isidor Straus‡ and his wife, going down together locked in each other's arms. "We have been too long together to be separated now," said this aged daughter of Israel, as she stepped back from the lifeboat into which they tried to force her. So might Rebecca or Rachel have spoken—no heroics, but with the quiet dignity of her averent race, and so they faced Jehovah together. There was gloom and mourning through all the land, but pride, too, and renewed faith in human nature. Three babies have been born since then to women whose husbands went down. One woman married again only a few months after the disaster, and one, I just read, is engaged to a man who was one of the few to escape with his womenfolk.

Nor have I said anything about the history made, the new party, in American politics—the "Bull Moose" party, which started to be a joke but isn't now, as if anything can be a joke with Roosevelt at the head. And for the first time in years the Democrats have come into their own. Wilson was sworn in last week, and everyone expects great things of him.

Jewish in the South: "In Dixie Land I'll Take My Stand"

For German Jews like Helen, whose families had immigrated to America in the midnineteenth century or before, being a Southern Jew was as natural as the rust-red color of Georgia clay. In many respects it was more than natural; it

---

*Major Archibald Willingham Butt was a top military aide to President William Howard Taft and to his predecessor, Theodore Roosevelt.
†John Jacob Astor IV, a prominent millionaire.
‡Owner of R. H. Macy's department store.

was downright good. In spite of the South's Protestant fundamentalist tradition and its reputation of intolerance, Jews found that they could take root in the Southern landscape. Antebellum Southern Jews, although few in number, had paved the way for their Northern and immigrant coreligionists in the postwar period. There had been some anti-Jewish feeling during the Civil War, but Southerners knew Jews—or at least knew of Jews—and for the most part their experience had been good. Jews had proved their loyalty during the South's most trying time. Many had served in the Confederate Army and had fought for The Cause. Moreover, they were from the same stock as their Gentile neighbors—they were white—and they had a history of taking care of their own. They were, in short, good neighbors who had something to contribute to their communities and their country.

Southern leaders after the Civil War wanted their "New South" to have a postagrarian economy, one that would rely on commerce and trade and even manufacturing instead of the slavery-dependent plantation life that had been the South's antebellum mainstay. It was a bold idea, but it was one for which native Southerners did not possess all the skills or the resources to implement. They needed educated people who knew banking and finance. They needed people who knew business and who had money to invest. They needed these Northern and immigrant Jews. Ironically, though, when they came, their arrival fed a traditional stereotype. "Where there are no Jews there is no money to be made," the *Richmond Whig* proclaimed in 1866. "Where there are no rice-fields there are no rice-birds; where there is no wild celery there are no canvas back ducks; where there is no trade there are no Jews."[12]

Enter Atlanta—then as now a boom town. When General William Tecumseh Sherman torched the city in 1865, only about 15,000 people lived there. By 1880 the population had grown to more than 37,000, and by 1900 it was over 90,000 and still climbing quickly. The number of Jews in the city grew along with the rest of the population. Although the percentage of the Jewish population remained relatively stable—a little under 2 percent in 1870; a little over 2 percent in 1900—in raw numbers that meant growth from merely 300 or 400 Jews in 1870 to 2,000 in 1900.[13] Whatever the numbers, as Atlanta's population burgeoned, its Jews thrived along with everyone else. There were opportunities in Atlanta, money to be made. Among its settlers were Sigmond, Jonas, and Jacob Selig, who arrived from Germany in the 1870s and soon built a bonnet factory. (Their young sister, Alice, who would become Helen's mother, arrived shortly after them.) It did not take the brothers long to become successful and prominent Atlanta citizens. By 1880 their factory employed about one hundred workers, sometimes more, and was producing $50,000 worth of goods.[14]

By the turn of the century the Seligs had settled near the new state capitol, an area that boasted wide tree-lined streets and relatively large Victorian homes. Most of Atlanta's German Jews lived in that neighborhood, although they were a minority there; this section of the city was prime real estate for upper-middle-class Gentiles, too. Socially, the situation was similar. Kept out of the most exclusive social clubs in the city, Atlanta's economically successful Jews did not despair. They formed the Standard Club as a place to gather and socialize among themselves, while also joining nonexclusive organizations such as the Elks and the Freemasons in large numbers.

In a scene that was repeated throughout the South, a Jewish subculture developed in Atlanta, one that felt very much a part of the wider, non-Jewish community. Jews built factories that employed many workers. They opened stores, from small shops to large department stores, which supplied the city with dry goods and groceries. They were elected to public office and held positions of civic leadership.* In other words, Jews socialized among themselves but blended well into the fabric of their city's life. And religion was no exception. Atlanta's first synagogue, the Hebrew Benevolent Congregation, was formed in 1867, the outgrowth of the Hebrew Benevolent Society, which had been established in 1860 to secure a burial ground for Atlanta's Jews. The vast majority of the synagogue's membership was German- or American-born, but this did not mean that the members were of a single mind theologically. Although many of them, or their parents, had brought "reform" ideas with them from Germany, others heard a more orthodox calling, and for nearly three decades the congregation vacillated between orthodoxy and "reform."

Stability came to The Temple, as it came to be known, on September 6, 1895, in the form of David Marx, an American-born twenty-three-year-old recent graduate of Hebrew Union College, Reform Judaism's rabbinical school. Elected to the pulpit by the narrowest of votes—37 to 34—and facing a congregation that had chewed up and spit out not one, not two, but six rabbis in the past thirty years, Dr. Marx (the honorific he preferred to "rabbi") nonetheless pushed his flock steadfastly toward Reform. "The way could not have been easy for the new rabbi," Janice Rothschild Blumberg, the granddaughter of a nineteenth-century Temple rabbi and the widow of Dr. Marx's successor, wrote in a centennial history of the synagogue. "Although the 'reformers' within

*Helen's father was a founder of the public schools in Hawkinsville, Georgia.

the congregation had won the war, they left it to their new general to win the peace, to put into effect the decisions for which they had fought, and to establish harmony with those whose opinions had been defeated. David Marx did this, going about it from the beginning with the same firm, decisive steps and determination which dominated his personality in later years."[15]

In other words, Dr. Marx was a man with a mission: Reform Judaism, which had begun in Germany but was finding its home in America. With its roots in the Enlightenment, Reform Judaism championed the use of reason, and it used reason to scrutinize traditional Jewish life and ritual. By the time David Marx assumed the pulpit at The Temple, the theology and beliefs of what became known as Classical Reform Judaism were coalescing. "They took the Bible very seriously," says Daniel Zemel, a Reform rabbi in Washington, DC. "They made a distinction between Biblical principles and rabbinic accretions. The latter were not important. It was like an onion: You could peel away and discard the outer layers to preserve the essence."[16] Reform Jews like Helen found Judaism's essence in the ethical laws of the Ten Commandments, loving one's neighbor as oneself, and monotheism. The rest—from the use of Hebrew to the wearing of yarmulkes—was commentary, and unimportant commentary at that. These concepts were what Dr. Marx brought to Atlanta, and it was not long after his arrival that the English-language *Union Prayer-Book* was adopted for worship, men no longer wore hats during services, Bar Mitzvah was eliminated, and the rabbi stopped dressing in what had been the traditional rabbinical garb.

It is easy to see why Classical Reform caught on in the United States. The theology conforms with the nation's loftiest principles of liberty, and with the American belief that people are in control of their own destiny. "It's what America is about," says Rabbi Zemel. Classical Reform stressed *being* American and minimizing differences with the wider society. Judaism was a religion, Dr. Marx taught—a great religion, to be sure, but just one religion among many others. Its followers, therefore, were Americans who happened to be Jews, just as their neighbors were Americans who happened to be Christians. As such, Jews could and should participate in the society at large. Their religion was their own private affair.

This was an appealing message to Atlanta's German Jewish community. These Jews considered themselves citizens in every sense of the word, and to the best of their ability they conducted themselves accordingly. Moreover, they were willing to bend religious traditions—religious laws—to participate in Southern life. If the wider society demanded that commerce be conducted on Saturday, the Jewish Sabbath, then Jewish-owned stores would remain open and services would be held on Friday nights and not solely on Saturday mornings (at one point, there were even Temple services on Sunday). Dietary restrictions were abandoned, and children attended public schools. As Louis Schmier of Valdosta State University in Georgia puts it, these Jews "eliminated the language of differentiation." After all, he says, "it's not the Gentile majority that has to change and adapt; it's the incoming minority."[17]

In the late nineteenth and early twentieth centuries, however, the "language of differentiation" changed. The change came not from The Temple's German Jews but from the wave of Eastern European Jewish immigrants who started coming to America in the 1880s. Before long, they had made their way South. In 1870 only 3 percent of Atlanta's Jews were Russian-born; by 1896 the number was nearly one-third,[18] and four years later the Russian-born Jewish population of Atlanta had nearly doubled.[19] The arrival of the Eastern Europeans "produced a profound reaction on the part of the established Jewish community," author Steven Hertzberg explained in his 1978 history of Atlanta's Jews, *Strangers within the Gate City*. "The very foreignness of the newcomers, their Yiddish language, Orthodox religion, Old World ways and physical appearance threatened to give the word 'Jew' a connotation that the older settlers had struggled for decades to outgrow."[20] Atlanta's Jews divided into the established "Germans"—the Reform Jews who belonged to The Temple—and the immigrant "Russians." The Germans distanced themselves from the Russians as much as they could. They excluded them from their social clubs and attended a different synagogue. But to the Gentile majority the distinction was not always so clear.

The established German Jews were ambivalent toward the new Russian immigrants. On the one hand, the Germans looked down on the Russians, with their strange ways, foreign culture, and more Orthodox beliefs in Judaism. On the other hand, they felt a certain kinship—albeit a distant one—that presented them with obligations that they felt compelled to fulfill. So Helen, as a young woman of twenty-two, signed on to teach them English. On October 1, 1908, she wrote to Day about her experience:

> I went to the Boys Night School Tuesday night and was intensely interested. I bet I learned more than my pupils. I had two in my class, one from Jerusalem, one from Russia; the former must have been 25 years old, and the other was 20. Both are brilliant, and we

were soon talking politics, religion, etc. They are the most advanced pupils in the school, as most of them have just gotten here and can't speak a word of English. My two boys speak so I can understand, with the aid of signs, etc., but I surely had to laugh at their grammar.

They are very ambitious and enthusiastic, and all the young men like America, but the old ones seem despondent. It is pitiful to watch them. They are unanimous in saying that there isn't as much "liberty" here as they expected. For instance, they say they can't even sing on the street or sit down on the curb without a policeman telling them to "move on." That, they say, isn't "liberty," and *liberty* is their watchword and lode star. They begged me to come every Tuesday and Thursday, and I shall try to go when I can. I had no idea I could teach, but was surprised to see how easily I adapted myself to it. Such work as that I love, and I really think I'd make a good settlement worker, as one can always do well the work one's heart is in. Still, I'm afraid I couldn't hold out, as I simply couldn't stand to see suffering. Positively when I see one in pain, physical or otherwise, I feel it keenly myself, and I don't think I'd ever get hardened to it. It's a great work, though, helping and encouraging these poor people, and I wish I had taken it up sooner. Doesn't it seem a shame how "we shut ourselves up in our own little citadels of well being, while the storms of life rage around our refuge"?

Jews still made up only a small percentage of Atlanta's population, but they played a disproportionate role in the city's economy. Factories like the Selig brothers' bonnet company helped fuel Atlanta's continuing boom. In the countryside, plantation life had given way to sharecropping, which in Georgia clay was a meager existence at best. Rural Georgians made their way to the cities to work in the new factories, but they soon discovered that urban life had its own hardships. Labor laws were virtually nonexistent, and child labor was rife. Wages were barely subsistence for those fortunate enough to obtain jobs. The average worker in 1902 took home only $300 per year, and, although that figure had risen to $464 by 1912, the cost of living had kept pace; there had been no gain in real wages.[21] In 1914, when Helen and Day moved back to Atlanta with their baby daughter, they found a city that was continuing to grow exponentially.* It had a large number of uneducated, rural-born,

---

*In 1910 there were 155,000 people in Atlanta; by 1920 there would be more than 200,000.

fundamentalist Protestants; a German Jewish neighborhood much like the one that Helen had left five years earlier; and a "Russian" population growing faster than the "Germans," although Helen's "crowd," as she called it, was still intact and still prosperous.

Between 1913 and 1915, two events conspired to shake Atlanta, and especially the city's Jews, to the core. First was the strike at the Fulton Bag and Cotton Mills. Founded in 1889 by Jacob Elsas, a German Jewish immigrant, the company had become Atlanta's largest textile factory. In 1913 several hundred workers went on strike. They soon returned to work, but in the meantime they had joined a union. Elsas responded by firing union members and hiring undercover "operatives" to spy on employees. Jacob's son Oscar took over the company in 1914, and in May of that year there was another larger strike. One union organizer called it "the first big strike of organized workers in the cotton mills of the South." That was not exactly true—there had been others—but the strike did mark the first time that the United Textile Workers Union and the American Federation of Labor had poured significant resources into a Southern strike.[22] And it brought to light what was really happening in Atlanta's factories.

As the strike was exposing the horrid working conditions of the Jewish-owned Fulton Bag and Cotton Mills, a second event in Atlanta brought anti-Semitism to the fore. On April 29, 1913, Leo Frank, a manager at the National Pencil Company, was arrested for the murder of fourteen-year-old Mary Phagan, a worker at the factory. Frank was born in Paris, Texas, reared in Brooklyn, New York, and educated at Cornell University. He moved to Atlanta to work for his uncle at the pencil factory, and he quickly moved up in Atlanta Jewish social circles. He became president of the local chapter of B'nai B'rith, and in 1910 he married Lucille Selig, Helen's first cousin.

Much has been written about the Leo Frank case. Suffice it to say here that if Frank's arrest stunned Atlanta's Jews, his trial did so doubly. Press coverage was widespread. Some newspapers were on Frank's side, and some covered the story with commendable objectivity. But there was demagoguery, too, especially from politically ambitious Tom Watson, whose newspaper, *The Jefferson*, regularly called Frank a "jewpervert," among other slurs.* Atlanta's impoverished, oppressed workers heard the demagogue, and he inflamed their passions. Crowds shouted outside the courthouse. At least one juror later

---

*Watson's ambitions paid off in 1920 when he was elected to the U.S. Senate.

confessed that he feared an acquittal would cost him his life.[23] Frank was convicted and sentenced to death.[*]

From death row, Frank appealed for clemency to Governor John M. Slaton. It was the end of the governor's term, and he could have ignored the case and handed it over to his successor. But he did not. He took it seriously, studying the entire trial transcript and conducting his own interviews. He concluded that Frank was innocent. On June 21, 1915, just before Frank's scheduled execution—and days before Slaton was set to leave office—he commuted Frank's sentence. The governor told his friends a full pardon was likely after the public learned the facts, and he had the prisoner transferred to the state prison in Milledgeville. "Feeling as I do about this case," Slaton said, "I would be a murderer if I allowed that man to hang."[24] It was a fateful decision. It ruined Slaton's political career. It also briefly put his life in danger. Thousands of people stormed the governor's mansion in protest. The mob was so vicious that the governor had to call for the National Guard for protection. Slaton escaped harm, but eight weeks later twenty-five men abducted Frank from his prison cell and lynched him. Their identities were well known, but no one was ever convicted of the crime.[25]

The Fulton Mills strike and, more important, the Leo Frank case stunned not only Atlanta's Jews but also Jews throughout the South. No matter how much they believed that they had integrated into the wider community, evil was lurking below the surface. A local newspaper quoted a woman after Frank's arrest as saying that even though this was the first time a Jew had been charged with a serious crime, everyone was willing to believe the worst.[26] But the established German Jews of Atlanta and elsewhere in the South did not protest or shout their concerns. Instead, they tried even harder to assimilate, to be just like their neighbors. And they tried even harder to be inconspicuous.

It is not so puzzling, therefore, that Helen scarcely mentioned Leo Frank even though he was a first cousin by marriage. Her only reference was on the eighth anniversary of his death; the memory prompted her to pick up the diary again after a four-year hiatus. Of course, one reason that she did not write about the events at the time they occurred was that she did not write about *anything* then; with her new baby, as she put it, she was "too busy *living* life to write about it." But there was also a deeper reason. Southern Jews like Helen knew about Leo Frank and thought about him, but they kept quiet. The

---

[*]The most damaging testimony against Frank came from Jim Conley, a black janitor at the pencil factory who later would be identified as the actual murderer. Leo Frank was pardoned posthumously in 1985.

entire incident was too disturbing because it went against their unending desire to be like their neighbors. And by allowing themselves to think of the
Frank case as an anomaly, which in fact it was, they were able, in their own
minds at least, to continue as part of the Southern society in which they lived
and prospered.

Readers of this diary may find it curious that so little in it is identifiably
"Jewish." In some ways, of course, *everything* in it is Jewish. Judaism was behind Helen's clearly liberal social conscience. Her religion not only guided her
views of life and death but also shaped her views of duty and responsibility.
She talks about Judaism in her first diary entry, writing that she would light
candles every Friday night. She started a Sunday School class in Tampa in 1910.
She was active in Jewish women's organizations throughout her life, and Day
was a leader of the Reform synagogue in every city in which they lived. Helen
was proud to be Jewish. "How some Jews can be ashamed of being Jews has
always seemed to me inexplicable," she wrote. "In me burns the ancient pride
of race."

On the other hand, Helen, like so many other Southern Jews of her time—
like so many American Jews today—did not think of herself primarily as a Jew.
She saw herself as a Southern American who happened to be Jewish, decidedly *not* as a Jew who was merely living in the South. She loved the South. She
loved the easy, friendly pace of life, the culture, the chivalry, the Florida
beaches, the cool, green southern Appalachian mountains, the sweet smell of
orange blossoms, the acceptance she felt from the wider community. When
she saw the Stars and Stripes or heard "Dixie," her heart swelled with pride.
Judaism was her moral compass. America was her country and her native land.
The South was the place of her heart. Helen was not less of a Jew for being a
Southerner, nor was she less of a Southerner for being a Jew. Both were part
of her core being. Another Southern Jew, Joe Isenberg, a former state repre-
sentative in Georgia, once summed it up this way: "There's a lot of Jew in this-
here Southerner, and a lot of Southerner in this-here Jew. And there's no
separatin' the two."[27]

NOTES

1. Telephone interview with Everett Lee, August 1997.
2. Telephone interview, August 1997.
3. Interview with Lee.
4. See Judith Walzer Leavitt, *Brought to Bed: Child-Bearing in America, 1750–1950*
   (New York: Oxford University Press, 1986).

5. Figures provided by the National Center for Health Statistics, the Centers for Disease Control and Prevention, Public Health Service, and the U.S. Department of Health and Human Services.

6. Leavitt, *Brought to Bed*, 19–20.

7. George B. H. Swayze, M.D., "Reluctant Pregnancy," *Medical Times* (November 1909): 321. Quoted in Elaine Tyler May, *Barren in the Promised Land: Childless Americans and the Pursuit of Happiness* (New York: Basic Books, 1995), 72.

8. President Theodore Roosevelt, "Sixth Annual Message to Congress," December 3, 1903. Quoted in May, *Barren in the Promised Land*, 61.

9. May, *Barren in the Promised Land*, 64.

10. Ibid., 70.

11. Ibid., 69.

12. Quoted in Steven Hertzberg, *Strangers within the Gate City: The Jews of Atlanta, 1845–1915* (Philadelphia: Jewish Publication Society of America, 1978), 34.

13. Ibid., 232.

14. Ibid., 40.

15. Janice Rothschild Blumberg, *As But a Day: To a Hundred and Twenty, 1867–1987* (Atlanta: Hebrew Benevolent Congregation, 1987). Revised from the original 1966 edition.

16. Telephone interview, September 1997.

17. Telephone interview, September 1997.

18. Hertzberg, *Strangers within the Gate City*, 239.

19. Ibid., 68.

20. Ibid., 69.

21. "Dixie Conditions Stir Unionists—Description of Actual State of Atlanta Textile Workers Make Delegates Weep," *Textile Worker* 3 (December 1914): 21, quoted in "Atlanta in the Progressive Era: A Dreyfus Affair in Georgia," by Leonard Dinnerstein, in *Jews in the South*, ed. Leonard Dinnerstein and Mary Dale Palsson (Baton Rouge: Louisiana State University Press, 1973), 173 (hereafter this chapter is cited as "Dreyfus Affair in Georgia").

22. For an interesting examination of the strike, see Jacquelyn Dowd Hall, "Private Eyes, Public Women: Images of Class and Sex in the Urban South, Atlanta, Georgia, 1913–1915," in *Work Engendered: Toward a New History of American Labor*, edited by Ava Baron (Ithaca, NY: Cornell University Press, 1991).

23. *New York Times*, February 15, 1915. Quoted in "Dreyfus Affair in Georgia."

24. *Atlanta Constitution*, June 21, 1915, extra. Quoted in "Dreyfus Affair in Georgia."

25. For more on the Leo Frank case, see Leonard Dinnerstein, *The Leo Frank Case* (Athens: University of Georgia Press, Brown Thrasher Books, 1966; reprint ed., 1987).

26. Hertzberg, *Strangers within the Gate City*, 178, quoting the *Atlanta Georgian*, May 28, 1913.

27. Quoted by Louis Schmier in September 1997 interview.

⁂ Chapter 3 ⁂

At "Home," at War, the Roaring Twenties— and Alice (1913–1925)

⁂ *Alice Apte is born in St. Louis on July 20, 1913, and Helen and Day move back to Atlanta with their daughter. They first live in Helen's childhood home, with her mother, at 394 Washington Street and then move a block away to 429 Washington Street. Soon Day's parents also are living in the neighborhood at 489 Washington. In Atlanta, Day joins up with J. Cohen Loeb, a longtime friend, to form a food wholesale business. Helen is once again in her element with her family and her old friends, Day is successful, and together they move up in Atlanta's social circles.*

The first entry in this chapter is from Toccoa, Georgia, a mountain town. Helen and her family, like other Atlantans who could afford it, often escape the summer heat by vacationing in the higher, cooler mountains only a few hours to the north. Helen is thirty-one years old when she picks up her diary here.

Toccoa—Monday, August 13, 1917

Four years since I have touched this diary. I have been too busy *living* life to write about it. O, I have suffered since I last wrote here, but I have had divine joy also, and now that my life is running in quiet, peaceful grooves, I can stand aside and watch it, and take time to write about it.

Then, too, in this great crisis in the world's history something impels me to write, to make some record of what transpires from time to time. History is being made now; the fight for democracy is on. Our glove is in the arena, and we must win. It's a case now of "my country right or wrong." Whatever we think or feel, it is too late now to rebel. We must stand by our president and our government. It were treason to do otherwise. But O, how terrible, how truly awful that we should have become involved in this holocaust. We were so peaceful, so prosperous, and now the era of horror is beginning for us. Who knows, who knows where it will end? The flower of our manhood must go, the very foundations of our lives, both individual and national, are attached, and we must win. We cannot be slackers now. We must all do our best. And the great God sits on high, listening to the prayers of the German and the French and the Russian and the Turk—and now the American—all, all praying for victory. And He sits on high and listens. I know He listens, and I know it will work itself out for good, as all things do. His divine hand is uplifted, and soon it will fall someplace, but fall it will, and then we shall know. He carries us all in the hollow of His hand.

Alice and I have been in this little mountain town for a month. Day is in Atlantic City, and I just got a letter asking me whether I remember the love letters he used to write me from there since the time he was seventeen. He says that love was like water unto wine for the love he feels for me now after eight and one-half years of married life. God bless him, my dear, dear boy.

And to think this is the first time this book has ever heard of *Alice*. My little daughter, heart of my heart, flesh of my flesh. Since I am here, I have destroyed the diary I was keeping for you, little girl. I was going to give it to you on your eighteenth birthday. It was called *The Heart of a Girl*. I read it over and I destroyed it. It was hard to do. It was like tearing out a part of myself as I tore each page, slowly and reluctantly, but I had to do it. My hair almost stood on end, and I shuddered as I read what I had put on paper where only a frail lock had kept it from curious eyes. Why, with the naive egotism of youth I had written out my very soul—those soul experiences, which I thought so unique, my friends' experiences, my own adventures in the realm of adolescence. *The Heart of a Girl*? I should have called it *Every Girl*, for now I see what I thought was my own Great Adventure, my own problems, my struggles, my prayers, my hopes, my fears, was only the common adventures of every girl, the same dreams, the same sorrows, the same joys, just youth finding its niche in the great world.

And so, my darling, you must fight your own fight without the help of that little book. The same fight will be yours. I can only try to make your mind and body strong to meet it. And now that I am older (thirty-one, good gracious) I can write with more reserve, and maybe I shall not destroy this book and can make it fit to be put into your hands when the time comes. You will find lots about your sweet self in it, for you are my life, and so even though I record some of the big things going on in the world about us, it cannot help but be a record of you, because each day, each hour, each minute of you is too precious to waste, and I wish I could immortalize your sweet, sweet babyhood, you little bit of heaven!

I wrote once in my other diary, where so many of my other ideals crashed around me, "Dear God, everything is failing me, so few dreams are left me, but I have still my dream of motherhood. O, please, please don't let that fail me, don't let that fall short of my ideal." Little foolish girl, what could you know? How could you imagine what motherhood really means? How could I ever tell? But this I can say—it *has not failed*. It is more glorious, more divine, more soul-satisfying than my girlish heart could dream of.

I last wrote here, I see, in March 1913, and Alice was born in July of that year. No wonder I didn't write anymore after March. Those four months—how could anyone live through such agony, I often wonder. The nights that I sat through in my rocker, in that little stifling room, gasping for breath, unable to lie down. The days of misery, of pain, of fear, because the doctor gave me so little hope, and yet I'm so glad I was brave. I *never* complained, I stood everything that came unflinchingly. All my folks said what worried them most was my angelic disposition! The heat was as unbearable as only St. Louis heat can be, and I was so weak I could scarcely lift my hand, and yet I smiled through it all. How happy I am I can say that now. It may help you some day, little daughter. And you were worth it all. Cheerfully I'd go through it all again to have you. Remember this someday, when your time of travail comes. I won't dwell too long on my time of agony. It was shortened, after all, because they took me to the hospital before it was time and forced you into the world, so that we both might have our chance for life. And it was such a miracle that you lived at all and that I lived. It was a marvelous piece of work Dr. Crosser did, and the Lord was on our side. He wanted me to have you, and so every day of my life I thank Him for His gift.

A Hospital Delivery

To be born in a hospital in 1913 was unusual, but to be born in a maternity hospital was almost unheard of. So Alice's birth at St. Louis Maternity Hospital on July 20 of that year was rare indeed. Although upper- and middle-class women were starting to turn to hospitals for delivery, hospitalization did not put an immediate end to the high maternal death rate (see p. 58). At general hospitals, infection, one of the main causes of maternal death, often was carried from one ward to another, and entering a hospital for delivery actually could be more dangerous than staying at home. Although doctors knew about the causes of infection, there were no antibiotics (penicillin was discovered in 1928, and antibiotics did not come into widespread use until the 1940s), so avoiding infection was essential. Some physicians were beginning to call for segregated maternity facilities—either special maternity wards isolated from the rest of the hospital, or separate maternity hospitals altogether.[1]

However, that was not the reason for the creation of the St. Louis Maternity Hospital. The hospital was founded in 1908 by some prominent St. Louis women to help young, unmarried expectant mothers who had drifted to the city from the countryside and were unable to find care. According to a brochure published on the hospital's third anniversary, "some of our leading physicians and ministers" told the women "of the overcrowding of our city institutions, and of the absolute lack of provision for the care of those unfortunate girls who, having made their first error (misplaced confidence), seek to lose themselves in a large city. This class of patients, being ineligible to our city institutions, becomes prey for unprincipled doctors, midwives, etc., and are forced, through necessity, into a life of shame." Despite the hospital's stated mission, about half the patients were married. But it remained a charity facility, vowing that "at no time shall more than one-fourth of the total number of beds be occupied by private patients," and only 20 percent of the patients (Helen among them) paid for all of their treatment.[2]

Helen never explains why she went to the hospital to give birth. Her doctor probably required it because of her complicated pregnancy and because he induced labor. But whether she knew it or not, giving birth in a specialized maternity hospital also gave her some protection against infection—and no doubt was an important factor in the "miracle" of her and her baby's survival.

Atlanta—Thursday, November 29, 1917

Thanksgiving Day. The *Journal* had a cartoon of another planet, and the inhabitants looked down on this one and said, "I'm thankful because I don't have to live down there." Alice said she was thankful for the turkey, and that's indeed something to be thankful for these days, when it's forty cents a pound. We had a nice ride, a beautiful day. Day is up at his folks' now. His father grows more feeble every day, poor old man.

I was to have gone to the Alliance* to serve coffee to the soldiers, but was too tired. Life is very strenuous now, not with bridge and movies, either, but with real work. For the first time in the world's history women have been called by the government—"The Women's Committee of the Council of National Defense"—and we are working shoulder-to-shoulder with our men. Womanpower, with its vast resources, has been organized, and in this war, women do not have to "sit and wait." There is weeping, God knows, but no waiting with folded hands. One hardly sees a woman's hands, unless they are flashing with knitting needles, or rolling bandages, or trench lights, or making gowns for soldiers. The man in khaki is every-where, and the sight of a U.S. Army uniform used to be a rare sight. We were at Camp Gordon last Sunday, and one of the officers showed us around. A wonderful sight. We have a soldier for dinner every Sunday. Some of our guests are pitiful objects; one wonders if Uncle Sam can ever make a sol-dier out of such material. So many Jewish faces among the soldiers one sees; some have only been here from Russia or Austria a few years. Some have to fight against their own brothers in the German Army.

I am recording secretary of the Council of Jewish Women. Dr. Ashby Jones spoke at our last meeting. He said he has been struck with the look in women's faces lately. They have attained a look of dignity, he said, a new dignity and a new earnestness. Men no longer flatter us; they expect us to do our bit. On our ride this afternoon we passed many houses flying the new flag of service—the white flag, with the red star, showing that that household has sent an inmate to France, in the service of his country. I hope it comforts some mother's heart.

The English have cut a big gap in the Hindenburg line, but the most serious thing at present is the Russian situation. If they make a separate peace, it will be terrible. Poor Russia is torn asunder. What travail the whole world is in, and the end is not in sight.

Atlanta—Wednesday, September 11, 1918

Yesterday our soldier boys went away. Where, we do not know, but they are on the way to someplace "over there." All three of them—Henry, Leonard, Maurice—brave and gallant and gay, and all with smiles on their lips. Our smiling, singing army—that's the way they will go down in his-tory, I believe. "The Singing Army"—God bless them, and O, God, keep

*The Jewish Educational Alliance, a community center.

my brothers in Your care, help us to be brave, and to keep the home fires burning. Maurice looked so pale, and the smile on his face was sadder than tears. I—well, I can write no more.

Atlanta—Saturday, September 14, 1918

We have heard from the boys en route. They were in Baltimore half of Friday but could not phone Sis, and she is heartbroken. We moved into our new apartment September 3, the very day we heard the boys had to go, so it was not a happy beginning, and it is hard for me to take any interest in it yet.

Tomorrow Yom Kippur begins. All of Day's folks will be here for supper. I have a new cook who wants to know do I have company "regular." Alas, I suppose I will as long as Day's folks are at the hotel. I had so looked forward to this winter, having Mama on the corner to run back and forth and to see the boys every night. It was too good to be true how they came home from Camp Jessup every night. When they reach their final destination and we hear from them and learn at least what country they are in, we will feel better, but what days of suspense we must live through. Mama has aged eighteen years, and I feel at least fifty. Alice prays every night, "God bless our soldier boys in France and bring them back safe and sound." Pearle and Dorothy are here. The baby is darling, but not *nearly* as smart as Alice at twenty-one months. Alice began dancing lessons this week.

The war news is encouraging, we are gaining every day, and everyone is hoping it will soon be over, but the government doesn't encourage the idea. The most the leaders will say is that it is the *beginning* of the end, but in New York last month I met Congressman Joshua Kahn of California, father of the draft law, and he said the government is making every preparation for a five-year war! Lloyd George said after a big victory, "We are *nearer* the end of the tunnel." Pershing said after this last offensive in which we gained five miles, "We have had some success." Lukewarm I call it. Must be some reason for it.

Atlanta—Wednesday, September 25, 1918

We haven't heard from the boys yet. As soon as we hear of their safe arrival, I am going to brace up, but the suspense is hard to bear. How wonderful it will be to get a letter from over there, and at least to know what country they are in. A new literature has sprung up—those letters to the folks at home. Such letters! And from boys whose worst ordeal was to write a "composition" or a "theme." At last, in the great school of experience they are learning to express themselves. Their young, eager, ardent souls are expressed in those letters from over there. They breathe a spirit of idealism, of high courage—yes, of fatalism, too. "The Young Crusaders" is the way I often think of them. They all start out with the Crusaders' spirit.

The more I see, the more I marvel at our American army, and our three boys are typical. I can picture them all, facing danger, doing brave and gallant deeds. Maurice—was there ever a greater "pacifist"? He loved *peace* more than any man I ever saw: peace in his home life, with his neighbors, in his business. It was really his chief characteristic, and now he looks every inch a soldier. I can see him facing danger, with his head held high, a sort of "noblesse oblige." "I *must* not, *cannot* fail, for the honor of my family, for the honor of my own soul." I can see Leonard, not only facing danger, but seeking it out, with his reckless, debonair gallantry. I can see him rushing into the fray, a smile on his lips, and saying to himself, "What does it matter, anyway? I have only one life to live and this is my fate." I can see Henry, his eyes steely blue, his lips together, his head erect, making a stand against all odds, and I can hear him say, "I do this thing because it is *right*, because it is my duty, and I *shall* not fail." And so I say my three brothers typify the whole American Expeditionary Force— Maurice, who though afraid, rises above that fear; Leonard, who knows no fear and never counts the cost; Henry, with a fine spirit of idealism, doing his duty because it is *right*.

Patriotism—we Americans never knew the meaning of the word. Of course, we loved our country, but that love had never been put to the test. We took it for granted. Now, like all love, it has proven itself only by standing the test, it is going through fire, and it will come out purified. The first time after the boys were in khaki that we heard "The Star-Spangled Banner" played, the tears sprang to my eyes as I watched them. Down to their sides went their hands, up went their heads, back their shoulders, and thus they stood at attention till the song was ended. We are so unused to those sort of things. We always fought shy of any sentiment, but not now. America has found her soul. "Our sons have shown us God," as Mr. Britling says.*

*From H. G. Wells's *Mr. Britling Sees It Through.* " 'God . . . is the only King.'. . . Then after a time he said: 'Our sons who have shown us God.' "

Atlanta—Tuesday, October 1, 1918

Today we heard of the boys' safe arrival overseas. Thank God.

Atlanta—Thursday, October 24, 1918

On October 21 we got the first letters from France—somewhere in France, but we think it is Bordeaux. Not a bad place to winter. They are all well and happy, and not a line was censored, which is quite unusual, but our boys are too good soldiers to break any rule. The discipline won't hurt them, and their letters showed deep feeling and thinking. Yes, Bubba is beginning to think! It looks like peace is coming, although the papers warn us not to be too enthusiastic. Germany says she is willing to stop, but will they accept Wilson's strict terms? We are waiting now for an answer. Germany wants to quit before her sacred land is invaded, but how our boys hate to give up the idea of marching down Unter den Linden and planting the Stars and Stripes in Berlin.

It is marvelous how the American frame of mind has changed. Those who were most bitter against the war now cry, "There must be no peace yet, not till the Hun is beaten and beaten forever." The boys from France write home and say, "Don't talk peace yet. Just back us up, and we'll fight till we get to Berlin." All the papers say the same thing. It is the American spirit, and yet I wonder if there isn't a little of the savage joy of the fight in it, if the blood hasn't gone to their heads like wine and victory made them see red. Peace can't come too soon to suit me, and yet I realize it must be decisive so the world will indeed be safe for democracy.

Spanish influenza has taken a terrible toll all over the country. Thousands of boys have died in the camps, and so many sad deaths everywhere. It seems to take the young. It is awful and everyone is depressed. Movies, schools, churches are closed. Day and I had it in a mild form.[*]

Atlanta—Monday, March 10, 1919

My tenth anniversary! It takes such a great event for me to write. I often think of my diary, but just haven't the time. Sister's baby was born last

---

[*]The flu outbreak of 1918 was the worst epidemic in U.S. history, claiming about five hundred thousand American lives, or nearly five of every thousand people in the country (1996 *Information Please Almanac*, 402 and 826.)

Saturday, March 1, but only lived 36 hours. Sis is doing fine. The poor little baby tried so hard, and I shall never get it out of my mind—the little blue limp body. The soul—what of it? Was there a soul in that tiny thing? *Something* breathed and protested, struggled and lay still.

Alice asked me the inevitable question today: "Where was *I* ten years ago today, Mother?" God meant me to have her, I realize that more every day, else why is it she survived the terrific fight she had to get here? Why did she survive, and Sister's baby didn't? Those things don't happen by chance. I see the Divine Hand in it. How much, how very much of happiness these last ten years have brought me. In spite of trials, worries, much sickness, and a great deal of petty aggravations, thank God I can say today on my tenth anniversary that I am happy.

I want to record it, as the fleeting moment of happiness is too evanescent to trifle with. It is too rare, too precious. Today you have it, tomorrow it is gone, and so I say, today I'm happy. I have my husband's love, I love him, I have my child, my home, we are all well, our boys are still Over There, but in good health, and so thank God from whom all blessings flow!* I just heard in "strictest confidence" that we will have a "surprise party" given us tonight, so I can add "love of friends" to my list. And O, my husband bought a new Dodge machine today, and I'm going to learn to run it.

Atlanta—Monday, November 10, 1919

Tomorrow we celebrate Armistice Day. We have just put a bronze memorial tablet in the Temple to the memory of our heroic dead—Roy Baur, Lynis Jacob, Aran Cohen. Tomorrow night at the Auditorium we will celebrate the day of victory and have memorial services for the dead.

One year ago, November 11, 1918, was a wonderful day. I'm sorry I didn't record it in here when impressions were fresh, but never shall I forget that thrilling moment when the bells and whistles pealed forth, and the extras proclaimed, "The War is Over. The War is Over." What joy, hope, relief, and prayer those words echoed in every heart, and what pain in the heart of those whose dear ones made the supreme sacrifice.

---

*This seems to be an unusual Christian allusion—to a doxology, the closing stanza of the morning and evening hymns by Thomas Ken (1637–1711):
   Praise God, from whom all blessings flow;
   Praise Him, all creatures here below;
   Praise Him above, ye heavenly host;
   Praise Father, Son, and Holy Ghost.

We went to New York, where we met the boys on their return. Another wonderful day I should have recorded. They came on the steamship *Tara* July 28. Alice, Day, and I watched the big boat dock and helped to welcome the hundreds of khaki figures who waved back to us while the band played and people cheered. Then came our three soldier boys, clean and erect and well, just as they went over. Thank God. We spent that afternoon with them at Camp Merrit, and then Alice and I went to Asbury Park and Day came home after a wonderful two weeks in New York. While there we saw the big parade, when Wilson arrived from France. We stood on Fifth Avenue and had a good view of him as he passed, bowing and smiling. I thought he has a very sincere and earnest face, and that he really seemed to enjoy and be glad of the cheers and plaudits. It was the zenith of his power, and now it seems he is descending.

A year ago, and we are still not at peace with Germany, though indeed the war is over. Peace with victory is a glorious thing, yet now we ask ourselves, What did we accomplish? Is the world now safe for democracy? Will nations lay down their swords and all dwell together like the Biblical lion and lamb? Alas, we seem further than ever from universal peace. Russia is a seething hotbed of hate and lawlessness. Austria is broken, suffering, dying. Our own America is torn with strikes, dissentions, and grave labor troubles. The "League of Nations" is still the bone of contention in the Senate, and President Wilson has been ill and incapacitated for weeks, the helpless subject of sneers and innuendoes.

We are prosperous, it is true, but business is unsettled. "We don't know where we stand from day to day," the businessman declares. Pessimists say we are rocking on the edge of a terrible chasm and predict everything from a general strike to Bolshevism, but we optimists think it is the natural reaction from the Great Conflict and that matters will soon be adjusted and a greater America arise. I see that the coal strike has just been declared illegal and ordered off.

Atlanta—Friday, August 17, 1923

Today is the anniversary of Leo Frank's death. I thought of that when I looked up the date to enter here. I was lying on the bed, reading, when suddenly I thought of my diary and had a desire to read it. I had to search for it. Don't know why I haven't written in four years. Much of interest has happened, and my personal life flows on in pleasant channels, but the world is sick. Europe is in chaos. Will our country be able to keep its isolation from political affairs over there? Germany is in the throes of civil war, France and England hate each other, and no one exactly understands what is happening in Russia. President Harding died in San Francisco August 2, and Coolidge is just beginning his term.

Atlanta—Thursday, September 13, 1923

This is Minnie's day off, and I let her go early. I am never so happy as when everyone goes out and leaves me alone. I seem to relax and feel free. I must be of a very unsociable nature, but I surely enjoy my own company.

Alice started school Monday in the fifth grade. If she does as well this year as in the past, I'll have no cause to complain. She has led her class ever since she started school, and when I hear the children say, "Alice Apte is the smartest child in our room," it is music to my ears, exquisite music! But in a way I am a little disappointed in Alice. There is nothing of the prodigy about her, and she did give promise of that as a baby. What does become of all those infant prodigies? Alice must have a brain above the average because she has gotten an "A" in every study every year, and has stood at the head of her class in every grade. "A" is from 90 to 100 and means excellence. She has a very quick, bright, and retentive mind, a clear, accurate intelligence like her Daddy's, but what I miss in her is imagination. She doesn't like poetry, and fairy tales bore her. When I remember the soul-satisfying joy I got from poetry, I grieve for her. Of course I'd rather she have Day's brain than mine. She is just exactly like him, even to her taste in literature. She isn't like me in a single way. I am glad, and I'd rather she had her happy, bright, straightforward disposition than mine. I was rather a morbid little thing, but I did get some thrills out of life and many a "great adventure."

Alice is not at all temperamental. Her great ambition is to be an "authoress." That is the one thing she inherits from me, and it is my dream and ambition for her. How I did want to write, how I still do, but no chance. I realize more each day how vast my ignorance is. I will see that Alice gets the education to fit her for it. I had to stop school when I was sixteen because of my wretched health. My old enemy! I am stronger now than ever in my life and have more endurance, but I never know what it is to really feel *well*. Headaches and indigestion, neuritis, etc.

Atlanta—Wednesday, January 9, 1924

Another year—may we be written down in the book of life for good. I can't complain of the year that is gone. We kept reasonably well, and business was satisfactory, and I had one great adventure! "How mad and bad and sad it was, but O, how it was sweet."* I can't write it out, but I must mention it in this record, because it was an epoch in my life. It is wonderful to a woman nearing middle age to feel she is admired and desired by another man not her husband. It thrilled me, it rejuvenated me, it made me joyful, but it did another thing to me—it brought me up with a jerk with the realization that my youth is passing, is almost gone. It made me want to hold it back with both hands. It made me look with horror in the mirror and to passionately dread what I saw there.

I had never thought before of growing old. I *feel* young. Life to me still is a beautiful adventure, but the fact remains that I am not young. Just a few more years and it will all be over—the fire, the passion, the sweetness of youth. Old age may be a beautiful thing, but it does not seem so to me. It seems desolate and sinister, and I cannot feel "grow old along with me, the best is yet to be."† No, the best *has* been, and to feel it is almost over has been my portion ever since that eventful week I spent in Dallas last spring, when Henry was married. I have no regrets for what I did—it was sweet, it brought joy to me, it hurt no one else, but it made me want to desperately hold on to my youth and to wonder if I had gotten all out of it I could. It made me realize what I never had before.

How pathetically some women try to keep young. I had always rather held them in contempt. It was the superb confidence of youth, but now I *know*. I am looking in the mirror now—there isn't a line on my face, but my hair is quite gray and my figure decidedly dumpy. I look like a nice, settled matronly woman, but I don't feel that way at all!

Alice is getting so big, I can't believe she is my baby. Her little breasts are developing, she has lost all her baby contours, and I can wear her shoes. Her individuality is also developing, and I no longer know her every thought, or rather think for her! She thinks for herself, and she expresses her opinions very freely. Of course I don't like it. I am jealous of it, I want her to belong all to me—body, mind, soul. I suppose every mother resents

*From Robert Browning's "Confessions":
    How sad and bad and mad it was—
    But then, how it was sweet.
†From Robert Browning, "Rabbi Ben Ezra" (1864).

the birdling trying its own wings, but we can't hold them back. We teach them to fly, and then don't want them to try their wings.

Two days after her tenth birthday her cousin Constance was born,[*] and I had to tell her the truth. "Where do babies really and truly come from, Mother?" I knew I should have to answer that, but I dreaded it. Ignorance is not beautiful, but innocence is, and I had made up my mind not to tell her until she asked me point blank. I have always believed in the *theory* of telling children, but the practice was not so easy. It tore my heart, and while she took it beautifully, I came to my room and cried bitterly for her lost babyhood, the lost innocence. Children who believe in fairies, who believe in Santa Claus, who think that the stork brings babies have always seemed to me the sweetest thing in life. And yet the realities of life are beautiful, and I tried to make them seem so to Alice. When I had finished she put her arms around my neck and said, "Mother I think that is the most wonderfulest thing I ever heard, and I thank you for telling me." So I felt repaid.

Just lately I have been wishing I had a son. I never had before. Alice had always seemed all-sufficing. But lately I have wished passionately that I had a boy—after all, it is a wonderful thing to bring a man-child into the world. I suppose it is the ages-old desire of every woman.

Atlanta—Wednesday, March 12, 1924

My fifteenth anniversary on the 10th (Monday), and such a happy day. I got such nice gifts and letters and phone calls all day, and at 6:30 we had a wonderful "surprise party," everyone bringing goodies, the table laden, and everyone so happy. The crowd was the sewing club girls, with their husbands, the Loils and Corinne. I was so touched and proud of such attention, as was Day. Afterwards we played mah-jongg, and they stayed until midnight. Day gave me a beautiful Maxfield Parrish picture and Alice gave me American Beauty roses. It was a very cold day with flurries of snow. I went to town in the morning with Sister.

I can say as I did on my tenth, thank God—the years have given me more of joy than sorrow, and I am happy. But sometimes the divine unrest of my youth comes over me and I feel a vague regret, a gentle melancholy. Could I have gotten more out of my life? Have I made the most of it? I lead

*Maurice's daughter.

a *happy* carefree existence, I attend to my little household duties, I play mah-jongg two or three afternoons a week, I go to the movies and pay calls, but sometimes it comes over me with a tremendous force that I'm not leading at all the kind of life I really like. I love clever, rather eccentric people and stimulating conversation and unusual situations. No one I go with ever discusses anything—we women have a continual round of petty gossip, not malicious, but just gossip. When we go out at nights, the men go at once to the card table, and there is no talk at all. Verily, conversation is a lost art.

There is a little thing I loved to quote as a girl, and really thought I meant it: "I'd rather go down in the raging sea than drowse to death by the sheltered shore." I smiled over that later and wrote in my diary about that presumptuous girl who wanted something more of life than peace. That was when my heart was resting after the storm and wild unrest of my girlhood. I thought there could be nothing more beautiful than the peace I had attained. Now, looking back from my middle age, I don't know. Maybe there are more beautiful things in life than a quiet peace. Am I drowsing to death by the sheltered shore?

Atlanta—Monday, March 31, 1924

My beautiful spring is here. Again, I feel rejuvenated. Yesterday we rode out in the country and gathered peach blossoms. Atlanta is really beautiful in the spring with the peach trees in bloom and the dogwood trees a mass of white blossoms. The surrounding country is rolling and lovely. The good old red clay hills of Georgia always give me a thrill when I return from a trip—they mean "home."

Not a word have I said of our wonderful trips, and we have had some worth recording. Ever since we've been able to afford it at all we've managed to go away at least once, sometimes two or three times a year. Day says he will only pass through this world once, and he intends to see all he can before he leaves it. I agree with him. Last winter we left here Christmas Day in our car, driving to Florida. Stayed in Jacksonville two days with the folks and then down the East Coast to Miami, where we stayed a week with Bill and Bessie, and came leisurely back January 6, as Alice had to get back to school. The year before that I took the same trip with Day and George Berend from Jacksonville to Miami, and then Day and I went over to Tampa for the first time since we left there fourteen years ago. Lots of water has gone under the bridge since then. In April I went to Dallas, where I spent my momentous week.

In June, about the 12th, we left with Alice and Ruby Diamond for our Western trip, which was surely an event. We went from here to Memphis, where we spent the day with Lucile Frank,* then to Kansas City, Denver, Colorado Springs, San Bernardino, Redlands, Riverside, Los Angeles and surrounding beaches, Pasadena, Fresno, Frisco, Portland, Hard Rivers, and Seattle, where we took a boat to Victoria and Vancouver. Then the magnificent trip through the Canadian Rockies, stopping at Lake Louise and Banff, Minneapolis, Chicago, and got home July 12. We were royally entertained all along the route by business friends of Day's. We were well every minute, made charming acquaintances, and saw *everything*—a marvelous lot for such a flying trip. It was great for Alice, and she is very observing. I forgot to mention Hollywood, where we dined at the Montmartre and saw many movie stars, and a long ride through Oakland, Alameda, and the Santa Clara Valley to the heart of the cherry orchards.

I think I liked Frisco the best of any city. It has an air! Los Angeles vaguely repelled me. I always *feel* a city as soon as I enter. I either like the atmosphere or I don't. I can't explain it. The Columbia River Highway rivaled the Canadian Rockies. We rode seventy miles to the Hood River, where we were met by friends and lunched at the Columbia River Gorge Hotel, then drove out to Mt. Hood, majestic and snow-covered.

The Western people are as hospitable as fiction makes them. We are always much entertained in the East, but with this difference. The New Yorker will greet you this way: "So glad to see you, how about a date for Wednesday evening, dinner at 6:30, good-bye." When you let them know you're in New York, they seem to feel it an immediate and painful duty to show you some attention. Money is no object; they enjoy showing you what an evening's entertainment costs in New York. When it is over they tell you good-bye, and leave you abruptly with a "Be sure and look me up again next time you come to the big city."

Out West it is a real joy for the natives to entertain you. We had men take whole days from their business to be with us. When they'd leave, they'd always say, "Well, what are your plans for tomorrow? Can I do anything for you? How about your tickets? Shall I see about reservations for you? What will the ladies do while you are busy? I'll send my car for

*Leo Frank's widow.

them to take them any place," etc. When we reached the hotel in Frisco, I found lovely roses in my room from the Hawaiian Pineapple Company, with the president's card. All sorts of little attention to make our trip memorable and keep us from feeling strangers in a strange land. Magnificent country—the best, awe-inspiring, breathtaking, but I also like the sophisticated East and hope to go up this summer.

Ruby was so lonesome for her mother on the trip, and now she has gone forever, having died suddenly Friday, March 28. Poor Aunt Hennie, she did so love life, or rather the little things that went to make up her life.

Alice just got her report card and again stood first. I know she must be above the average child, because to stand at the head of a class of forty-odd means something, but I am so ambitious for her that I am always looking for a sign of genius, or at least talent. Perhaps it is absurd to expect anything extraordinary of a ten-year-old child. She adores reading and devours books as I do, and she always has a paper and pencil in her hand, and has written stories, but I must admit I can find no signs of genius in them! Her outstanding trait now is her frankness and her unflinching honesty. She hates deceit, and injustice nearly kills her. The neighbors all tell me she is the best-behaved child on the court where they all play. One lady told me she watches them, and Alice is so "fair and square." That she is, God bless her. She looks me right straight in the eyes with her own hazel eyes wide open, frank and candid eyes like her Daddy's. I dread the day to come when a girl will come between those honest eyes and my searching ones. She will have secrets from me, of course. Even now I feel sometimes that I do not know her every thought, and I am jealous of the growing years that are taking my baby from me. She is so big, not only tall but developed almost as much as I was when I married. I was just a scrap of humanity, with a figure like a boy's. She is long-waisted and athletic looking, and she "adores" sport clothes. No fluffy ruffles for her.

I am reading *Jurgen*,* and while I don't care for allegory, Cabell is a master at it, and I am getting many good laughs out of it, as I did out of *Figures of Earth*. He says, "The moment you are no longer young, the years of vain regret will begin." Looking back on my life, I don't really regret anything—only, if I had to go through it again, I'd get more joy out of my youth. I would get more thrills. The girls of today are looked upon with horror. There is something rather horrible about their lack of re-

Jurgen, Virginia author James Branch Cabell's 1919 book, was a medieval romance that was suppressed on obscenity charges.

serve, their utter lack of reverence, their eager searching for a new thrill, their promiscuity. No, "promiscuous" I could never have been. It sickens me. But in my few little love affairs, I gave so niggardly, I regretted every kiss I allowed. I worried and suffered over every liberty taken with me. I felt degraded, impure. There was nothing impure about those little affairs; it was only Nature crying out in me for expression. We were only toys of Nature, we boys and girls. We had the same instruments as the young folks of today—sex crying to sex—but we were taught to think it wrong. I was afraid and ashamed of passion. The young folks of today are a reaction. The "petting parties," the "late dates," the utter freedom and license that exists is wrong, of course. It would kill me if Alice would do it, but I hope before she is grown the pendulum will swing back—not to the old ideas, but maybe a sane and normal way can be devised for these young, seeking souls. So, if I had to live my youth over again, I would live it gaily and joyfully, not cry myself to sleep because I had kissed or been kissed, not pray to be forgiven for my thoughts which were not impure thoughts, only natural ones, not feel abandoned and forsaken because Nature was using me. But how can youth know these things? No, one must *live* life to really understand it.

Atlanta—Tuesday, July 22, 1924

On May 17, my precious mother passed away. Without warning she was snatched away from us, and we are desolate. That I should have to write such a thing in here, that we should go on living our lives as if nothing happened seems incredible. If anyone had told me last year that I should have been so bereaved, I would have said, "I couldn't stand it," and yet I am standing it. After the first terrible shock and almost unbearable grief and heartache, I took up the threads of my life and went on. So I have found out another thing by living it—grief does not kill; it only sears. Either we have to lie down and die with our loved one, or we have to go on with our lives and adjust ourselves. Outwardly, we are the same, but O, the dull, constant, really physical ache in our hearts, the lump in the throat. A dozen times a day I want to tell her something. I catch myself saying, "I must take that to Mama." She is with me every single minute of the day and often in my dreams.

Her memory is a blessing to us; her deeds live after her. She needs no eulogy, but the one that best suits her would be: "She served." That expresses it, but O, so mildly. Her life was always one of service to others. Her work was done. She lay down to rest. Her poor tired heart just stopped. Bitter tears are falling from my eyes, my mother, but not all bitter either, because I have the blessed memory of your goodness, your sweetness, your tender care. And nothing can take that from me.

When I think back on her life and of how she has passed away like the grass that withereth, it seems terrible that her deeds should be made to live engraved in stone or marble. A great life, a heroic life, and yet she leaves no record except in the hearts of her children. She led a childhood of bitter poverty, orphaned at the age of twelve, shortly after sailing from Germany alone to join her brothers here in Atlanta. Imagine the little lonely child at sea coming to a strange country, and mine, almost at her age, so carefully guarded that she scarcely crosses the street alone. Her brothers were doing well and established her in a comfortable home, but in payment she baked and cooked and cleaned. How she worked I know, I who knew her proud spirit.

She married my father when she was about twenty-one, and went to live in Hawkinsville. Those were the happiest years of her life. There she gave birth to a child every two years, there she saw my father grow to affluence, loved and respected by the whole community, the founder of the public school system there, working always for the betterment of the community, a proud father and a loving husband. When Sister was twelve, and Pearle was the baby, they decided for their children's sakes to move to a city, where we could have more advantages and be thrown more with Jewish people, for although we went entirely with Gentiles and knew no difference or no prejudice, my parents remained intensely Jewish, and they wanted us raised as Jews. So he sold out his large interests, really vast for those days, and we came to Atlanta, staying long enough for Leonard to be born, then going to Richmond, Virginia, where he bought a large clothing business.

The hospitable Virginians received us with open arms. My parents were charming and always welcomed into any society. We children were known for our good manners and our almost painful cleanliness. We were always being scrubbed until we shone, and while we had every attention, we were also disciplined. We were taught to respect our elders and to obey unquestionably and immediately. We had Gentile neighbors with whom we were on intimate terms. We lit our candles on Friday night, and my mother blessed them with the ancient blessing of the women of Israel. My father read the Sabbath eve service, and we all touched the cup of wine to our lips. Our neighbors thought it beautiful. We in turn respected their Sabbath, and we children had to keep very quiet on Sunday, nor would my mother be seen sewing at the window or the maids be allowed to do any unnecessary work. They joined the exclusive Jewish clubs and went out to the theatre and dances, whenever we children were well, but, of course, we indulged in every disease known to childhood—six of us at a time with measles, mumps, chicken pox, etc., so they really couldn't go very much. But they loved their home and always had company.

Almost from the first the business did not go well. Papa had been cheated by his best friend. He had paid much more than the business was worth. I was too young to understand much, but I know he never got bitter. He struggled on for five years (Henry was born the year before), then he gave up. I was nearly twelve. I remember well that awful night May 18, 1898. He gave his life that we might live. All that was left after every debt was paid was his insurance. There was my mother, not as old as I am today, with six little children and barely enough to live on. Did she repine? Did she lie down, give up? No, with courage beyond words, with no heroics but with a stern resolve, she wound up the business there and came with us to Atlanta, where there was a piece of property left from the wreckage.

Now begins the history of remarkable years. Of how she fought and struggled and *lived* for us, I have just begun to realize. She built five houses on that piece of property, supervising every bit of the work herself. She asked very little advice; she used her own judgment; she asked pity or help from no one. Men respected her and dealt fairly with her. We lived in the best of the houses on Washington Street, which was then the most desirable part of Atlanta. We had every comfort, many luxuries; we children were always well dressed and had *every* advantage. She must have made superhuman efforts to do it. When we know now how little money she had, we just don't know how she did it.

She held us all together by the sheer force of her will. We never heard her complain. Work was her salvation. She was too busy to do much thinking. She never took a single recreation. In these days of bridge and the movies it seems hard to believe. There were no movies, but a lot of card-playing. She never touched a card, she never went to a matinee because she'd rather we went. She never took a meal away from home, but she cooked many a one for us, and gave us many a party. She had only enough clothes to look decent. I never remember her staying in bed a day. The household would have stopped without her. She kept the wheels moving, and the only mistake I can see is that she didn't demand more of us. It was so easy for her to do things that she just went ahead and did them. She was so independent, so capable, so efficient, that nothing remained undone.

Our home was known as "Liberty Hall." She was wise enough to know that home must be made pleasant for children or they wouldn't stay in it. It was a great thing for the boys, especially. There they brought their friends, raided the icebox, played in the yard or all over the house. We each had "our crowd," and how we girls fought over the "sitting room." On Sundays we had open house; sometimes we counted sixty people there. She was never too tired to fix us a party. The boys and girls confided in her, trusting to her sane judgement, her cheery common sense. Before we were up in the morning she had done a day's work.

Many a cookless day she had, but the meals were cooked, good and nourishing, six lunches put up for school, the furnace seen to, because that was her job. To save coal she did it herself, making countless trips a day up and down the steps. Is it any wonder she wore out, poor darling? I could write volumes of her daily sacrifices, her cares, her heartaches, but I could never tell it all. I can write no more. My heart is breaking, my whole being cries to her, but she is gone—forever.

Gainesville, Georgia—Saturday, August 2, 1924

I have been up here a week, and a little peace has come to my aching heart. We went to New York and Atlantic City on June 30 and stayed two weeks. Day thought the change would do me good, but I was miserable. I think the gaiety clashed too much with my mood. The music in the hotel drove me mad, and when I stood and looked at the ocean, which has always thrilled and obsessed me, I could have screamed aloud in abandon. I would look out at sea, and it looked cruel, and my heart would cry out, "Mama, Mama, where are you?" She seemed so far away. Here she seems nearer to me. In the quiet of the "Eternal Hills" I have found some comfort.

Day comes up every weekend, and I count the nights. They are lonesome, but my days are full. I can read and write and sometimes be alone. Sister and Pearle, Bessie and Bill, and Mother are here, but I manage to slip away, and now I am sitting in a little Japanese pagoda down by the camp. I feel more intimate with the infinite. Mother has come for a long visit, and if I were home, I'd not be a minute to myself, so I will stay here as long as I can but must get home to move on September 1. Brenau College, where we are staying, is a charming place, with quite an atmosphere. The building is old and crumbling, and I have carefully stopped up the cracks against mice, but I like the air of culture and learning.

The historic Democratic Convention was going on in New York while we were there, and Day hung over the radio, getting the latest news. After the longest session in history Davis was nominated, and now we await November, but everyone is betting on Coolidge.

I met Sidney for tea at the Ansonia one day, leaving Alice at the hotel with the Silvers. We spent a pleasant hour over the tea table, but it was not satisfactory. One can't say much with a waiter at one's elbow. He said I was even sweeter than he had remembered me, etc., and wanted to know if he could come to Atlantic City and spend the weekend after Day went home. I promised to let him know, but I never wrote him because I decided to go home with Day. I was not in the mood for philandering. I couldn't even get a thrill out of the situation.

Atlanta—Saturday, October 4, 1924

Today is said to be the holiest Sabbath of the year and the Day of Atonement. I didn't go to temple because I wanted to stay home and relax. Besides, it tears me to pieces to say the Kaddish prayer with all eyes upon me. I can't control my grief, and I'm one of those who, when they grieve, want to crawl into a dark place alone. These holidays have been very sad, of course, for all of us, with our dear one gone. I'll be glad when they are over, and yet these solemn days are beautiful. Though we modern reformed Jews have drifted away from the rites and ceremonies of our faith, "There is a mystic tie that binds the children of the martyr race." The sound of the shofar thrills me more than any aria from grand opera. It touches something way down deep in me, something fundamental. It reaches the soul—our own heritage. How some Jews can be ashamed of being Jews has always seemed to me inexplicable. In me burns the ancient pride of race. I am glad, proud to be called "Jew." It holds no opprobrium for me even though it is meant that way. It is a terrible thing that anti-Semitism is growing in this country. It will hurt worst those Jews who are ashamed of their religion. Me, it cannot touch.

I have been delving a little into the realms of psychology. It is fascinating, but it overstimulates my mind. It takes a mighty well-balanced mind to wrestle with the problems of the self-conscious mind, the "Science of the Soul" it is called. Especially interesting is a book I just read—*The Doctor Looks at Literature*, by Joseph Collins. He discusses the psychology of the sick soul, or psychotherapy. Abnormal things hold a strange fascination, reading about these things excites one, but a little of it goes a long way with me. Instinctively I turn away from it and crave for the normal. Some try to tell us that those other instincts are the natural ones, that civilization and custom has made us overcome them, but no, every instinct in us cries out against those unspeakable, perverted things. Normal people want decency, gratification of normal instincts. Only sick minds and souls can believe the other. Leopold and Loeb were declared to be not legally insane, yet they are surely the victims of sick minds. They are surely not normal human beings, so I think the judge was wise to give them life imprisonment, though he was much criticized. I believe scientists will yet find things of great interest in them that will help to solve the problems they are working on. There is a mysterious borderland between insanity and those poor victims of "a sick soul."

Alice and Mother have gone to temple. Yes, Mother-in-law is on her annual visit. I don't know if Freud said anything about the relationship between mother-in-law and daughter-in-law, but I don't need him to tell me that it is a "psychological" relationship. They are two very different "complexes," and I doubt if there has ever been real love between the two. Something prevents it. Call it jealousy or whatever you want: It is as if the wife and the mother are each, even though unconsciously, fighting for supremacy. Each one says, "He is mine." I can understand her feelings even though I haven't a son. My instinct tells me how I'd feel if I had a son and had to give him up to another woman. I am fond of my mother-in-law. She is fond of me, but—!

We have gotten on better than usual this time, because I made up my mind not to be any more unhappy than I had to be, and because "Mother" is to me a sacred name.

Atlanta—Monday, November 10, 1924

My guest has gone home. How good to be alone once more, not having to account for every act, no spying eyes always upon me. She is going to keep house with Aunt Dordy, surely the best solution of her living problem, but

I don't expect it to last long. We are having a very warm fall, not a cold day yet.

Well, life—one d__ thing after another! The latest is that Pearle has gone to Dallas to live, leaving on the 6th. I haven't realized it yet, but it is awful. How we shall miss her, her sweet personality, her bright smile, her cheerful disposition. She was my greatest comfort, and we are truly congenial spirits, but I will have to forgo her companionship and get used to this loss as I must get used to a greater one, but it is hard. And little "Billybo," my sweet baby. She says she loves me more than anyone in the world, but soon she *will* have forgotten me entirely. Sister is as heartbroken about it as I am. I only hope Alvin will do well there.

I must record a date of importance to Alice—September 12. On that day she crossed the brook where womanhood and childhood meet. Poor baby, barely eleven. I cried my eyes out, but what's the use—it's inevitable as much so as death. I was only ten. Thank goodness she looks and feels fine. She is doing well with her music, reading quickly and accurately, and grasping her teacher's instructions instantly. Mrs. Moore says she has never had a pupil learn more rapidly, but I can't see any real musical talent. She just does it easily and conscientiously, as she does everything she undertakes.

Atlanta—Monday, December 8, 1924

A dark, dreary day. I awoke half-stifled and with all my feelings of a storm brewing. I can always feel one in my bones! Now it is pouring in torrents, so that I can hardly get over to Sister's, and she wants me to come for lunch. We are both lonely, but she has absolutely no resources in herself, and I can always find something to keep my hands or brain occupied.

I just read *Women in Love*, by D. H. Lawrence—vile, obscene, nauseating, but interesting anyway. It's a pity some of his characters could not have had the benefit of gland treatment, poor, perverse creatures. Following it, I read *Psychoanalysis and Gland Personalities*, by André Tridon. Fascinating and illuminating. I've had several doctors tell me I need some gland treatment, but I don't know which one and have never done anything about it.

On days like this I see constantly before me that lonely grave at the cemetery, rain beating upon it, so desolate, so alone, and my heart breaks. Poor darling, sometimes she seems so far away, and yet there are times when she is right with me. We sit and almost talk together, and the other day when Sis and Lee were having one of their trivial and interminable arguments, I looked straight into her eyes, and we exchanged one of our knowing, quizzical looks, as plainly as if she were sitting there before me. It did not seem uncanny to me. Somehow it comforted me.

Atlanta—Wednesday, December 31, 1924

New Year's Eve—pouring in torrents, Day in Miami, so blue that I could positively *scream*, but what's the use. I must just keep my balance and try to get through tonight when the little bells and whistles blow and I am alone. None of us has gone out anyplace at all since our bereavement, and it is getting on our nerves terribly, this constant sitting around, doing nothing. I know we should take some recreation, but I for one just can't. It is an obsolete custom, keeping such strict mourning, but I haven't the least desire for mah-jongg or cards or movies, so I am following the line of least resistance—just to stay at home.

I read far too much for my physical good. I guess I average a book a day, but it is like a drug to me. I steep myself in it, and I swear I can read chapter after chapter, and when I'm through, I couldn't tell a thing I've read. I just intoxicate myself with words. Reading has always meant that to me. I spring into a book and simply devour it. That's why I haven't gotten much good from the vast amount of reading I've done since I was seven. I don't read word by word; I just devour whole lines at a time. Often I go back and read pages over, just as one skims over a much-prized letter to get the first news of it and then goes back and reads more thoroughly. I can pick up a story, start it in the middle or read it backwards and get just as much pleasure out of it. Day can't understand it. I read Balzac at the age of eight, law books, tracts, treatises, anything. Of course I didn't know what I was reading, but it was just *reading*. It's a wonder I haven't gotten more out of it, but I have a very poor mind—no memory, no retentiveness, so unobservant that I can be with a person all day and when I leave not even know what they have on. Just a poor dreamer and an encumberer on the face of the earth!

I am reading H. L. Mencken's *Prejudices**—startling! Sometimes, though, I do remember what I read, but it is in phrases, sentences, whole

*H. L. Mencken's acerbic essays between 1919 and 1927 were collected in six volumes called *Prejudices*. At some point Mencken met Helen's future son-in-law, Daniel Rosenbaum, perhaps in connection with Dan's 1930s newspaper syndicate, "The South Today." When Helen died, Mencken wrote Dan a note of condolence.

paragraphs that sing themselves through my brain—words, words again, but they give me infinite pleasure, and I have at least gotten that out of books. "And ride in triumph through Persepolis."* I don't even know where I read that, but I love it—just the sound of it. This morning, I picked up *The American Grocer*. Dry reading, yes, but listen to this under Import Prices:—

"Spices and Tapioca":
Pepper, Singapore
Pepper, Zanzibar
Pepper, Mombasa
Ginger, Cochin
Mace, Batavia
etc.

If I can get drunk on that, it is surely a harmless dissipation.

Reading and Reality: A Life from the Pages of Many Books

Before television, before radio, before movies, when telephones were a curiosity and travel was difficult, books had little competition for the leisure time of educated, cultured people. In today's multimedia environment, that era seems quaint. But if at the turn of the twenty-first century too much television can lead today's youngsters to blur fiction and reality, too much reading could pose a similar danger for their ancestors at the turn of the twentieth century.

Helen was a voracious reader all her life. In July 1901, for her fifteenth birthday, she received a blank journal. Called *Books I Have Read*, it allotted two pages for logging each book. The left-hand page was for Helen to record the book's title, the date read, its author, publisher, "Department of Literature," and, if she wanted, a brief sketch about the book. The right-hand page was for Helen's "Comment and Quotations." By June 1904—about three years after she started keeping the journal—Helen found herself running out of pages. She quit keeping the log.† But in those three years more than one hundred entries give a wealth of insight into her mind. What's more, because those were her impressionable years (fifteen-to-eighteen years old), her reading affected her beliefs for the rest of her life.

*From Christopher Marlowe's *Tamburlaine the Great*, Part I.
†She resumed her log in April 1906 and continued to keep it for about a year, but because there were only a few pages left in *Books I Have Read*, she stopped making comments and merely listed title and author.

Helen read a little of everything (for excerpts of her journal see Appendix B, pp. 193–208). Although plenty of melodramas and lesser literature appear on her list, she kept returning to the romantic fiction of the great nineteenth-century authors, especially novels with a strong female character who is forced to choose between some overwhelming duty and some passionate desire. Suppressing these desires is never easy; they are strong, even overpowering at times. But by choosing duty over desire the character maintains her dignity because she "does what is right"—even though the tales often end in tragedy. For instance, in George Eliot's *The Mill on the Floss*, which Helen "ranks among the first of the books I love," Maggie Tulliver, the protagonist, is pulled in many directions—by her love for Tom, her brother; by her respect for her father (and his memory); by her sympathy for Philip, the crippled son of her father's sworn enemy; and by her passionate, magnetic attraction to Stephen, her best friend's fiancé. In a weak moment Maggie starts to run away with Stephen, and then she stops. Duty compels her not to go further. She returns home, but her impulsive surrender to desire causes Philip to discard her and Tom to reject her. Resigned to her fate, she dies trying to rescue her brother in a flood. Her life may be unhappy, her death tragic, but she is honorable. She has done what is right. Duty has conquered desire.

Here are some other examples that brought Helen's praise:

- Sir Walter Scott's *Ivanhoe*, which she calls "the greatest Romantic Novel ever written" (she read it before *The Mill on the Floss*). Rebecca, the beautiful, virtuous Jew, is caught in her own struggle between duty and desire. She loves Ivanhoe. He is attracted to her, but he is betrothed to another. Besides, he is not Jewish, and she has a responsibility to marry within the faith. So, like Maggie in *The Mill on the Floss*, Rebecca conquers her desires, submits to her duty, and thus "comes nearer my ideal than almost any other character in fiction."
- Tennyson's *Idylls of the King*, the ultimate love-triangle story (Helen also liked poetry, especially poetry with a romantic theme): "Lancelot is an ideal man, though—'His honor rooted in dishonor stood, / And faith unfaithful kept him falsely true.'"
- Shakespeare's *Othello*: "Desdemona [is] a fine specimen of womanly devotion."

Helen's romantic idealism also led her to books with a social message. The quotation that she selected from Victor Hugo's *Les Misérables* is instructive: "As long as three problems of the age are not solved, namely, man's degradation by the ill-adjusted labor question, woman's ruin through hunger, and children's wasting away through lack of light; so long as mental asphyxiation is somewhere possible, in other words, and from a wider view, as long as the world cherishes poverty and ignorance, books of this kind cannot be useless."

Helen did not like books with weak female characters; she may have appreciated Dickens's plots and social message, for instance, but she would have liked him better "if only he wouldn't make his women either fools or dolls!" She did not particularly enjoy books with no women characters at all, such as Richard Henry Dana's sea tale, *Two Years before the Mast.* She objected when authors painted an unreal picture of things with which she was familiar, such as George Eliot's portrayal of Jewish life in *Daniel Deronda.* And she detested stories in which desire and passion trumped duty. *The Rubaiyat of Omar Khayyam* is a good example. With its sensual poetry, this book was, in effect, a renunciation of the Victorian concept of duty and a celebration of a seize-the-day attitude. Helen's reaction? "His philosophy is simply repulsive. His beliefs, or rather his unbelief, takes away much of the pleasure found in the real greatness of the poem." Despite the negative comment, however, her reaction to *The Rubaiyat* reveals another aspect of Helen's reading—her appreciation of aesthetics. She loved good writing, so she could appreciate the book even as she rejected its content. Many of the quotations in her journal seem to have been chosen simply because they were beautiful, not because of their meaning. Note her comment about Oliver Goldsmith's *The Deserted Village* (p. 196).

Helen's appreciation of good writing is also reflected in the quality of her own prose, as is her concern for others less fortunate than she. Most important, however, Helen's attraction to Victorian fiction confirmed her belief that life is a struggle to control passions, to suppress desires, and to perform one's duties. When she read *The Mill on the Floss,* she wrote: "Never have I felt such affinity for any character in fiction as I have with Maggie Tulliver." Such were Helen's feelings as a teenager, but throughout her life she saw herself as just such a character from a novel—a Maggie Tulliver caught in her own never-ending struggle between duty and desire.

Atlanta—Wednesday, December 31, 1924 (continued)

Day went to Miami Saturday night after being elected president of the Club. I was so proud of him, as everyone said such kind and praising things. He made a wonderful speech, sincere, earnest, enthusiastic, like himself.

He was also offered the presidency of the National Brokers' Association, but refused. He is on many committees, called on in all civic things, a member of all civic organizations, and he stands high in the business and social life of the city. But he is not making any money, and he ought to, as he surely has the ability. He deserves more than a mere living. I told him I'd be perfectly willing to move to Miami if he saw a good future there, and he has gone to look things over. People are moving to Florida by the thousands.

Atlanta—Wednesday, January 21, 1925

I must quote something from *Prejudices* because it is rather in line with my own thoughts lately: "God, if He exists at all, is neither good nor bad, but simply indifferent—an infinite force carrying on the operation of unintelligible processes without the slightest regard either one way or the other for the comfort, safety and happiness of man." A long way from my childish faith, when I asked God not to let it rain, to make me a good girl, to make me beautiful. How naive, how stupid. Anyone who thinks at all must see that God is not interested in our little affairs. I still believe in some great, irresistible force, some mysterious, universal plan, some Power above, but what are we in it all—grains of sand, struggling ants, less than the dust. Here today, gone tomorrow—

> Like snow on the mountain,
> Like mist in the river
> Like the bubble on the fountain—
> gone and forever.*

What's it all about, what is the reason for it all? The mystery, unsolved. Will death solve it? I doubt it. I wonder if it is a presentiment that I always feel death so near, so inevitable, that in the midst of any plan for the future, something in me asks, What's the use? It will all be over so soon. I don't really think it is a presentiment of my own passing away. I suppose everyone feels that way, especially when death has been brought

*Probably from Sir Walter Scott's "Marmion":
  Like the dew on the mountain,
  Like the foam on the river,
  Like the bubble on the fountain,
  Thou art gone, and forever!

so near them. Nothing seems really to matter so much when one has been brought so close to the great adventure.

"I have a rendezvous with death."* Those words seem to re-echo in my brain. Morbid, I know. I wish I could feel all the "Pollyanna" things I used to feel. "Life is real, life is earnest" and "I know I cannot drift beyond His loving care." Those are the sentences my mind used to say, but when I try to say them now, the little imp jumps up in my brain or soul or some such part of my anatomy and grins, "O what's the use, what's the use." I read in *Janet March* (that really *immoral* book, no other word describes it)† that when things go wrong, just say to yourself, "It's a crazy world," and you will feel better. Well, maybe it is rather crazy, but it is a wonderful thing just to live in it, to love, to laugh, even to suffer. But it is all over so soon!

NOTES

1. See Leavitt, *Brought to Bed.*
2. *St. Louis Maternity Hospital: An account of three years' service in a new field,* published May 1911. From the archives of the Missouri Historical Society, St. Louis, Missouri.

*From Alan Seeger's "I Have a Rendezvous with Death."
†*Janet March*, by Floyd Dell, published circa 1925.

Helen's wedding picture, 1909. "I was perfectly passive and remember my start of surprise when I saw how well I looked in my handsome white satin gown, made in the Directoire style and with a long train, my first. I looked very tiny in it, but I think and was told that my face looked better than ever in my life."

Day Apte, in his prime. "The more I think of these years of married life, the happier I feel. Who am I to have had such a husband, such love showered on me, such fidelity, and such faith in me! I say it in all humility, and sincerely say it—Day is much too good for me."

Day and Helen about the time of their engagement. "I married him with doubt and reluctance, though with an instinct that I was doing the right thing and that all would be well."

The house at 394 Washington Street, Atlanta —Helen's home from age twelve to her marriage. "Our home was known as 'Liberty Hall.' . . . It was a great thing for the boys, especially. There they brought their friends, raided the icebox, played in the yard or all over the house. We each had 'our crowd,' and how we girls fought over the 'sitting room.' On Sundays we had open house; sometimes we counted sixty people there."

Tampa's Hyde Park neighborhood, 1910. "Tampa agrees with me well. . . . We like Tampa so much and are enjoying our lives, taking in every amusement, and there is always someone in town we know." *Courtesy Special Collections, University of South Florida Library*

The Ballast Point Pavilion on Tampa Bay. "That night . . . we rode out to Ballast Point and had the whole place to ourselves. A strong breeze was blowing, making the baby waves almost like ocean swells breaking on the shore. The moon shone, not brilliantly, but with a gentle soft blue light, and my heart fairly ached with the beauty of it all, until my husband's arms around me, his dear understanding of my mood swept away the ecstatic pain with which such nights fill me and left only peace and contentment in its place." *Courtesy Special Collections, University of South Florida Library*

Joseph Jacobus, Helen's father. "Almost from the first the business [in Richmond] did not go well. Papa had been cheated by his best friend. He had paid much more than the business was worth. I was too young to understand much, but I know he never got bitter. He struggled on for five years, . . . then he gave up. I was nearly twelve. I remember well that awful night May 18, 1898. He gave his life that we might live."

Alice Jacobus, Helen's mother. "There was my mother . . . with six little children and barely enough to live on. Did she repine? Did she lie down, give up? No, with courage beyond words, with no heroics but with a stern resolve, she . . . came with us to Atlanta, where there was a piece of property left from the wreckage. When we know now how little money she had, we just don't know how she did it. She held us all together by the sheer force of her will."

Charles Apte, Day's father. "I almost go wild when I try to read and write and the folks talk to me the whole time. I weep bitter tears when I get up at 6:30 to eat breakfast with my husband alone and my mother-in-law joins us. I almost go into hysterics when at last I am alone with Day at night and we are just beginning sweet confidences, and Father calls in from the next room to find out if Mr. Jones bought any cigars."

Helen with Alice, age four months. "My little daughter, heart of my heart, flesh of my flesh."

A family portrait, June 4, 1917, on Sister's wedding day. *First row*: Henry, Leonard, Maurice (Bubba). *Second row*: Alvin Cohn, Pearle, Alice Apte, Day. *Third row*: Lee Strasburger, Sarah (Sister), Helen. *Top row*: Alice Jacobus.

Leonard, Henry, and Maurice (Bubba), *left to right*, 1918. "Yesterday our soldier boys went away. Where, we do not know, but they are on the way to someplace 'over there.' All three of them—Henry, Leonard, Maurice—brave and gallant and gay, and all with smiles on their lips. . . . God bless them, and O, God, keep my brothers in Your care, help us to be brave, and to keep the home fires burning. . . . I—well, I can write no more."

Alice, about age twelve. "In a way I am a little disappointed in Alice. There is nothing of the prodigy about her, and she did give promise of that as a baby. . . . Alice must have a brain above the average because she has gotten an 'A' in every study every year, and has stood at the head of her class in every grade. . . . She has a very quick, bright, and retentive mind, a clear, accurate intelligence like her Daddy's, but what I miss in her is imagination. She doesn't like poetry and fairy tales bore her. When I remember the soul-satisfying joy I got from poetry, I grieve for her. Of course I'd rather she have Day's brain than mine. She is just exactly like him, even to her taste in literature. She isn't like me in a single way."

"After all, forty isn't so old!"

The house Day and Helen built at 601 N.E. 58th Street, Miami. "Our house is beautiful, . . . and we have a lovely, complete, comfortable home. But it leaves me cold. . . . What on earth do I need a big house for when I am alone all day from 8:30 until 5:30? It is so far out and so lonesome. I can't even walk to a store. Alice has six miles to get to school, and every day there is a discussion as to how she will get home. I have to keep two servants, and, of course, our expenses and responsibilities increase in every way. . . . To own a home is a luxury for a very rich man, one who can gratify every whim, but to own a home and feel it a strain to keep up—no, I can't see it."

Day and Helen with Alice at her high-school graduation. "On Friday night, June 5, we went to the Bay Shore Park to see our daughter graduate—our tall, slim, young daughter, with her candid gray eyes, her erect trimness. She looked lovely in her long white satin dress, fitting very tight over her hips, and flaring to the bottom, a soft draped neck in front, and cut to a low V in back. She wore a wrist corsage of roses and looked very young and pure and virginal."

The siblings at Dot's wedding, 1940. *Left to right*: Maurice (Bubba), Sarah (Sister), Henry, Helen, Leonard, Pearle.

Joan, Sister's daughter, and her husband, George Lavenson. In 1944 a trip was "marred by news of George's death. He was lost in the plane bringing back eighteen wounded soldiers. He had been wounded in the hip in Normandy, six days after D-Day."

Joseph Jacobus, Bubba's son. "On January 16 we got news of Joseph—died in action in Belgium. Impossible to realize. We are all heartbroken; twenty-four years old and gone forever."

Helen and Day with David. "I could fill the rest of this book talking about David, but I won't. I'll only say he is the most adorable, beautiful, perfect baby ever born!"

⊸❧ Chapter 4 ❦⊷

Pioneering in Miami (1925-1929)

❧ *By 1925 the Florida Boom is in full swing. Helen and Day are thirty-nine years old, and Day, an aggressive businessman, decides to take his chances in Miami. His brother, Bill, has preceded him and seems to be doing well. For her part, Helen is willing to take a chance, too. With her mother dead and her siblings moving away (Leonard joins them in Miami), there seems less reason to stay in Atlanta. Besides, it is the Roaring Twenties. There is excitement in the air. There are adventures to be had. There is money to be made.*

Miami—Tuesday, March 3, 1925

We have been here in "America's playground" since February 5 and expect to remain until May. Day is trying his luck, and I hope he will get his share of the general boom and prosperity. Miami is indeed "The Magic City." People talk in millions, fortunes are made overnight, hotels spring up like mushrooms. It reminds me very much of Los Angeles—the whole atmosphere of it somewhat like Atlantic City in the downtown section. It is really fascinating in the height of the season—the crowds and the music. I don't know how I'd like it to live here—too much sameness, I'm afraid, too glary and artificial. We are all so widely separated. Sis is in Dallas. Henry writes he is going to Europe in May.

I miss going to the cemetery. My heart is still heavy, heavy. There is a graveyard near here, right in the heart of the city. It was once the suburbs, but Miami is spreading, leaping in all directions. The graves are badly kept, many with no stone. I often walk over there and put flowers on some lonely grave. It doesn't help the poor souls there, but it helps me. The other day, I put flowers on the grave of "William Fox—Born in Odessa Russia 1897, died in U.S. Naval Air Force, 1917." What a story there!

We are staying with Bessie and Bill. If things turn out here as Day expects, we will move here in the fall. Alice is in school—High 6. Plenty to do here if we wanted to go out, but I still cannot bring myself to do it.

Miami—Tuesday, April 21, 1925

Our Florida visit is growing to an end. We leave here Thursday and reach home Saturday. On the whole it has been a satisfactory trip. We have all kept well, Day has made almost as much money as he makes in Atlanta in a year, and I feel a little more cheerful and a little lightening of the awful depression. Alice weighs ninety pounds, as much as I weighed when I married! She got two report cards, leading her class both times. Her teacher sent me word she ought to be in junior high, as the sixth grade was too easy for her. I don't think the schools here are very good, and that is the main reason I'm not anxious to come back here. Besides, there are no Jewish children here her age, and she is growing older now and ought to have a social background.

In one way, though, it would be a relief to get away from the petty jealousies, the envy, and rivalry that goes on there. Everyone is afraid their child won't be as popular as the other one. People are moving here by the thousands, and soon there will be a new crowd here. I suppose we will come back, as I really think Day can make big money here. In Atlanta things seem dead. It is fascinating to watch Miami grow. It is interesting to take part in the upbuilding of a city, and I know Day can soon become as well known here as he is at home. Sister will take it very hard, and I feel sorry for her. She is so alone and so dependent on me.

Atlanta—Wednesday, May 6, 1925

We got home on the 23rd of April after a very uncomfortable trip, as I had such as cold—a nice souvenir to bring home from Florida. It is good to be here. After all, as it is *home*, and Atlanta also has her charms. We went to ride in the country the day after we got back, and the air was sweet with honeysuckle and green, growing things. In place of the palm trees, we have the stately oak, the pine, and the poplar; instead of the hibiscus and bougainvillea, the dogwood and the peach blossoms. I love the sensuous smell of the grapefruit and orange blossoms. I thrill to the exotic beauty of the tropics, the dancing bright blue water of the bay, the calm ocean, lap-

ping so gently the white and sandy beach, but there is also something very
beautiful in the rolling hills of my native state, something fresh and wholesome in the clean breezes, in the earthy smell of the woods. Miami is like
a languid, Spanish beauty, Atlanta like a young and wholesome matron.
We received a cable yesterday from Henry of their safe arrival in France.
They have planned a lovely trip. All seem glad to see us, but Day is determined to go back in the fall. I am satisfied, as I can adjust myself to any
change and thank Heaven I can see beauty anywhere.

Atlanta—Wednesday, July 8, 1925

Alice is at Girl Scout Camp "Civitama," and Day is in Miami. I am all
alone, and I feel somehow "incomplete." Everyone has been so nice to me,
and I have been invited out for all meals. The nights are bad, though, as I
miss my sweetheart so. He writes that he is perfectly miserable without
me and that the longer we are married, the more he needs and wants me.
He wired and phoned me to come down there, but I just can't. Alice will be
home Saturday, and I can't leave her. Besides, I have been almost pros-
trated from the heat and can't bear the idea of the long hot trip to Florida.
Day will come home as soon as Bill goes back, and then we will start selling out and get ready to go back for good. The Miami paper had an article
about Day, welcoming him there and telling about his high standing in the
business and social world of Atlanta. I am sure he can become prominent
there, as he would never be satisfied to remain a nonentity.

Alice is delighted with the camp, all pep and enthusiasm. She is a
good sport. Carlyn is homesick and says the food is bad, the girls snobbish
and prejudiced. Alice says the girls are lovely to her, the food is fine, and
she has never known the meaning of anti-Jewish feeling, and I hope she
never will. Some people seem to invite it, and that family especially. I am
glad Alice is happy and satisfied, but I somehow feel a little piqued that
she doesn't miss me more! Alice is going to be a self-reliant and independent girl, and of course I want her to be, but where is my baby who up
until a year ago never had a thought I didn't know? She has changed since
the physical change took place in her. She is sometimes nervous and out
of sorts, and I ought to have more patience with her—I, of all people, who
understand so well—but there are times when she irritates me and, yes,
when I irritate her, times when a slight antagonism comes between us and

I can see her appraising and judging me. It makes me furious, but I can understand.

Miami Beach—Saturday, August 29, 1925

We left Atlanta August 11, in our new Rio sedan, Leonard coming with us. A hot, tiresome trip, and I had not intended coming down so soon, but since Day lost his mother, I thought my place was with him. The poor soul passed away July 21, after a three-day illness. We were all with her at the end, and it was sad, sad. I had not realized how fond I was of her in spite of our little irritations, and I have truly grieved for her and for her poor life, so ruthlessly snatched away, just as she was getting the material things she had always craved. Almost her last words were of Alice, to whom she left all her jewelry. She will appreciate it someday, but when I showed it to her, she said, "Mother, it doesn't mean a thing to me. I guess it's worth a lot of money, but I'd rather have my Grandma back than all the money in the world."

We are staying at the Wofford until we can find an apartment, which seems impossible. The situation is acute. People moving here by the thousands, and no place to live. We can get a one-room kitchenette apartment for $150 a month, but how can we live in one room? It reminds me of the gold rush to the Klondike—plenty of money, but no comforts. People are living without telephones, without hot water, without servants. When I think of how easy I had it at home, I wonder if it's worth it. Miami is not the pleasant place to live it was last winter—it is like a madhouse, dangerous to cross the street, dangerous to drive a car, almost impossible to get a bite to eat without standing in a line. Men rush madly about, with the lust for money in their eyes. Everyone seems to be snooping around, trying to listen in, and I'm so tired of learning real estate I could *scream*. I am on the porch with the ocean just across the street, but it scarcely thrills me. This is not *my* ocean. No, my ocean is a thing of moods. This one is always the same. A hard brilliant blue, it shimmers and sparkles and gently laps the shore—hardly a wave or ripple. The water is hot, and curiously enervating. No, not *my* ocean at all. "Rain"—I think of "Sadie Thompson" and those other strange characters, marooned in that tropical inn.* It gets one, that steady drip, and they say the rainy season has begun here. It has been

---

*A reference to "Miss Thompson," the 1921 short story by W. Somerset Maugham, which takes place on a South Sea island.

pouring steadily since yesterday, but it is a relief from the steady glare and heat.

Miami—Saturday, September 12, 1925

We moved into this tiny apartment on N.E. Miami Court September 1. It has one bedroom, a dressing room in which Alice sleeps, a kitchenette, and a bath—$200 a month until November 1, then $250.* We are looking for something larger but so far no success: I do all the work, which isn't much, but the cooking is hard for me, as I'm not used to it and I don't like it. It is strange to think Day is making more money than ever in his life, and I am having it harder. Never have I done without a servant, but I think it will really do me good. I was getting fat and lazy, and not that I gained in weight, but I *felt* fat. I now weigh 126 pounds, Alice 92 pounds. She swims nicely, which she learned at camp. Her counselor wrote in her autograph book, "You are a good scout, Alice, and that's saying a lot." Another wrote, "To the best scout and the best sport I know." She helps me a lot in the house and saves me many a step.

Miami—Thursday, November 26, 1925

Thanksgiving Day—yes, lots to be thankful for—all in good health, money coming in easy, a nice roomy apartment at last. We miss our departed ones, of course. Day's birthday yesterday, and of course he felt sad, as his mother was always with us on that day. It has been very cool all week— went down to 44°, the coldest November in years, but today is warm and beautiful, and we will take lunch and go over on the beach.

Miami—Monday, November 30, 1925

Rain—mild, gray, relentless rain. It has poured steadily since last night, and much damage has been done. There are six inches of water in the office, and Day and Leonard had to come home, drenched. I was glad to have them for lunch, as Dora didn't come and I was lonesome. Yes, I who never knew the meaning of the word am often lonesome here. It used to aggravate me to have Sister call me a dozen times a day, but I'd like to have her call me right now. I've been playing the gramophone—*William Tell, Storm Overture*—but it was too realistic. I am just beginning *Swann's*

*$200 is the equivalent of about $1,800 in 1998; $250 is the equivalent of nearly $2,300. Figures based on the Consumer Price Index.

Way by Marcel Proust. Read Sherwood Anderson's *Dark Laughter*. It may be art, it may be life, and I may be narrow, but it left a bad taste in my mouth, almost physical. Still, deep down in me, something responds, certain instincts stir.

Day was very sick Friday with one of his kidney colic attacks. He suffered agony all day, and it tore me to pieces to see his suffering. He had morphine five times. It is four years since he last had an attack, and I do wish they could find some permanent cure. The next day he was down at work. Men have such quick recuperative power.

Have I ever said Sidney is married? Well, he is and so, "finis."

Miami—Tuesday, February 16, 1926

I have been in bed several days with intestinal grippe. Feel weak and nervous. Sister, Joan, and Lee just completed a visit with us, and we had a lovely time together. We were invited out every day, and I surely had my fill of parties, but Sister adored it. We took in the races, the jai alai games, the dog races, etc. Plenty to do in Miami. Everyone says it is a miniature New York. Tremendous development is going on, but there is a great lull in real estate. Things are very quiet, and all are disappointed. Day, as always optimistic, says it is a healthy situation and things will pick up, but there are some sick and worried people here, chiefly those who invested too heavily and are not prepared to carry the investment. I now like it much better here than I did. We had a fine visit home Christmas, and I came back feeling more satisfied. I have gotten over the faint nostalgia I felt for Atlanta.

Miami—Wednesday, March 10, 1926

My seventeenth anniversary! How incredible it sounds. Happy years on the whole, until our recent sorrow. I can say again—thank God for such a husband. We will not celebrate in any way, as our hearts are full, thinking of our dear ones. I went to our newly organized club at Marcella's this morning. I am the treasurer. Then went to market with Ethel and came home to lie down, and have one of my headaches. Will read a while after dinner and so to bed!

Spring is here again, but there is no difference here. The same bright sunny days and a few cool ones. A faint suspicion of grapefruit blossoms, but the scent is not as strong or potent as the orange blossoms I used to love in Tampa. Since Sis was here, Roberta has been here, and Uncle Julius, Aunt Mena, Bessie and Bill. One is blessed with company in Miami. Day gave me a gorgeous emerald and diamond bracelet and a dinner ring to match. I never thought I cared for jewelry, but I'm no different than other women. I adore these, and I'm proud and happy Day can afford to give them.

Miami—Saturday, March 20, 1926

Alice has gone to a picnic with her school class, and I am miserable. When she asked my permission last night, my heart began to sink, but of course I said yes, for why should the child suffer for my cowardice and morbid fears? I hate for her to go any place without me, and can hardly wait until she gets home, but I always let her go, and try not to let her know how I feel. How she is so fearless is a mystery to me, and she is so dependable I can always trust her. When she left, she said, "Now Mother, don't worry. I won't do anything I know you don't want me to." I want her to go to camp this summer, as it will be good for her and good for me.

Henry's baby, a boy, was born March 12, and I feel like a grandma, as it seems yesterday I held him on my lap and rocked him to sleep. Yes, we rocked babies in those days, and he *was* a darling. I am eleven years older than Henry. He is so proud and happy—and Mama not here to see it.

Tonight we are going to the Biltmore for dinner. So many lovely places to go here, and we go out to dinner quite often. We had a very cold spell last week, but now it is beautiful. I don't believe I'd go back to Atlanta to live if I could. I lead the freest kind of life here, go and come when I please. I don't know why it always irritated me so, for anybody to ask me where I was going, as I never went any place the least bit out of the ordinary, but I used to catch myself at home trying to slip out the back way, just to go down to the store, but no use, always a head would be poked out of a window and someone ask, "Where you going?" I would want to scream out, "None of your business," but of course I never did. Here I take a childish delight in the most irregular hours. Sometimes I eat my lunch at 11, sometimes at 3. I go downtown at the most outlandish times, slip into a movie, wander through the shops, sit in the park and listen to Pryor's band. It gives me a thrill of adventure, very absurd, but for the first time in my life, I can do it, and as a child I always dreamed of the day I could be independent, *free*, and no one to question me!

Alice is taking art lessons and is doing remarkably well. As with her music, I don't see any genius, but whatever she undertakes, she does well.

Miami—Sunday, May 2, 1926

Day is in Atlanta on his way home from Cincinnati, where he went to get a new rabbi. He wired they were successful,* but it is no more than I expected, as Day never set out to accomplish a thing yet that he didn't do it. It amuses me to see how he can do this. At the annual meeting of the congregation, by sheer force of personality, he swept them all with him and carried every point, though many started out opposed to him.

I have not felt well and was in bed a week during April, as Dr. Hutson found some trouble with my heart. I just went to another doctor, and he says there is absolutely nothing wrong with my heart, so which am I to believe?

Everyone has been so nice to me since Day is away, and I have been invited out every day. I often wonder why people are so sweet to me. It seems to me they are always nicer to me than I deserve, and I do appreciate it. Friday, when I went to register at the courthouse, I found a line about a mile long, but a man in back of me got me a chair and pushed it all the way down the line for me, and I was the only person to sit down and wait my turn. I never get on a crowded car that a man doesn't offer me a seat, and I have always found men courteous and polite. I like them!

New York—Hotel Knickerbocker—Thursday, July 22, 1926

We have been here since last Friday. I spent my fortieth birthday in Clayton, where we went to see Alice in camp.† She loves it and has won several honors. I hated to leave her and miss her, but know it is best for her, though she spent her thirteenth birthday away from me—my precious baby!

---

*Temple Israel dispatched Day and two other men to Cincinnati—the headquarters of Reform Judaism in America, housing Hebrew Union College and the Union of American Hebrew Congregations—to find a new rabbi. Told that a local rabbi, Jacob H. Kaplan, might be interested, the three men went to hear him preach, liked what they heard, and hired him for $8,000 a year. Rabbi Kaplan became a good friend. Day served as president of Temple Israel from 1928 to 1934. Rabbi Kaplan remained at Temple Israel until his retirement in 1941. (See Charlton W. Tebeau, *Synagogue in the Central City: Temple Israel of Greater Miami, 1922–1972* [Coral Gables, FL: University of Miami Press, 1972], 62.)

†The camp in Clayton, Georgia, was run by Lillian Smith, the noted Southern writer.

It is very hot here, and I spend most of my days in my room. We have seen *The Shanghai Gesture* with Florence Reed, Lenore Ulric in *Linda Belle*, and Saturday will see Mae West in *Sex*. Chinese, Negro, and white lust—it's all the same. *Linda Belle* positively nauseated me. I don't get shocked, but I was repelled. New York is full of oversexed women and bored men looking for a new sensation. Sex is in the very air.

Yesterday was a year since Day's mother passed away. We went to temple yesterday morning. It is open fifteen minutes every day, a wonderful idea—just a breathing space, a relaxation in the mad day, but how few take advantage of it.

We drove out to Long Beach last night with some friends. The man who sat next to me couldn't or wouldn't make his hands behave. It was a hot, moonlit night, and after all forty isn't so old! We expect to leave here Sunday on a boat to Boston. Day is my lover, my wonderful companion as always. We are having a second honeymoon.

Miami—Thursday, November 11, 1926

Armistice Day—a glorification of peace! Alas, what a farce: There is no peace. Yesterday at the council meeting [National Council of Jewish Women] my committee had charge of the program, and we women pledged ourselves to work for peace and to end war. I am chairman of the Peace and Arbitration Committee.

Cool today, and looks like fall. Alice is at the parade and will stay to go to a movie with Helen Klein. Day will come home to lunch. I have no servant and have had none since we moved in October to 534 N.E. 23rd Street, right on the bay and a nice apartment. I like being alone and the little housework, but I hate the cooking and dishwashing at night. Dora promised to come back Monday for half a day.

Literally speaking, a lot of water has gone under the bridge since I last wrote, and a lot has gone over the bridge and over the causeway and over Miami! Yes, we have lived through the hurricane of September 18,* the most disastrous this country has ever known. Alice and I had only been back six days, and we were at the Dallas Park Apartments, a fine concrete building, so our experience was not as bad as many others, but it was bad enough when that ten-story hotel rocked like a cradle, when the windows

---

*The 1926 storm left the city in ruins. More than one hundred people were killed.

blew in. Water leaked from every conceivable place—gas, lights, and water gone, the river at our very door. Yes, it was bad enough. For twelve hours the storm raged, and it is a great experience to feel that any moment might be one's last. It surely seemed that between the water and the wind we were doomed, and it was interesting to see different people's reactions. Our little family came out of it creditably, I think. I was afraid dreadfully, but I didn't show it. I don't believe Alice or Day felt any fear. They were wonderful and calm, cheerful, doing everything to aid and cheer others. If I needed any proof of their characters, I had it that night and day of terror. They are just exactly alike. While other children whimpered and cried, Alice never uttered a word of fear or complaint.

We had another fright October 20, when a hurricane of equal ferocity was predicted. We went down to the Roberts Hotel, where Maurice was staying, and with hundreds of others who were taking refuge in the large buildings we sat up all night, waiting, but it did not materialize.

Poor Miami. Almost prostrate from the collapse of the real estate boom, it had to stand that battering. But more than ever it deserves the name of the Magic City, for it is little short of marvelous how it has come back, and scarcely a trace of the catastrophe to be seen. The day after, all felt that the end had come, the sights were pitiful, the wreckage indescribable, but after the first awful depression, everyone got to work, and when I came back from Palm Beach a week later, I could not believe my eyes. We have been through a lot in this sunny city, but it has been worth something to be a pioneer. It has given us experience and adventure. Day lost a lot of money, of course. Everyone is crying hard times, and last year money was no object.

I wrote last in New York. That was only the beginning of our wonderful trip. We went to Boston, on the train to Portland, Poland Spring, Montreal, Lake Placid, Buffalo, and back to New York. Wherever we went we had a lovely time, and people are always so nice to us. In Lake Placid the folks at the hotel made the biggest kind of fuss over us. It is a gift for which we are thankful. You either have it or you haven't it, and it's a gift from heaven, no less. I can see why Day is so popular. He is excellent company and can hold a whole room full of people with his conversation. He is genial, interested in everyone, forceful and interesting. By sheer force of personality he can sway anyone to his side, and he loves it. Like all strong characters, he is very egotistical. He loves authority, and he hates to ever admit he is wrong. I am so different. I have not the least desire for authority, and I have an abhorrence for mixing in anyone's affairs, or for giving advice. Day rushes in where angels fear to tread, and while my friends do not love me as his do (they would die for him), I have no enemies. People either love or hate him, but even his enemies are forced to admire and respect him.

Miami—Friday, December 24, 1926

Christmas Eve dawned bright and fair with the thermometer at 77°. Natalie is visiting Alice, and we are going on the beach to go bathing, the first time since the hurricane. For a long time I could not even look at the bay. That anything so beautiful could be so sinister is beyond imagination. Last year this time, we were in Atlanta.

Miami—Thursday, January 6, 1927

Another year! We spent New Year's Eve and Day in Palm Beach. O, it was cold as only Florida can be cold. I just hate it here when we have that sort of weather. Still cool, but much more pleasant. We went to the new Pennsylvania Hotel to watch the New Year in. Something must be wrong with me, but I never have a good time on that night. I can't help from being terribly bored, as I just can't see the fun of screaming, blowing horns, ringing bells, etc. Lord knows we need the spirit of youth and fun, but it just isn't my temperament to enter into it. I wish I could be gay all the time. Day says it is all he misses in me. He wants me to laugh and smile all the time, and I just can't. I can be happy in my own way, and it seems the happier I am the quieter I get, with a deep inner glow. I am just made that way.

Everyone got drunk and then very sick. The room was so crowded that it was impossible to dance. Men and women swayed in each other's arms, jostled each other, stepped all over one's feet. No, I didn't have a bit of fun. I wish I could enter into things as Day does. How seldom I do the things I really want to do. O, for just a few interesting, congenial people. Life is passing, and what am I getting out of it?

Sister is in Dallas. I hope to go in June. Day goes to Chicago next week and to Cleveland as delegate to the convention of Reform congregations. He is perfectly satisfied with his life, and I try to interest myself in the same things. I am secretary of the Sisterhood,* but it takes up little of my time. I only have Dora a half day so I can have something to do, but still there is a lapse. Yes, I very much fear I have reached the "dangerous age." Early autumn. Physically, I feel well. I am still taking the gland tablets, and I think they help. I am much stronger than I was as a girl. Nature tricks us so.

Miami—Tuesday, March 22, 1927

My eighteenth anniversary passed very pleasantly. Eighteen years of love, of sweet companionship, of mutual respect and understanding. Who could want more? Thank God, again I say, for such a husband. But—life is so short!

Miami—Monday, October 10, 1927

I came home September 4 after a wonderful vacation. Alice went to camp in June, going to Atlanta ahead of me. I spent two days there, thence to Dallas, where I stayed two weeks. It was so good to be with Pearle and see Henry and all, but it was very hot. Day joined me and was sick with ear trouble the few days he stayed. All were so nice to us, and we were so shocked last week to hear of Mr. Marcus' death.† He was in perfect health when we were there. We went to St. Louis for two days about July 10, and were much entertained and glad to see old friends. Got to Chicago on my birthday and spent four delightful weeks at the Stevens Hotel—America's newest and largest. Ran up to Minocqua, Wisconsin, and stayed three days there, but I was glad to get back to Chicago. I like the big "Windy City." Just as Miami reminds me of a young Spanish girl, Chicago seems to me a big virile young man, full of the joy of life, full of sex, but in a cleaner way than New York—fresher, not so enervating. I did not realize I knew so many people there, and we were royally entertained. They made an awful fuss over us, and I could have been dated up every minute, but I kept lots of time to myself, to wander around and to read, etc.

We went to Louisville to the apple shippers' convention August 10. That's a very commonplace, uninteresting town to me. I could not find any atmosphere. Day stayed in Atlanta two days, then I ran up to Clayton

*Many Jewish congregations have service organizations for men and women called Brotherhoods and Sisterhoods, respectively.
†Theo Marcus, Henry's father-in-law.

to see Alice. Found her so well and happy. How she loves camp life! It never would have appealed to me as a girl. I only stayed two days, as I just can't stand the country. I am surely "urban"—the noise of subway and elevator I can stand, but the deadly quiet of the country nights gets on my nerves. Every snap of a twig sounds like a pistol-shot, and the mysterious sound of birds, insects, and strange beasts terrifies me!

I am a lucky woman to have such wonderful trips, such complete relaxation, and so much attention showered upon me. Yes, it is good, but to come home with a singing heart is best of all. However, it takes a long time to get adjusted to the humdrum life of housekeeping. It's hard to come back to earth and get back on the job again. It's like going barefooted all summer and then trying to wear the old shoes again. September is the worst month in Miami—rain, heat, mosquitos, and the fear of a storm in the air.

Miami—Monday, March 26, 1928

My nineteenth anniversary was spent in Cuba. We left here, Alice, Day, and I, March 8 on the beautiful new steamer *Iroquois*, staying three days in Havana. A lovely trip, none of us seasick a minute. Havana is interesting for a few days, but that's enough. We saw all the sights, went to a wild (?) cabaret, the casino, Chinese theatre, and "Sloppy Joe's." That interested me most of all. Drinking and eating together were the high and the low, the rich and the outcast, sailor, derelict, millionaire, white, and black. A very cosmopolitan and democratic city, but decadent, erotic, too gay. We were invited to a real Cuban home where I got the real atmosphere. The wife was an American girl, and she told me some horrible things, which made me abhor the Cuban men and pity and a little despise the women.

This winter has flown. We had a good season, the best since the Boom. The future of Miami is still incalculable. The days drift by, luncheons, bridge—the same old thing. We could have an awfully good time here if we had a congenial little crowd. Our best times are when the visitors come. Business is good with Day, and he is well satisfied. The temple was finished and dedicated. I was a delegate to the Sisterhood convention in Palm Beach.

Quite a cold winter, but I have enjoyed my little bungalow, even though I did come near freezing at times.

Alice is on the basketball and track team at school, so I don't see much of my child. She continues to get an "A" in every study. She is going back to camp.

Miami—Saturday, December 22, 1928

Lying in bed in my new home, where we have been two weeks. I have a bad cold and fever, which anyplace else would be called flu, but since we don't have that in Miami, I suppose it is only a cold. A beautiful summer day, but a cold spell predicted tonight, and I dread it, as we have had two this month and I almost froze to death. I expect Sis, Lee, and Joan on Sunday and will be so glad, though I am really not settled yet. The day we moved I developed an abscessed tooth, and then Day had two attacks of kidney colic. The doctor wanted him to go to hospital, but he passed a tiny stone, which we think and pray may end his trouble.

Our house is beautiful, but the sickness when we moved and a lot of exasperating details of finishing up took away much of the pleasure. Workmen are still all over the place, and it is impossible to finish cleaning up. Some of our furniture has not come, but what has is beautiful, and we have a lovely, complete, comfortable home. But it leaves me cold. I know I ought to be ashamed. I know most any woman would consider herself lucky. But I never wanted to build and still feel we made a mistake, but it was Day's dream and ambition, and I felt I could not deny him.

I believe I have good and valued reasons for not wanting to build this house, and I cannot help feeling we have made a mistake, but now that we are here, I want to get all the pleasure I can out of it and help Day enjoy it, though I believe he has misgivings himself, but he would not admit it. What on earth do I need a big house for when I am alone all day from 8:30 until 5:30? It is so far out and so lonesome. I can't even walk to a store. Alice has six miles to get to school, and every day there is a discussion as to how she will get home. I have to keep two servants, and, of course, our expenses and responsibilities increase in every way. The conditions in Miami today do not seem to justify the expenditure of $30,000.* To own a home is a luxury for a very rich man, one who can gratify every whim, but to own a home and feel it a strain to keep it up—no, I can't see it, especially since rents have come down so much and we could have rented anyplace in town for $100 a month. I could be just as happy in a little

---

*$30,000 is equal to nearly $285,000 in 1998, based on the CPI-U.

apartment, only the three of us now that Leonard is going to Dallas to live. How I hate his leaving, and how we shall miss him, but it is for his good. It has been a comfort to have one of my own with me.

I am a strange person, but home to me can mean one room, just one room I can call my own, can close my door and be alone. I can go into a bare room, put out my few personal belongings, a few books and magazines, *close the door*, and lo, I am *home*. I love pretty things, but I can be happy just to look at them. I don't have to own them. I have never coveted anything in my life, or envied anyone, anything. My wants are few and simple, and I do not crave material things, but I do crave that inner beauty of spirit, which sometimes I feel I have missed.

Another lovely trip last summer, which I must record. We spent my birthday with Alice at camp, drove by bus to Asheville, train to Norfolk, boat to New York, where we met Henry and Dorothy and spent four delightful weeks. We went to theatre together and dined together, they staying at the Warwick, we at the New Victoria. Stayed in Atlanta until September 1. Alice, after camp, visited Janice in Macon. Some shows we saw in New York—*Show Boat* (charming), *Bachelor Father*, *Trial of Mary Dugan*, *Coquette* with Helen Hayes, *Royal Family*, *Three Musketeers*, and that strange morbid enthralling thing—*Strange Interlude.**

I had to open this book again to record something that amused me very much. Since I am in bed, I have entertained men in my boudoir all day! The painter, the plumber, the contractor, the carpenter. The electrician was just here to connect the heater, and as he left, he came back to the door and said, "I just had to come back and tell you you look like a doll baby, lying there."

Well, an achievement I call it, to look like a doll baby with a cold in the head!

Miami—Sunday, July 14, 1929

In the midst of packing, but must record my birthday, a very lonesome one with Alice at camp.

I see I did not write on my twentieth anniversary. It was a lovely occasion. We gave a dinner for thirty at the Florida Hotel, champagne, etc.—it really was a fine affair. Got many nice presents, telegrams, etc.

---

*Eugene O'Neill's nine-act play about the emotional and sexual reactions of a woman who subconsciously hates her father.

I have not had a cook for weeks and have enjoyed being alone, but it is very dull here, and I will be glad for a little change. Everyone is away. Weather delightful, have not felt the heat once this summer. Have read a book a day, but nothing very interesting except *The Well of Loneliness.** I have gotten more adjusted to the house and do find it comfortable and homey, and I have made up my mind not to worry about it next winter, nor to take it so seriously. It is perfectly absurd to worry about housekeeping and I know it, but when I try to neglect one little thing, it seems that generations of thrifty German hausfraus must rise up in me and demand perfection! So while in theory I know I should not worry about it, it is, like many other theories, only a theory!

I shocked Day very much by telling him I did not think it essential for married couples to be faithful to each other. The theory of freedom and self-expression is fine, but I'm like Day and his reason for not eating ham: He says he has absolutely no religious scruples against it, he thinks it ridiculous *not* to eat it, but he was brought up *not* to eat it and he "just can't." So it's that way with me—"I was brought up not to and I just couldn't!" And I have reason to know I couldn't, too! Such a funny little affair. I wish I could write about it. I can't do that, but it has made a little excitement for me and much real amusement.

*Radclyffe Hall's novel caused a sensation because of its sympathetic portrayal of lesbianism. It was banned in Britain, and sales were temporarily suspended in the United States.

◈ Chapter 5 ◈

Like Not Eating Ham (1930–1934)

◈ *Day prospers, and he and Helen continue to travel, taking their daughter to Europe for a summer-long trip. Alice graduates from high school and then goes off to college. A dangerous world becomes more dangerous—the Depression, a war in Europe, and temptations at home. As this chapter begins, Helen and Day are forty-three; Alice is sixteen.*

Miami—Wednesday, January 29, 1930

Alice has gone to the beach, as she is out of school this week, being exempt in all exams. She is having a nice time, going out with a few boys, and while I'm glad she has met boys to go with and knew it had to come, I also hate it. I know I can't keep her locked up in a glass cage, and she has to try her wings. What can a mother do these days but talk frankly to her daughter, make her feel you are her confidante, and then trust to luck, or to God? Alice is good, simple, frank, but she is also a modern girl, whatever that may mean. Of course girls are and always have been the same, but it is ideals, standards that have changed. For instance, she told me last night, when she went out in a two-seat car with four people, that she had to sit in a boy's lap. I asked her why the girls didn't sit in each other's laps, and she answered, "O, Mother, it just isn't done." I asked her how that boy behaved, and she said, "All he did was keep his arm around me, and if that gives him pleasure, why should I mind?"!

Who am I to preach! Just last week, such an experience! I guess I'd better not write anything about it, but I can't resist it. Samson phoned me Saturday night. He was only in town for a few hours and was coming out. I was so happy, as I've not seen him in years, and while I waited for him the years rolled back, and once more I felt the magic of that summer night, when he and I were boy and girl together. I could see the soft Southern moon, the giant oaks of Grant Park, the lake, the rustic seats. O, young love, young passion, always to me so poignant and so sweet. I have thought of that night so often, but did not dream he had remembered. He spoke of it at once, and of how he had thought of me constantly through all these years—twenty-five years! He remembered every minute, almost, of that summer he spent in Atlanta. Told me things I said and he said, which I had entirely forgotten, swore he had always cared, etc. I had told Alice to be home at ten o'clock, and to the minute she was here—none too soon! It flashed through my mind that it was really irritating how prompt Alice always is, and why must she always do exactly what I tell her! Well, it's just as well. I guess we had one hour together, and not everyone can have their hour. After he left, she said, "Mother, I think he's nice, but he likes you too much, and you like him!" He is just the same as he was as a boy—strong, virile, ruthless, and sensual, and of course fascinating.

Day came home from Chicago Monday after a ten-day absence. We missed him terribly and how happy to have him back. He brought us beautiful presents. Gorgeous weather and a good season.

Miami—Friday, March 14, 1930

Monday was our twenty-first anniversary. We were invited to Roth's Restaurant for dinner and sat at a table with "Miss Illinois" and "Miss Florida," who were here to take part in a beauty pageant. Day is the director of that event—what he will be next, I don't know! We were also present at the Directors' Ball at Coral Gables and had a box sent us for the big night. After dinner we went to see *Vagabond King*, supposed to be the last word on movies, but to me only another rather banal musical revue. The more I think of these years of married life, the happier I feel. Who am I to have had such a husband, such love showered on me, such fidelity, and such faith in me! I say it in all humility, and sincerely say it—Day is much too good for me. What have I ever done, what have I accomplished? But if I have made him happy, have satisfied him in every way, then I have not lived in vain, and perhaps that has helped him to do his work so well and to accomplish the good he is always doing. We are trying to get reservations for Europe for June and know we will have a wonderful trip.

On February 23 I left with Dr. and Mrs. Kaplan for Tampa to a Sisterhood convention. On the way, his car skidded and turned over, all escaping with minor injuries. I broke a bone in my wrist and had a very black eye. I feel so thankful that I am not even nervous. My nerves have never been as strong as this winter, and I don't know when I felt so well. I weigh 120 pounds. The house is a real pleasure to me now, since I ceased to take it so seriously. I don't worry about anything, just take things as they come and try to get as much out of life as possible. What a pity I did not do this sooner in life. Middle age is really an interesting state—one is able to stop for a while at the top of the hill, look around a bit, and take a deep breath, before starting to go down the hill on the other side. That's what I dread— the going down!

Miami—Wednesday, April 23, 1930

I am getting my house in order for our trip. Took down the draperies and am packing things away. We have gotten passage on the *France* June 17, and return passage on the *Sumaria* September 3. Have not completed our itinerary, so more of that later. For the first time I am really thrilled over a trip. I always enjoy myself after I go, but never have the pleasure of antici- pation, as a peculiar form of nervousness always makes me depressed and afraid, but I don't pay a bit of attention to my apprehension, as I recognize it for what it is—just nerves.

I am terribly afraid of the water—it has a fascination and a horror for me, and every time I think of our trip I can see one of those "swell" movie shipwrecks, and I shudder! But, I know it's going to all be great. Bill and Bessie go with us, and I do hope she and Day will agree not to argue too much!

Alice and I plan to leave here May 30, the day school is out, and I will go to Atlanta to shop, until Day joins us there, then a few days in New York. I promised Samson—well, what *did* I promise him exactly, anyway?

Miami—Tuesday, September 30, 1930

Well, let me take a deep breath. This has been, in many ways, the most momentous summer of my life. Some of it cannot be said, and all about our wonderful trip is in my other diary, *My Trip Abroad.** It seems like a dream, and my impressions are all jumbled, but it was a great experience. To see eight different countries, make contacts, absorb the atmosphere—

---

*This diary is truly just a travelogue, a detailed account of where they went and what they saw, with some historical notes about what they learned.

what a privilege. As usual, our trip came out just as Day had planned it, almost to the day, though we made a few changes in our itinerary. We all kept well, though I had two miserable colds and was often too tired to enjoy things.

Time each day is recorded in *My Trip Abroad*. I only want to mention a few highlights—my birthday in Venice, the gondoliers singing my adored *La Bohème* under the balcony of my room at the Royal Danelli, the cable from Samson, Day's gift of red roses from the glass factory. My funny little experience in Paris, which was so unexpected, and rather sweet. The visit to Hechtsherm, my mother's birthplace; not often in a lifetime does it come to one to stand in a sacred place and be overcome by such pure and holy emotions. The trip up the Rhine from Mainz to Bonn, and somehow I felt such affinity with the broad and gracious river, the tiny towns, the hills, and the vineyards. I suppose it was because there is the home of my ancestors, and there are the roots of my being.

Berchtesgaden—what precious, tender memories. To think of meeting Mort there, as if by a miracle. The years roll back, and we feel the same to each other as we did twenty-five years ago. How well we understand it all now out of the depths of experience. Our true and devoted friendship, which we loved to call platonic, our horror when we found it was not platonic after all, our struggle against passion, and our brave decision *not* to let it interfere with our friendship. We knew there could never be anything more between us. Was I not bound to Jim and he to Viola? How well we understand it all now! Of course he says the obvious thing—that it was I, not Viola, whom he loved all the time but did not realize it then. Dear boy, I was shocked when I first saw him. He looked old and very thin, and worn. I had still been thinking of him as twenty-one, young, handsome, and so strong, and I suppose he had the same shock when he saw my gray hairs. He is very happily married, the father of two children and stepfather of two more. Dear, dear boy, my friend and confidant. He and Doris have promised to visit us this winter.

I was with Samson in New York once on my way over, once on my way back. I had lunch with Sidney at the Pennsylvania Hotel on our return. We did enjoy talking together again, and I'm sorry I have not been phoning him these last four years. He says I am just as he has always remembered me, sweet and fascinating!!

Hard to get back to prosaic housekeeping again! I got back on the 21st, just in time for New Year's. O, I wish I could get some real joy and consolation in going to temple. I used to get real comfort out of prayer, and now I simply cannot pray at all. The longer I live, the more presumptuous it seems for me, *me*, to offer prayer to ask for favors. Who am I, what am I, that God should listen to me? I know that's the wrong way to look at it, but I can't help my feelings. Perhaps that is one of the penalties we pay for sinning—losing our power to pray. One thing I am surer of than ever, though, is that we do pay, if we sin. There are certain inexorable laws, and if we break them, we pay. Some pay in one way, some in another. We pay by suffering, we pay, as I said, by not being able to pray, and a thousand other ways, but pay we *must*. Every normal person has a sense of right and wrong, argue though we may in the modern fashion. You *can't* get away with it!

Miami—Tuesday, November 11, 1930

Just listened to an Armistice Day Program from Washington—two minutes of silence at 11 A.M., prayer by Dr. Abram Simon, and address by President Hoover. All cry for peace, but the president said, "How can we countries who have been made from war say there is never just cause for war?" Personally, I believe the only justification of war is for freedom, which, of course, means defending ourselves from attack, and how can we do that without being prepared? O, if all men and all countries would only "turn their swords into ploughshares." But what did we see in Europe— Italy, a military nation, soldiers everywhere and ready to spring at France. France hating everyone, but the only prosperous nation today, practically no unemployment, and their chief industry seems to be exploiting Americans, whom they look upon with ill-concealed contempt—insolence. Germany struggling, prostrate, and lately becoming inflamed with anti-Semitism and Hitlerism; Austria ruined, hopeless. England in terrible financial and economic stress; and just now comes news of its repudiation of Balfour Declaration, which has caused a storm of protest throughout the world.*

We are invited to take lunch today on the Munson liner *Munargo*, and Alice, having a holiday from school, will go with us. Had our first cold spell the first week in November, which only lasted two days, and now it is delightful again. Just got my house in order and draperies up.

---

*The Balfour Declaration of 1917, named after then-British Foreign Secretary Arthur J. Balfour, stated that Britain favored "the establishment in Palestine of a national home for the Jewish people."

Miami—Sunday, January 18, 1931

I expected to be in New York today, but instead Alice and I are spending a lonely Sunday at home. I was ready to leave for Philadelphia with Day last Monday when she developed the mumps, which she caught in Dallas. I have been in the house with her all week, and have been so blue. The weather has been cold, rainy, miserable. Never have we had such a winter—even the elements seem to have it in for poor Miami. A great deal of depression is still felt over the closing of Citizen's Bank, and everyone was looking forward to the "season," but it seems to be a poor one, the whole country being in throes of terrible business Depression. Alice had a fine time in Dallas, and all raved about her.

New Year's we went to the Roman Pools. A gay crowd, and there I had the strangest experience, which I still cannot explain, so an evening I had expected to find dull turned out to be very exciting.

Miami—Wednesday, February 25, 1931

Nearly March, and hard to believe the winter is nearly over. A cold, rainy disagreeable season such as we have never had in Miami, but it has passed quickly and pleasantly for me—that is, if not all pleasantly, at least excitingly. Yes, two "strange interludes," but that's all, only interludes, just to break the monotony and make life a little more interesting. But there is only one man in the world whom I love and who holds my heart in the hollow of his hand—my husband.

A great fascinating game, the game always being played between men and women, but it's a dangerous game, and a woman must keep her wits about her. But how foolish to play with fire, what danger of being scorched, because to men there is only one culmination, and they are not satisfied, as women are, just to have a little thrill of excitement. Before one knows it, one is involved too deeply, one way or another. Yes, it is far best to walk the straight and narrow path and never to stray, but of course you miss a lot of fun!

Physically, I have never felt better in my life, never had more endurance, never felt stronger. Everyone tells me I look younger and better than they ever saw me; some go so far as to say I am better looking. After all, fire is a good thing, even necessary to life. Only be careful to merely warm your hands. Don't go near enough to be scorched!

Miami—Saturday, May 2, 1931

Such an anticlimax after the last paragraph! I see I wrote on February 25.

On March 15 I was stricken suddenly with terrible pain and nausea. Sent for the doctor and had two hypodermics with no relief. Spent a terrible night, and early the next day Dr. Dolerin brought out Dr. Adkins, a surgeon, and I was sent at once in an ambulance to Jackson Memorial Hospital. An intestinal obstruction was at once suspected, and the next few days I have only the haziest memories of. They were working on me constantly, and I was in agony. Had six doctors in consultation, and all advised an operation, but I begged so hard not to. On Friday the 29th I ceased to object, because I realized I could not live in the condition I was in. By that time I didn't care what happened or what they did. At 3 P.M. I was on the table, taking spinal anaesthetic, a wonderful but rather terrible thing. They found an internal rupture, and I heard them say I could not possibly have lived another twenty-four hours. As they lifted me from the table, my respiration became affected, and for an hour they had to pump my lungs full of carbon dioxide. The next few days are like a nightmare. I was desperately ill, pulse, heart, lungs, extended with gas and unable to get relief. Stomach pumped twice, Lord knows what else! I knew I was dying and was reconciled to it. This is the second time in my life I was near to death, and I can truly say that to face death is not hard.

"O," I thought, "how blessed it would be to just close my eyes and rest, *rest* for ever, no more pain." I wanted to ask the doctors to leave me alone and let me die in peace, but I knew it would do no good. Everything that medical attention could do was done for me, no expense spared, no attention too much for me, and who shall say whether it was that or the prayers of my friends that saved me? I could not pray for myself, but my whole being is a prayer of thanksgiving now. Some miracle saved me, or it was God's will that I live? I thank Him for saving me, and O, I thank Him for the love, the tender sympathy, the wonderful attentions of my family and friends. I did not realize how many friends—true, real friends—I had. Words can't express what they did for me. I can't begin to write it. Many stayed at the hospital day and night. I had so many flowers we could not get them in the room. I had the deep, sincere love and prayers of all, and I feel humble and unworthy of it all.

It is six weeks yesterday since the operation, and I get stronger each day. Last night I went to temple and I was downtown last week. My knees are still rather weak, and I have pain in my heart but otherwise can't complain. Dr. Kaplan said a beautiful prayer of thanks for my recovery last night. He and I have grown closer than ever since my illness. A rare and beautiful friendship, a sweet relationship exists between us. Others might not understand it, but that does not matter.

"My Constant Physical Weakness and Low Vitality"*

Readers cannot help but notice that for most of her life Helen was not healthy. She was so frail as a teenager that she quit school. Later, as an adult, she had so many problems that Alice returned home after college to help take care of her. And when Helen died, she was in Miami for a doctor's appointment. But what were these illnesses? Were they really as debilitating as Helen implied? Did they have a psychological component, too? Were they, perhaps, just one more difficulty that Helen, as an imaginary character in a Victorian novel, felt she had to overcome?

Answering these questions requires some speculation. There are no medical records, and there was no autopsy, or, if there was, there is no record of it. But there is the diary, and, although it contains nothing definitive, it does offer clues that allow for some sleuthing. Four "detectives"—a gynecologist, a gastroenterologist, a psychiatrist, and a pharmacologist, who also is a medical historian—read the diary and convened for a roundtable discussion in late 1997 to offer their thoughts about Helen's illnesses. They found several likely diseases, some of them serious, including iron deficiency anemia as a young woman, fibroids throughout her life, a hiatal hernia in middle age, and, exacerbating all of these problems, a mild depression. The mild depression perhaps stemmed from her father's apparent suicide when she was a child, or perhaps was linked to the frustration that she endured from the limitations imposed on her because she was a woman. Appendix C is an edited transcript of the roundtable discussion. (See pp. 209–15.)

Miami—Wednesday, May 20, 1931

Two months today since the operation, and I feel much stronger. The pains in the heart have ceased, and I have gained back nearly all my weight—

*August 11, 1932, diary entry, pp. 146–47.

much to my disgust. I must have lost twenty pounds, and now I weigh 118 pounds. I weighed 124 when I went to the hospital. I go out a little each day, but still rest a lot. Weather is delightful—pleasant days and cool nights. I don't want to go away until July 15, and then don't know where we will go.

Alice graduates June 5. She is editor-in-chief of the annual and was selected to the National Honor Society. She has been accepted at Goucher, and how I hate the idea of her leaving us. She was wonderful during my illness, brave and strong, and learned to market and do things around the house, which she never knew before. Poor Day is busy paying doctor bills, which were tremendous. I have been so much trouble and expense to him, but he never complains and says I am worth it all and more—bless him!

Miami—Saturday, June 13, 1931

On Friday night, June 5, we went to the Bay Shore Park to see our daughter graduate—our tall, slim, young daughter, with her candid gray eyes, her erect trimness. She looked lovely in her long white satin dress, fitting very tight over her hips, and flaring to the bottom, a soft draped neck in front, and cut to a low V in back. She wore a wrist corsage of roses and looked very young and pure and virginal. It was a typical Miami sight— large, tropical moon, waving palms, a myriad of colored lights and fluttering ribbons. Alice was so matter-of-fact about it all that I could not get emotional. She hates sentimentality, so I try not to bore her with any gushing, but of course my heart was full, as it always is at the thought of youth so sweet and pure (at least in theory, as girls of today are not always symbols of purity, alas!), so confident, so eager, so untouched by life's burdens. Alice is indeed the personification of clean youth. She is sincere, honest, dutiful, dependable, unwavering in her ideas of right and wrong. She is a girl any parents could be proud of, but sometimes I could wish she were just a little *softer*, not *quite* so uncompromising. I think it would give her a little more charm. She was on the honor roll, standing fifteenth out of a class of 360. She could easily have been first if she had tried. Next week, on the 20th, she expects to leave for Atlanta. I don't want to go away for some time, as I am enjoying it now, taking things easy, and going to the beach. I feel much better, but some days am quite weak. Weather not too warm, and my house always delightful.

Miami—Saturday, July 4, 1931

I am listening to a holiday program on the radio. Last year this time we were in Interlaken, Switzerland, after a trip over the Rhône glacier, and that night we attended fireworks at the Kursaal. Wednesday night we listened to the landing of Post and Gatty after their eight-day, fifteen-hour trip around the world.* Alice is having a good time in Atlanta, in spite of terrific heat. Miami is a real summer resort.

Miami—Saturday, July 11, 1931

Tomorrow is Leonard's birthday and mine Tuesday. I simply cannot realize I will be forty-five years old—a middle-aged woman, but I feel younger than I did at eighteen. When I was a young girl, I carried the weight of the world on my shoulders. Everyone told me their troubles, and I took my responsibility so hard, and O, how serious life was. Life is no longer serious to me—I take it as it comes, and I find it sweet. Everyone comments on how young I look. In spite of my gray hairs, all tell me I have not a line in my face. I weigh 120 pounds, and while I think I am much too fat for my height (5'1"), I *have* been told that my figure is girlish!

I have been told a lot of nice things lately, and I think that's the one thing that keeps me feeling young. It's funny, but women don't find me good-looking. Only men have told me so, and even if one can't believe them, still it makes one feel good to hear their foolish, sweet little compliments—bless 'em! I like men. I like their strength and their weakness, their little-boy shyness, and their grown-up wildness, so strangely combined. I like their funny, obvious reaction, and they all react the same way and to the same things. They are just perfectly sweet and lots of fun. Decidedly, I have reached middle age and am not a man-hater! Nor do they exactly seem to hate me. So I say that, even if they love to flatter and say silly things, still it sounds good to hear them. Especially when one is no longer young, one loves to be told, "You are my inspiration, my beautiful poem, my life's romance," or "You are like a spray of wild honeysuckle, so sweet and fresh," or how is this one—from a mere husband, too—"You grow more beautiful each day and sweeter and more desirable."

*American pilot Wiley Post and Australian navigator Harold Gatty were the first to circumnavigate the globe by air in their Lockheed monoplane *Winnie Mae*. Two years later, Post would do it solo.

Did I say middle age? Second childhood would be more like it, and O, wouldn't Alice be disgusted if she could hear the sweet nothings that are poured into my ears. She says someone is always "cooing over" me, and how can I stand it? Only to my diary could I admit that I like it!

Miami—Tuesday, July 14, 1931

Not such a pleasant birthday, as I had a headache all day. To a movie tonight. Sweet letters from Alice, Sister, Anna. Day gave me a check and ten boxes of Camels.

Miami—Wednesday, October 7, 1931

I carried this book around with me all summer without opening it. As usual in Atlanta, I am kept busy with luncheon dates, but this time I played no cards and felt better for it. Alice and I had a nice room at 1050 Ponce De Leon, such a lovely hotel, and the three weeks we were there were very pleasant, and we could be quiet and alone when we wanted. The last week in August we met Day in Washington, spent a day there, a day in Baltimore, where we made final arrangements at Goucher, and went on to the Barbizon Plaza in New York. We decided to come back with Day on the boat September 2. Hated the trip, but glad we decided to come home, as we had three weeks altogether, and Alice and I were together every minute.

O, how I hated to see her leave, but if she is happy and satisfied, I shall be repaid. The morning she left, September 28, when I went to wake her up, before her eyes were wide open, she murmured "O, Mama, I'm so scared." My baby! I had her back again for a few moments, when I got in bed with her and held her in my arms. Soon she was her calm self again and was brave when she said good-bye. She wrote that she guesses she is like Eddie in *Bad Girl*—"he doesn't say much, but he feels a lot, like me." Her letters are not as enthusiastic as I'd like, but I'm sure she will soon become adjusted.

In New York we saw *The Follies, Vanities, Green Pastures, Barretts of Wimpole Street* with Katherine Cornell, *Grand Hotel* with Eugene Leontwitch, and I liked that best of all.

I had lunch twice with S.; Day went up to Rochester for a day, and that day Alice went to a matinee. He wanted me to spend the day with him, but I decided not to. A rainy day and a lonely one, but I spent it alone at the hotel. What a good girl am I!

In Atlanta I went out with Alice once a week. We'd go to a movie, and then take a nice long ride. It was pleasant. Alice had dates every night, and for the first time had a man make serious love to her, but she does not care for him. She tells me everything.

Miami—Wednesday, November 11, 1931

I am celebrating Armistice Day by having my windows washed by two poor Jewish men who begged for work, so I couldn't resist. Have to stay home to watch 'em. Day is home, working on his papers. At 9:30 we went to the parade, having seats in the reviewers' stand. I had a nice lunch at home and am now listening to the radio. In spite of all the talk of peace, all the horror of war, still one is always stirred by the sound of martial music, of soldiers marching. We will go to a movie tonight. How we miss Alice!

Miami—Saturday, November 28, 1931

We celebrated Day's birthday Wednesday with a dinner party, and such a party it turned out to be! Our usually quiet and rather stiff crowd was transformed by a few drinks. What a difference liquor can make. One drink is all I can stand, and it doesn't make me feel good. I get just woozy. But the others! The food was very good, and the table looked beautiful, with my silk cloth I got in Vienna. One of my new crystal goblets was broken and the cloth a wreck, but everything turned out so nice I didn't mind. I have long ceased to worry about little things. We had sixteen guests.

Thanksgiving Day, we sat around with Bill and Bessie and turned on the radio for the Penn-Cornell game. What a thrill to know Alice was right there. She spent the day in Philadelphia with her roommate. I'm waiting for a letter from her now. She phoned Day Wednesday night.

Miami—Friday, Christmas Day, 1931

And such a day, gorgeous sunshine, and like summer. We have not had a cold day this winter, wearing sleeveless dresses and only covering with a sheet at nights. Alice has gone to the beach, Day is playing golf, and we will have turkey dinner at 12:30, and then Alice will go to a football game with Joe. One week of her visit has already gone! She is well, but very thin, and I'm trying to feed her up.

Miami—Monday, January 25, 1932

Nearly February, and the season on in full swing—that is, as far as company is concerned. Miami is having a very poor season, due in part to warm weather in the North, but mostly to the general Depression, which is getting worse and worse, and no one knows where it will end. Alice's visit is a pleasant dream, and she is in the midst of midterm exams now. New Year's Eve we went to Club Lido. Not a very gay crowd at Lido, and I hear no place else. People are just not in the mood for merrymaking. Each one has his own financial problems and feels the weight of the rest of the world. New Year's Day was joyous, though it had poured the night before. We stayed home all day, and I had a great thrill listening to *La Bohème* on the radio. Alice went to the football game in the afternoon, and Day and I went to sleep.

On January 12–15 we had the National League of Commercial Merchants' Convention, of which Day was the general chairman, and like everything he attempts, it was a great success. I was on the Ladies' Committee, and we all had a good time. Weather was perfect, as it has been all winter, and everyone was just delighted.

Yesterday I had X rays taken of my chest, and found "it"—whatever it is—much smaller, which is encouraging. It seems there is an enlarged gland in the chest wall, but I have not asked much about it, as what I don't know won't hurt me—for the present, at least. I have some pain in my chest and heart, but my general condition is good, and I've gone steadily back to my normal weight of 123 pounds.

Day was elected president of the Boy Scouts of Dade County.

Miami—Friday, March 11, 1932

Yesterday was our twenty-third anniversary. I could not write because I was engaged all day, in staying outdoors, to keep warm. After a glorious winter of summer weather, it has turned very cold, and of course disagreeable. Not much of a way to celebrate, but these days, with so many demands made upon us, we feel we must forgo celebrations, and just to be together is happiness. I said a little prayer of thankfulness before I closed my eyes, which is really the only kind of prayer I've made in a long time. I never ask for anything, only lift my heart in a psalm of praise and thanksgiving. Alice's coming home next Friday for the Easter Holiday will be my anniversary present.

It is now over a week since the Lindbergh baby* was kidnapped, and no clue as yet. The heart of the whole nation is torn.

Miami—Thursday, April 21, 1932

Day and I have both been ill with the flu. It is four weeks, and we are just beginning to feel better. He had infected ears and I pleurisy. One day I had 104° fever and had to have two nurses. Flu is a virulent and insidious disease. Everyone was lovely, as always—flowers, etc. Glad Alice had gone, so she was not exposed to it. We did enjoy her visit so much, and it *flew*. She is doing much better since she got back, and she finds the work easier. She had gained weight and looked much better than at Christmas. I only weigh 120 pounds now and hope I can keep off the few pounds I lost. The weather is cool for this time of year. Day and I are talking about going to Dallas next month, and I hope to be of some help to Pearle, who has so much trouble—financial and sickness—and who deserves it less than she?

Miami—Thursday, July 14, 1932

My birthday. Very warm, but I find Miami cooler than any place in summer. It was terrible in Dallas, where I went May 21 with Day. He went on to California, and I stayed three weeks with Pearle. Had a lovely time, and then to Atlanta for three weeks, where Alice met me. Day joined us for two days, and Alice and I came home July 2. Pearle, Alvin, and children reached here that afternoon, and will spend the month with us. Early this morning came a wire of congratulations from Samson, signed "with all my love." I was so surprised, as I have not heard from him since I was in New York last year. I went to town with Dot and Alice, and this afternoon we will go on the beach and stay for supper.

Miami—Thursday, August 11, 1932, 4 P.M.

Home alone, and while I like to be alone, I feel desperately bored today, as I so often feel. I ask myself the same old question: Why don't I do something interesting? But I don't know what to do. I ought to be ashamed to see my life slipping by and doing nothing, but what can I do, what am I

*Son of pioneering aviator and American national hero Charles Lindbergh and his wife Anne.

fitted for? Added to a naturally indolent disposition is my constant physical weakness and low vitality. All my life I've just had to nurse myself and conserve my strength, but I know if I had real force of character, real willpower, I could overcome that physical weakness, as many great writers and workers have. The only thing I know that I'd really like to do is to write, but I'll never be able to do that now. When I was younger, I could have studied, applied myself, to make up for my lack of education, but now it's too late. I am so ignorant, my mind so untrained. I can't even think logically.

Miami—Monday, October 31, 1932

I have been back two weeks today from a rather unexpected trip. I left with Alice September 29 for Baltimore, reaching there New Year's Eve. Bill and Bessie met us at the depot. We went for dinner, then to temple. Stayed in Baltimore until Monday at the Lord Baltimore Hotel. It was much fun, getting Alice settled at college and meeting her friends. "Alice, you have such a *cute* Mama" was the opinion rendered! I was also pronounced "OK."

Bill drove us to Dover, where I spent six very dull days. What a place. Bessie was as bored as I. We drove to New York on a Sunday, and I reached there with a terrible cold. Went to Memorial Services Monday (Yom Kippur). Saw *Of Thee I Sing* that night, had lunch with Mort Thursday, and Wednesday with Samson. I met him at the Republican Club, and in the afternoon drove to Brooklyn with him to see a client. He came up to my room a few minutes. He is the same as ever. We left Thursday morning, Bess driving me to Baltimore, where I stayed until Saturday, then home.

Miami is like a different place since Pearle is here. Also glad to have Leonard with us.

Miami—Thanksgiving Day, November 24, 1932

Waiting for Pearle and family. We will have a big turkey and all the trimmings. In spite of the Depression and worries, there is O, so much to be thankful for. I miss Alice terribly. She is going to Easton tomorrow. It's a lovely warm day, though we have had two cold spells so far. Last night we went to the opening dinner dance at the Biltmore. It was a brilliant sight, and all are hoping Miami will come back and be a real resort again.

Miami—Saturday, November 26, 1932

Yesterday was Day's birthday. I met him for lunch and bought him a pretty tie, then went to the temple, to help with a surprise supper the Sisterhood gave him last night. It was lovely, with a big cake, etc., and such tributes paid him that it was embarrassing, but they were deserved and, I believe, sincere. He was elected yesterday to the Rotary Club, and now I am a Rotary-Ann!

Apropos of nothing (or so it would seem) I am once more impressed with the utter naïveté of men. They are really too childishly funny and transparent. When in the throes of passion, nothing matters—not friendship, not loyalty, not vows of fraternal organizations—nothing! If for whatever reasons that passion wanes, their conscience immediately awakes. They remember that your husband is their best friend, that they are under obligations to him, their honor demands remuneration! Even H—, a vandal if there ever was one, asserted, when it became expedient, that "there is honor among thieves."* Dear foolish, guileless creatures! O, I forgot to mention that they also remember their wives, and how much they owe them, etc.

Miami—Monday, February 20, 1933

Last Wednesday was a historic occasion, and I in a measure participated. I was sitting on a grandstand in the park a few feet from Roosevelt, when the dastardly Zangara fired five shots, missing the governor, but hitting five others, including Mrs. Gill and Mayor Cermak, who had been sitting directly in front of me all evening. Thousands had gathered to greet our president-elect, and it was a thrilling sight—soft-colored lights overhead, a warm breeze from the bay, a happy crowd. Suddenly the shots, which I saw, and then pandemonium. The radio is just announcing that Cermak is out of danger, Mrs. Gill still in critical condition.† I was greatly impressed with the kind and pleasant expression of Roosevelt, and he seemed so human. When the shots came, his face froze into a mask of horror.

---

*"There is honour among thieves" is from Sir Walter Scott's *Red Gauntlet*.
†Anton Cermak, the mayor of Chicago, and Mrs. Joe H. Gill, the wife of the president of Florida Power and Light Company, were the most seriously wounded of the five people shot on February 15. Although Mayor Cermak (pronounced SUHR-mack) seemed to be in better condition immediately after the shooting, he died from his wounds about a month later.

Miami is having its biggest season since the Boom—hotels filled, streets crowded—and everyone says this is the brightest spot in the country today, but conditions are serious here and everywhere. We seem to be sitting on the edge of a precipice, and no one knows what to expect.

Cermak and the Dastardly Zangara: Some Questions and Answers

Q: Why was Franklin Delano Roosevelt still president-*elect* in February 1933? And why was he in Miami?

A: Roosevelt was first elected in November 1932, but because the Twentieth Amendment of the Constitution had not yet taken effect, he was not inaugurated until March 1933.* In the weeks before his inauguration, Roosevelt took a combination victory tour and vacation, and tropical Miami was an understandable February destination.

Q: Why was Anton Cermak, the mayor of *Chicago*, in Miami with Roosevelt in February 1933?

A: Politics (predominantly) and Prohibition (probably).

There were three main political factions in the Democratic Party in turn-of-the-century Chicago, but by 1930, says Paul M. Green of Governors State University in Illinois, "the Democrats were fairly well consolidated, although there were lots of splinter groups—local war lords, really."[1] Cermak was an immigrant from Bohemia of Hussite† descent, but he married a Catholic and reared his children as Catholics. His mixed background, plus his political skill, allowed him to bridge the splinter groups, bring in the new immigrants, and maintain the Democrats' core support in the working class. By the time Cermak became mayor in 1931, he was the undisputed boss of Chicago politics.

Cermak, the recognized "wet" leader in Chicago, did not trust Roosevelt to repeal Prohibition. Even more important, says Green, "he didn't like a lot of the people around Roosevelt. They were too WASPy," and he dismissed blue bloods like Harold Ickes, a close Roosevelt adviser, as just "a rich boy from

---

*Until the Twentieth Amendment, the president was inaugurated in March of the year after his election. The Twentieth Amendment, which changed Inauguration Day to January 20, was sent to the states by Congress on March 3, 1932. Although it was ratified on January 23, 1933, the amendment set October 15 of the year of ratification as the effective date, so Roosevelt's 1933 inauguration was the last to be held in March.

†The Hussites were followers of Czech Protestant reformer John Huss, who lived in the early fifteenth century.

Winnetka [a wealthy Chicago suburb] telling Chicago what to do." In fact, Cermak had not supported Roosevelt's nomination in 1932, even putting up a favorite son to draw support from the eventual nominee, and he saw, in retrospect, that his action could lead to serious political difficulties down the road.

By early 1933 Cermak had to figure out a way to deal with the new president. He went to Miami while Roosevelt was there to make up for past indiscretions and to size the man up. High on his agenda were two items: First, how firm was Roosevelt on repealing Prohibition? Second, could Cermak, with Roosevelt's help, finally secure the large loan he had been unsuccessful in seeking for Chicago from the Reconstruction Finance Corporation?

As much as Cermak wanted to make up to the president-elect, as much as he wanted to size him up, he also, Green says, wanted to deliver a message: "I am the boss of Chicago. I am the king of the hill. If you want Chicago, you have to go through me." It was an important message to deliver. And how fortunate he could do it in a nice place like Miami in February: sun, surf, and just a short hop to Havana, one of the mayor's favorite playgrounds during the dark, dry days of Prohibition.

Q: Why did Giuseppe Zangara take a potshot at Roosevelt?

A: No one knows for sure. Accounts from the time describe Zangara, who had immigrated from southern Italy nine years earlier, as deranged and having incoherent but clearly nihilist attitudes. "I'm sorry I didn't kill him," Zangara told police. "I want to kill all presidents—all officers. I don't know whether I shot Mr. Roosevelt or not but I want to make it clear I do not hate him personally. I hate all presidents, no matter where they come from, just like I hate all officers and everybody who's rich."[2]

Zangara was captured immediately. He was tried, convicted, and executed in scarcely more than a month (Zangara was executed on March 20). For some Chicago politicos, the speed of justice—coupled with their knowledge of Cermak's struggle with organized crime over control of soon-to-be-legalized alcohol—has led them to wonder whether Zangara had a connection to the Chicago mob. Paul Green says he has found no evidence to support any relationship. Nor have others who have disinterestedly examined the facts.* But facts do not always stand in the way of a good conspiracy theory. "There are still people around today," says Green, "who think Zangara shot the man he was aiming at."

---

*Cermak's biographer, Alex Gottfried, for one.

As for Cermak, he hung on for a few weeks but succumbed to complications from his wound on March 6. A special train brought his body back to Chicago, where he lay in state for twenty-four hours. Then there was a huge funeral with half a million people lining the route, followed by another ceremony in Chicago Stadium witnessed by twenty-three thousand people, and then a burial witnessed by fifty thousand. "In death," his biographer, Alex Gottfried, wrote, "Cermak was honored more than in life." In part this was because of what he reportly had said to Roosevelt after he was shot: "I am glad it was me instead of you." But it was also because of the political legacy he left behind, what Gottfried called a "virtually invincible" political machine.[3]

Miami—Friday, March 3, 1933

Twenty banks throughout the country have declared a moratorium, an unprecedented state of affairs. People are rushing away from Miami, some say; others say that Miami is benefiting, as thousands of dollars are being deposited here. The First National Bank seems safe, but who knows from day to day what will happen? Everyone is hoping that when Roosevelt goes into office tomorrow, he will spring some drastic measure. The whole world is in a state of unrest, alas, yet the world doesn't end, and I suppose things will adjust themselves, and life goes on.

This winter has passed pleasantly, with less entertaining than usual, but I've had lots of company. If I only could do things that really interest me. I have everything to make a woman happy, yet always there is that vague unrest, that faint nostalgia—for what? I don't even know.

Miami—Monday, March 13, 1933

My twenty-fourth anniversary last Friday, and a nice day. Went to town early for a manicure, and to Roney Plaza for luncheon, playing bridge afterward. At 9 P.M. Day went to the Doherty* dinner and I to see Mae West in *She Done Him Wrong*. He came for me at 11 P.M., and we went out to the Biltmore, where we had been invited to hear the broadcast, and it was most interesting—in celebration of "Doherty Day." He has done wonderful things for Florida, and we have had a good season, which promised to last through April, but of course the park situation drove thousands home.

*Col. Henry L. Doherty was an oil tycoon, public utilities and real estate magnate, and philanthropist.

Such crucial times as we are living through now! There is a bank holiday throughout the U.S., but no panic. Everyone is philosophical, feeling this had to happen and hoping for complete readjustment. Roosevelt has already gained the confidence and respect of everyone. Last night he spoke over the radio, a simple, sincere, and direct talk to the American people, as one friend to another. As I am writing (12 o'clock), news comes over the radio of his message just sent to Congress, demanding immediate repeal of the Volstead Act [Prohibition]. Truly history is being made these days.

Miami—Wednesday, May 10, 1933

I have been home two weeks after a most unexpected visit to Baltimore and New York. Dr. Welch insisted on my going out to his clinic for complete examination, and under X ray found a typical "hourglass" stomach with almost complete constriction. Day was going to New York anyway, so before I knew what had happened I was on the train to see Dr. John Kantor. It seems when Kantor examined me, my stomach was normal, and he said my stomach goes into a spasm when it gets pressure of gas from carbon, which is "most peculiar"! It is very large, long, and twisted, and comes up very high under my heart. Since I was born that way, there is little to be done except diet and certain treatment to keep away gas. I am surely willing to adopt his diagnosis, and everyone is much relieved. My trip up seems a nightmare, as I surely expected the worst, and I made up my mind I'd never go through a long and fatal illness, so I positively would not inflict such a thing on myself or family.

We spent a day with Alice, and as Day had to go to Dover, I went on to New York alone, and that night had a strange experience. Sitting in the lobby of the Governor Clinton Hotel, I was brooding over my condition and not in the mood to phone or think of anyone. Finally, I noticed a distinguished looking middle-aged man staring at me. I suppose I did not discourage him, because he came over, and we engaged in a strange conversation. Starting with general topics, it ended by his asking me to sleep with him, and trying to make the proposition very attractive. We talked over the situation, I explaining that I never did such things, and we ended up the best of friends, exchanging our views on life, sex, etc. He was really a gentleman and promised not to find out my name or annoy me. I can surely get away with things, but men are *so easy* to *handle*! I told Day something of it when he came next day, and he was furious that I'd let a man insult me. But to tell the truth, what woman is insulted, especially if she is middle-aged and plump, if a man finds her beautiful or desirable? Anyway, it cheered me up a lot that night, and gave me courage.

S. was angry that I had not let him know I was alone that night, but I purposely did not. He is not as easy to handle as most men. I had lunch with him once and spent another hour of the afternoon with him. Also had tea with Sidney. He looks old and has lost a lot of his charm. Saw two plays: *Dinner at Eight* and *Autumn Crocus*.

Alice was just elected treasurer of Goucher by large majority. I feel she must stand high there, and she is very popular.

While in New York we went off the gold standard, and there was much excitement, but I can't see what difference it makes, and no one is able to exactly explain it. Everyone concedes that conditions are improving, but Roosevelt in his speech last Sunday said not to be lulled into false security. He has surely endeared himself to all. He speaks directly to the people, as one friend to another.

Monday beer became legal in Florida. Day has the Rupperts account, and we hope it will prove a big thing, when prices are stabilized. It is now selling at twenty-five cents a bottle.

Miami—Wednesday, August 2, 1933

Must record my birthday on the 14th and Alice's on the 20th. I spent a pleasant day. Went to Ethel May's for lunch, and for dinner went to Garden of Allah. Alice had a lovely day, had lunch with Day at Nunnaljo, and at 7 P.M. had a dinner for twenty young folks at Garden of Allah, dancing, etc., and all had a good time. She went with Paul Marks, who sent her a gorgeous corsage. She received lots of nice gifts, and she looked so sweet in a pale blue crepe dress. It was the first large party she ever had, as we are always away on her birthday. When she was little, I always sent a treat to the Orphan Home in Atlanta instead of a party—altruistic, but she missed happy memories of birthday parties. Last week she had four wisdom teeth extracted, two badly impacted, but she stood it fine.

Henry just spent a week with us, coming on a boat from Galveston. He is so sweet, and it was wonderful to have him, our baby brother. Dorothy and the children are in Aster Park. Henry looks old on account of his gray hair, but he is very handsome and distinguished-looking. Joseph spent three weeks with us, and we enjoyed him, a fine boy and no trouble, but I

seem to have more company in summer than in season, and I am ready for
a rest and change. We plan to go away August 18, but have not decided
where. Day is worn out—what businessman is not, with such strenuous
times. He is now chairman of a committee to work out the new code on
the National Recovery Act, which of course is chief topic of conversation
and speculation now.

Miami—Monday, October 16, 1933

We have been home two weeks after a lovely trip. Drove to Highlands,
North Carolina, spending two weeks. I hate summer resorts. I was bored,
but it did Day lots of good. He golfed, and Alice rode horseback, and I just
sat around and gained two pounds! We then drove to Laurel, Delaware,
and stayed ten days with Bessie, while Day looked after tomato canneries.
A storm destroyed the crops, and they had a disastrous season after expecting to make big money. Spent a week in New York at the Edison Hotel,
and I bought Alice's clothes for school. Only saw S. once. Had lunch with
him at Ye Olde Tavern downtown. Went to Temple Emanu-El on New Year's,
and Governor and Mrs. Lehman sat near us. We heard that on Yom Kippur
the walls on the beautiful building were placarded thus: "The Jews Must
Go, The Pope Must Go, Democracy Must Go." What a combination, and
how significant of the spirit of hate and bigotry. The German situation
grows graver every day. They have just decided to leave the disarmament
allies to go their lone way. Can they defy the whole world? The conditions
in this country are not much better. The N.R.A.* has not succeeded yet,
but perhaps it is too soon to tell.

On October 10 I voted for Repeal. The law passed in Florida and seems
sure to pass everyplace.

Miami—Thursday, March 1, 1934

The date of my twenty-fifth anniversary draws near, and my heart is filled
with joy and gratitude. We have planned to go to Nassau from March 10–
14 to celebrate, as a steamship company offered us the trip as their guests,
and it will be an ideal way to settle the party question, as we didn't know

---

*The National Recovery Administration, the New Deal agency set up to oversee fair
business competition, was abolished in 1935 after the Supreme Court declared uncon-
stitutional the law that had established it.

whom to invite or where to draw the line. It has been a wonderful winter, more people in Miami than in the Boom time, and everyone spending money freely once more—such a joy after the years of Depression. Our obligations have been lightened, so I have decided to spend freely also, as for the last two years I couldn't spend a cent without worrying that someone else needed it worse. We have gone to all the nightclubs and entertained a lot. I have felt fine except for neuritis in my hand, which makes it difficult to write.

Alice has done wonderfully at school, getting two A's on her last report. She will come home Easter and was home Christmas for a lovely visit. Sis, Lee, and Joan also were here.

Miami—Thursday, March 29, 1934

We are leaving on a trip Sunday and I'm very busy, but must take time to record my twenty-fifth anniversary, Saturday, March 20th.

What a happy day. Gifts, telegrams, flowers, etc.—proof again of dear friends. At 7 P.M. we sailed for Nassau on the *Munargo* for four days at the Colonial Hotel, guests of the Munson Line. We had a lovely time, another honeymoon, and it did Day lots of good. He is worn out and nervous from a multitude of duties, but business is good and he is enthusiastic. We will go from here to Ocala, Jacksonville, Savannah, and make headquarters in Fairfax at the tomato canneries. Don't know how I will like it there, as I don't like country hotels. Alice will drive to Savannah with us and take a train to Baltimore. She has had a grand vacation and looks fine and so sweet.

Miami—Saturday, June 30, 1934

I've wanted to write in here ever since I came home on May 17th, but the book is almost finished, and I have a strange superstition about ending it, as if that will mean the end of all. I know that's foolish, and I shall just buy another book and start all over, calling this one, I suppose, "My First Twenty-Five Years."

Looking back on these pages, I can't see that I have changed very much; indeed, I feel even younger than I did as a bride. How serious I was, how introspective, how intense. I have changed in those things, I know. I have lost my simple faith, but I have acquired a Philosophy. I am not cynical, but I am surely much broader-minded. Day says I am too much so, but I simply cannot say that this is wrong and this is right anymore. What's right for one is wrong for another. Each one must work out his own life, in his own way, and who am I to blame or condemn anyone? "Live and Let Live" is a good motto.

I am not nearly as nervous as I was then, and in spite of *much* serious illness I am stronger, can stand more physical strain, though worry, excitement, and unpleasantness still tear me to pieces. I weigh 123 pounds, and I look very dumpy, as most of the flesh has developed into that middle-aged spread. My hair is gray, but everyone still tells me I haven't a line in my face and look young. People who have known me since I was a girl say I am much better-looking. I surely was an ugly little girl, painfully thin, very dark, though my regular features and good eyes somewhat redeemed me.

Now about the relationship between my husband and myself, what shall I say? I surely love him a thousand times better. I married him with doubt and reluctance, though with an instinct that I was doing the right thing and that all would be well. My very intense and romantic nature would have made me have doubts about any man. I don't think girls are like that anymore—expecting love to come with a great, blinding light, looking for the knight on his white charger to carry you away. Perhaps they still are that way under their veneer of hardness and wisdom. Day has made me a marvelous husband. He is so good, so much better than I deserve, that, as I wrote before, it makes me humble.

Does he love me as much as he did then? A year ago, I would have said yes, though it's almost unbelievable that a love such as his could have survived twenty-four years as adoring, as passionate, but it did. The last year, though he denies it, that adoration has given way to some criticism, some resentment, something intangible. That ardor is cooled, perhaps because we are older, perhaps because of the strain of problems men had to wrest with during a crucial financial period. Well, it is surely natural a man shouldn't be as passionate at forty-seven as he was at twenty-two. How many women can boast that they kept their husbands as devoted, as satisfied, as desiring for twenty-four years?

We were away seven weeks, four in Fairfax, with weekend trips to Pinehurst, Charleston, Augusta, Savannah, Charlotte, Columbia. We had a new Dodge car, which I named "The Boll Weevil," and we did have lots of fun. I stayed in Atlanta three weeks, the usual social life, the usual date with A. Everyone was lovely to me, but as usual I was glad to get back home. Alice has been here three weeks, and we do have such good times together. She has gained five pounds and weighs 111 pounds.

Before I end, I'd like to write a few highlights of my life.

Places I've Loved

Magnolia Gardens, the moon rising over Biscayne Bay, sunset on a lake near Orlando, Gigli singing in St. Mark's Square—the whole of Venice—goose livers at Hartmans in Vienna, the Church of the Madeleine in Paris, Lake Lucerne, Berchtesgaden, and the Konigsee, the dogwood in the spring near Atlanta, the hills of Habersham, the marshes of Glenn, San Francisco, Banff and Lake Louise, the waterfalls of North Carolina and of the Columbia River Highway. The thrill of standing at the cradle of liberty, Lexington and Concord.

The harbors of Boston and Havana. Paradise Beach at Nassau. My mother's birthplace near Mainz and the Rhine.

Hors d'oeuvres at the Royal Cafe in The Hague.

All of London and the English countryside.

The Cafe De La Paix—Sloppy Joe's. The Cathedral at Milan and Rheims, Temple Emanu-El in New York.

Books I Have Loved

I love anything to read except detective stories.

My best reading was done between sixteen and twenty, and I read Dickens, Scott, Thackeray, Balzac, Tennyson, Burns, Byron, Shelley straight through. I read at the rate almost of a book a day. Of the modern writers, my favorite is Galsworthy, and I have liked some of the weird modern poetry, "The Roan Stallion," "Tamar," etc. Also, the books of Dr. Joseph Collins, Bertrand Russell, and Ben Lindsey.

Plays I Remember

Viola Allen in *The Christian*, Maude Adams in *The Little Minister*, Marlowe and Sothern in *Romeo and Juliet*, the Metropolitan Operas that came to Atlanta every season with Caruso, Eames, Matzenauer, Ponselle, Farrar, Scotti, Martinelli. My favorite composer, Puccini; my opera, *La Bohème*.

Helen Hayes in *Coquette*, Lenore Ulric in *Lula Bell*,* Katherine Cornell in *The Barretts of Wimpole Street*.

Movies

The long ago Clara Kimball Young in *Hearts in Exile*, *The Birth of a Nation*, *The House of Rothschild*, *The Last Parade*, *Dinner At Eight*, Janet Gaynor and Charles Farrell in *Seventh Heaven*, though I've never liked either of the actors.

Miami—Thursday, August 2, 1934

We expect to leave August 11 for Atlantic City, to stay three weeks at the Ambassador, then to New York. Alice and I are busy getting clothes, etc.

On Alice's twenty-first birthday, the 20th, we had lunch at the Pools, and that night gave Alice a dinner at Cava Villa for seven couples, opening champagne we had been keeping. And what more auspicious occasion! She wore a brown mousse linen and corsage of roses. It was lovely.

So endeth my little book. When I come back in the fall, I hope to have another little book and lots of adventures to write in it. I am not too old yet, it seems, to look for adventure, and I hope I never shall be. Isn't even death itself a glorious adventure? I pray we will keep well and return in good health, and so good-bye, my confidante and friend.

Finis.

* * *

I must mention something of world conditions, because it seems to me, we stand on the edge of a precipice. Just twenty years ago exactly the World War started. How horrible to think that nations have turned to war again. Hindenburg is dying,† Dollfuss killed,‡ strikes all over the U.S.A., nations at each others' throats. O, I pray God we will keep out of it, such a monstrous, horrible thing, bigotry, hatred, and fanaticism. Why can't men live together in peace?

---

*She seems to have meant *Linda Belle*. Readers may recall Helen's mention of the play in her July 22, 1926, entry (see p. 125), when she wrote that it "repelled" her.
†Paul von Hindenburg, the German soldier and statesman, was elected president of Germany in 1925 and held the post until his death in 1934. In January 1933, Hindenburg bowed to pressure and appointed Hitler chancellor.
‡Austrian chancellor Engelbert Dollfuss was assassinated by Nazi revolutionaries on July 25, 1934.

NOTES

1. Telephone interview, September 1997.
2. Alex Gottfried, *Boss Cermak: A Study of Political Leadership* (Seattle: University of Washington Press, 1962), 322. Zangara's statements to the police were made through an interpreter and printed in the *Chicago Herald and Examiner*, February 13, 1933.
3. Gottfried, *Boss Cermak*, 328, 324–25, 332.

A War to Hate, a Grandson to Love (1934-1946)

➣ *Helen starts another diary, and this one is a real diary with blank pages to write on, not a modified daybook. Alice, who has given it to her, writes an inscription dated November 15, 1934: "Mother, dearest, I hope the rest of your life will be recorded here as happily as the first part." The tone and style of this second volume are very different from the first. The entries are scarcer and less revealing of Helen's inner thoughts. Perhaps it is just that she is getting older; she is now forty-eight. Perhaps her life and her thinking have become more stable. Perhaps, too, it is the terrible time of World War II. Whatever the cause, she is aware of the change. "I don't want to make this diary personal," she writes at one point. "It must be a record of these momentous times." Nevertheless, in this last chapter Helen continues to combine the personal with her observations of the world around her. The birth of her grandson changes her life. And as the war rages on, Helen reflects on its gut-wrenching seriousness and how different this war seems from World War I. Now she feels war's pain directly, and she demonstrates her uncanny luck in witnessing history firsthand.*

Miami—Wednesday, November 21, 1934

After finishing my other diary, I felt a hesitancy about starting another—not that I am superstitious, but I had a queer feeling when I ended my "First Twenty-Five Years." I can hardly expect to have another twenty-five years, but at least I can start it.

First, I must record my summer vacation, a most pleasant one. Day went up to Fairfax August 1, and Alice and I joined him in Southern Pines August 8 and drove to Baltimore, where we spent the night, then to Atlantic City, where Alice and I stayed three weeks at the Ambassador Hotel,

Day going to Milton, Delaware, and joining us weekends. I don't care at all for Atlantic City, but Alice had a grand time, and that is why I went. I met no interesting people and had not a single experience. But what a difference in New York, where we went Labor Day. We stayed three weeks at the Edison Hotel, and I could fill pages of this diary, but I won't, as it's not to be too personal! There is something in the very air of New York that stimulates me, and I felt and looked years younger when I left September 25, with Alice going back to school.

We reached home on October 22, in midst of the American Legion's big parade. Found my house full of unexpected and uninvited company, cleaned up, had painters, etc., and in a few days' time felt as if I never had a vacation. However, many pleasant memories remain. Miami is already crowded, and every day people are coming in who must be entertained.

Miami—Thanksgiving Day, November 29, 1934

A beautiful day, and our hearts are full of thanks. Pearle, Alvin, and Billy coming for turkey dinner tonight. Saturday was Day's birthday.

Miami—Monday, March 25, 1935

It seems we were just talking about the "season" beginning, and now it is over—a short life, but a merry one. We have been out practically every night since December, taking in all the nightclubs. We have entertained all sorts of people, gone to parties galore—in fact, all the things that make up a Miami season, though this is the most hectic one we've ever had. Alice was home Christmas, Bill and Bessie here at the same time, Sister in January, Dorothy and Henry in February. I think I'd have given out if I hadn't gone to Tampa one week to stay with Bessie while Day went to Chicago. It was great having Henry and Dorothy here, and they were most satisfactory guests, demanding nothing, and we were hardly home for any meals.

I have a chauffeur now, so am free to come and go, though do wish I could drive myself. Alice went back to school today, after her spring vacation, which she spent in Easton. We are looking forward now to her graduation, but have made no further plans for the summer. She and Day would like to go to Europe, but I wouldn't think of it with war clouds appearing. Yes, incredible, horrible as it may be, Europe is again in turmoil, and all I pray is that if war comes, we won't be dragged in.

We spent our anniversary quietly. Had Pearle and family to dinner.

Miami—Tuesday, May 14, 1935

I am writing this in bed, where I must spend half of each day. Yes, after going fine all winter I had to pop up with something. I became used to my symptoms of pain in the chest, accompanied by gurgling noises, but in addition to that, all winter I had a different pain and congestion in the chest and choking spells became more frequent. Dr. Welch insisted I come for X rays and found a rupture in the diaphragm, blood pressure 170, and he sent me to Dr. Nichol, a heart man, who found some trouble, I don't know exactly what, and put me to bed for two weeks. I didn't realize how much I needed it until I gave in. As usual, everyone lovely—flowers, books, candy, etc., and the time passed pleasantly. I read *Of Time and the River, Joshua Todd, A Few Foolish Lives, No Quarter Given*. I am taking good care of myself so I will be able to go to Alice's graduation, and we leave here May 31, I hope. She called me Sunday on the phone, for Mother's Day. Bill and Bessie are staying with us.

Miami—Thursday, May 30, 1935

We expect to leave here for Baltimore Saturday, and I am counting the days until we see Alice, praying I will feel well. Some days I am fairly well, then again, feel very weak. I will consult heart and stomach specialists in New York.

Miami—Tuesday, July 16, 1935

Day is packing, and I am lying on the bed. Very hot night, first time I've felt the heat this summer. We have had a nice breeze while the rest of the country is smothering in heat and drought. Tuesday was my fiftieth birthday. Incredible. I really do not feel old, with all my weakness, aches, and pains. We had a dinner at the Biltmore Pool, the whole family. Can't remember what I did last year, but I was in Atlanta, I know. I see I have not recorded a word, and I did have an eventful summer.

Alice's graduation was a thrill, but I felt too ill to do much. Quite a siege with doctors in New York—Kantor, Rothschild, Winkelstein, Vorlans, a coldhearted and mercenary bunch. Dr. Nichol had stated I had hardening of a coronary artery. They decided I did not, but all my symptoms came from the ruptured diaphragm. I felt miserable and still do. I have to rest half the time and did little entertaining this winter. Alice and I went to

Georgetown, South Carolina, with Day driving down, I with terrible pain from the sacroiliac joint, all strapped up. What a trip! Georgetown is a typical decayed Southern town, and dull as dishwater. Then to Atlanta, and in August I spent a week in Milton, Delaware, at a cannery. Then Alice and I went to Atlantic City, and in September to New York. We got back to Miami the first week in November, the day before the hurricane.

Yesterday, I got a card from Samson with very appropriate wishes. I had to smile.

We went to Jacksonville to attend Aunt Dordy's funeral. She died May 25.

Just bought a new Packard car.

Miami—Sunday, March 14, 1937

Our twenty-eighth anniversary was Wednesday. We went to dinner at the Irmey Hotel, taking Alice and Berney Wagner, with whom she had a date to go to the Royal Palms. We went down there with them, to see the new bar and the queer gambling tables, run like slot machines. We came home early, as Day has not felt well since his pneumonia in Chicago. I left with him about January 20, and we were three days getting to Chicago, on account of the floods at Louisville, Cairo, etc. I left Chicago on a Monday night for Rochester, Minnesota, where I went through all kinds of terrible tests, including esophagusaphy. I got back to Chicago on Saturday to find Day in bed with a 103° temperature. I thought he had the flu but got him two nurses and he got on fine, with his good heart and resistance. It was an awful ordeal, but I feel so thankful, as it could have been so much worse. Brought him home in an ambulance about February 10. All the doctors at Mayo could suggest to me was an operation, which they called imperative, but I won't have it.

Miami—Monday, March 21, 1938

I can't believe it is a year since I wrote here. I am thankful to say on my twenty-ninth anniversary I felt a little better than last year. I have my same pain and symptoms, but think I'm a little stronger.

Had a nice day on the 10th. It was a Thursday, so the maid was off, but I had six for lunch—split pea soup and toasted cheese. Guests—Pearle,

Dot, Yedda, Froma, Alice, and me. We had lots of fun. Dorothy and Henry were here this winter. Sis, Lee, and Joan were here for Christmas.

The season sped by with the usual stream of visitors and obligations, and I did a little more than last year.

Miami—Thursday, May 30, 1940

Memorial Day, and I just heard [H. V.] Kaltenborn tell on radio how the graves in France won't be decorated today. No, for the Germans are bombing those cemeteries today, and we may never know how many graves are desecrated. I wept over those graves. In 1930 I uttered a prayer for those boys who gave their lives to "make the world safe for democracy," and I prayed for peace "in our time," and for all time, and for all people. Futile, futile. The news is so depressing that I just had to shut off the radio, but I feel I must record some of the things I hear from day to day, as history is being made right now, and the fate of the world at stake. The English are escaping in small battered remnants [from Dunkirk] back across the Channel, the king of Belgium surrendered his army, Germans claim victory everywhere, the English admit the situation is desperate. I will write events as they happen from here.

Miami—Saturday, June 22, 1940

Another historic day. At 6:50 P.M. (German Time) the peace treaty with France was signed in the railroad car at Compiègne where twenty-two years ago the Allies laid down terms to the Germans. We visited this car in 1930, and little did we dream that in the next ten years things could happen as they did, and Germany would rise to almost rule the world.

The peace terms have not been made public, but everyone is expecting the worst, and all are praying the French fleet can escape. Meanwhile, fighting goes on and men are dying absolutely without cause. Horrible! I am writing with tears in my eyes for the utter waste of it all, and for beautiful France, prostrate under the tyrant's heel. In the U.S. there's quite an uproar, as Roosevelt appoints Stimson and Knox to his Cabinet,* and everyone is saying, "We can't keep out of it." The Republican Convention starts Monday. On June 10, Italy entered the war, "bravely" waiting until

*Henry L. Stimson was named Secretary of War; Frank Knox became Secretary of the Navy.

victory was assured and stepping in for the spoils, stabbing France in the back.

Last summer I must record our trip. Alice and I went to Jackson, New Hampshire, which we didn't like, so we went to Balsams, to the Dixville Hotel, which was delightful. Day joined us in August and stayed ten days. War came and he got restless, so we went to Boston for a few days, then to New York in the last of August and got nice apartment at the Park Royal, where we stayed until November 1.

On our thirty-first anniversary we had the family for dinner. Dot married May 14. Pearle and family left on a trip today. On June 18 we sold this house for $11,500 cash.* It's a small price, but I have no regrets. We will let next fall take care of itself. We have been most comfortable here and happy, but it's too big for us. I had two teeth pulled last week and feel weak and sickish. I fought it off as long as I could, and the bone was disintegrated and had to be scraped.

Miami—Wednesday, June 3, 1942

"I don't know where to start" is a trite expression, but after staring at this blank page, I can't think of any other way to start after a silence of two years. After selling our house, we went to the beach, to the Royal Palm Hotel, for a month, then to Lookout Mountain, where Alice got engaged to Dan.† Then to New York, the Dorset Hotel, and Alice was married at Hotel Warwick October 15 [1940]. It was a beautiful but quiet wedding, with thirty-three guests, lovely music, champagne, and a breakfast. Dan registered in the draft October 16 in Washington. We came home November 1 and went to the Dallas Park Hotel, where we spent a nice winter, enjoying steam heat, etc.

I can't remember what we did on our thirty-second anniversary, but in June we went to Atlanta, to a Kiwanis convention, and then to Mayo, where I had an operation on my neck for a crushed phrenic nerve and was in the hospital five days. Dr. Harrington still insisted on the big operation, but I couldn't do it. I suffered three months with very bad pains in my neck, but think the stomach condition was relieved some. We came back to Miami, I with a bad cold, and I think it was the last of August when we

---

*The house had cost $30,000 to build in 1928. The $18,500 loss in 1940 equates to more than $120,000 in 1998 based on the Consumer Price Index.
†Daniel Rosenbaum and Henry Jacobus's wife, Dorothy, were first cousins. Alice met Dan while visiting her uncle in Dallas.

went to New York and stayed until November at the Park Central Hotel. Pearle and Alvin were there, and Joan visited me. We had a good time. Day and I took a little trip up New York State, to Syracuse, Utica, Corning, etc., and it was my first visit to the Mohawk Valley and the lovely scenery upstate.

We moved into this little apartment December 3, 555 N.E. 66th Street, two blocks from Alice, and I wanted to be near her, in her pregnancy. Day and I went to Tampa in February and flew back here March 1, when Dan phoned us that Alice was in the hospital. My first air flight and my first grandchild, all on the same day. I could fill the rest of this book talking about David, but I won't. I'll only say he is the most adorable, beautiful, perfect baby ever born! He is now three months old, and I'm sure he knows me. I can't miss a day having him smile at me. But I don't want to make this diary personal—it must be a record of these momentous times.

Forgot to record Billy's wedding May 15, 1941. Henry and Dorothy and Sister came.

On December 7, 1941, I was lounging around the living room, papers all about, Day lying down on the lazy Sunday afternoon. About 2:30 I turned on the radio—just an idle, bored impulse—and just as I did, a voice broke in on the musical program and said, "The president of the United States announced that Pearl Harbor has been attacked by Japanese planes."

I stood, rooted to the spot. Day jumped up and we looked at each other, in stunned silence. Finally, I said, "Pearl Harbor. Isn't that Honolulu?" Then the reports came in thick and fast. We thought we were dreaming or as if some strange Orson Welles fantasia was being enacted. That is how war came to the U.S.A. that lazy Sunday afternoon, December 7, 1941. I have kept a record of newspaper headlines from January 1, 1942. They are in another book, and perhaps some day I'll incorporate them in this one.

I went back to Tampa to join Day when David was four weeks old. We stayed at the Bayshore Royal. I thoroughly dislike Tampa. It's a deadly dull town, and the people are small-town folks, narrow and provincial. I was very bored, and now Day says we must move there in the fall. I'll adjust myself, I'm sure, and must count it our war casualty.

We came back here March 7 for Bill's fiftieth birthday dinner. On our thirty-third anniversary we took them to dinner at the Thack and Shore Inn. Last night, Pearle's twenty-eighth anniversary, we had them, Leonard, and Froma to dinner. Tomorrow is Sister's twenty-fifth. I must go to dentist this afternoon to fit my new bridge. Yes, I came to it at last: false teeth! Disgusting!

Miami—Sunday, June 7, 1942

Six months ago today, the war started!

First month: Japan touches off war with Pearl Harbor attack, Wake Island falls after valiant defense.

Second month (January): A.E.F. Lands in Northern Ireland, twenty-one American republics sign unity pledge at Rio, U.S. forces slash at Marshall and Gilbert Islands.

Third month (February): Singapore surrenders, American task force raids Wake Island, route is set and work begun on defense highway to Alaska.

Fourth month (March): Allied forces overwhelmed at Java, U.S. troop convoys and Gen. MacArthur reach Australia, commandos raid St. Nazaire.

Fifth month (April): Bataan and Corregidor fall to enemy after heroic stands, Tokyo bombed by Maj. Gen. [James H.] Doolittle, Allied defense in Burma collapses.

Sixth month (May): U.S. wins Coral Sea battle, Russians beat Germans to punch in Ukraine with attack on Kharkov, R.A.F. armadas pulverize Cologne, Rostock, Essen.

Now, let us see how six months of war has affected our personal life! We are allowed one-half pound of sugar per week, per person, and must present rationing cards every two weeks. We got gas rationing cards, B, which allow us seven gallons per week. Dan is in draft class 3-A, but we expect him to get a questionnaire for reclassification.

Day registered in the draft calling for men 45 to 65. Income taxes are tremendous. Food is not much higher due to price ceilings. Sugar in the last war went to thirty cents a pound. It is now six cents a pound. We buy as many Defense Bonds as possible. We must drive with parking lights only. The street lights are dimmed. The beach is one vast camp. Miami seems depressing; there is a kind of tension. We are leaving for New York June 14.

Miami—Wednesday, July 8, 1942

We got back from New York Sunday, July 4. Had a nice visit to Wingdale, New York, in the Berkshires, and were at the Savoy Plaza. Saw two shows—

Let's Face It and *Angel Street*. New York is dimmed out, no Great White Way, not a light on Broadway or Fifth Avenue. Traffic lights are small crosses. Everyone is a little jittery, fearing sabotage.

Atlanta, four days. It's just the same, no dimouts.

Could hardly wait to see David. He had grown a lot, looks like a little boy instead of a baby, and is adorable. Very hot here.

Miami—Tuesday, July 14, 1942

My birthday, and still I don't feel old. What is this reach of "eternal youth"? Perhaps it is a contented heart, or if not *perfectly* contented, at least a heart full of thanks for the blessings that are mine, resources within myself, and quiet philosophy. And now that I'm a grandmother, I feel even younger, as it gives me a greater interest in life in watching his little life unfold. I have often heard of how one loves one's grandchild even more than one's own child. That isn't exactly true, as what love could be greater than a mother's, when she holds her baby in her arms? But there is something in love for a grandchild that is different from any other—a feeling of such exquisite tenderness, such deep and poignant adoration, that it brings tears to the eyes. Alice, Dan, and David left for Dallas last Saturday, and I'm counting the days. I went to market with Froma, and tonight Day and I will go out to dinner, a quiet celebration.

Miami—Wednesday, July 22, 1942

We drove over to the beach Sunday—about the last time, I guess, as gas rationing is on in earnest now, and we can only get four gallons a week. We took Lt. Gottlieb from Richmond to dinner, and then went to see *This Above All*. We came home very depressed. Soldiers everywhere, sentries, guns, drilling. It is so dimmed out that it is almost a blackout, really dangerous to be driving a car. It makes you realize the war is really on. We always pick up boys on the boulevard going back to camps out 79th Street. It breaks my heart, those soldiers standing all along the street, hot, tired, bored.

To anyone who remembers the last war, they will know this war is different. No glamour, no thrills, no singing. "Our Singing Army," we used to call the soldiers—trainloads of them, always singing—"Over There"; "My Buddy"; "Tipperary"; "Smile, Smile, Smile"; "Katy"; "Keep the Home

Fires Burning." These boys don't sing. They look grim, bored. Yes, this war is grim; it's a fight to the death.

Miami—Friday, August 14, 1942

A nostalgic feeling overcame me, as I read yesterday that the R.A.F. had bombed Mainz. I saw again the little town where my mother was born. I see the bustling city of Mainz, from where we took a taxi to drive to Hexheim. My heart was full to bursting as my feet touched the ground, as we left the boat. "The Rhine," I said. "This is where I have my roots, where my ancestors were born." Now, I feel no kinship for that soil, only horror, repulsion, and I'm *glad, glad* they bombed it. I hope it is in ruins.

Last night Apte Bros.* gave a party at the Clover Club for employees. There were twenty-six, and it was fun. We are being much entertained before leaving. Everyone is so nice, and O how I hate to leave Miami.

Tampa, Florida—Tuesday, November 10, 1942

Exactly eleven months after Pearl Harbor came the wonderful news of the second front. The Yanks in North Africa, a great surprise to everyone. We got back to Tampa October 14 after a stay of six weeks at the Savoy Plaza. We had a fine time. New York is depressing and exciting. The streets are dark, but there are tremendous crowds, and night clubs and theatres are doing better than in years. We saw *Show Time* with George Jessel, *Star and Garter* with Gypsy Rose Lee, Emlyn Williams in *Morning Star*, *Junior Miss*, *Count Me In*, Noel Coward's *Blithe Spirit*.

Moving tomorrow to a larger apartment here, at the Embassy.†

David is more adorable than ever. He knows me now, and laughs out loud, and holds out his little hands.

Weather hot—85°. One-hour blackout last week—Bill and Bessie were here to dinner. Coffee very scarce, meats scarce. Sugar still rationed, but we have never suffered any real sacrifice yet.

---

*Apte Brothers was the name of the food brokerage and canning company that Day and Bill owned.
†The Embassy Apartments, only a few blocks from where Helen and Day had lived in 1909 and 1910, later became a University of Tampa dormitory.

Tampa—Saturday, March 20, 1943

Our thirty-fourth anniversary we spent pleasantly. David was with me all afternoon—my greatest joy. He says au-ba (auto), choo-choo, bird, ba-bee, bye-bye, shoe, up-down. We think he calls me Nana. I was the first person he knew by name. He is my heartstring. That night I had the Baskers, Maas, Aptes, and Corinne over and served the last bottle of champagne. Day gave me a ruby and a sapphire band ring.

There are a lot of soldiers quartered across the street at Tampa University. They pass here three times a day, drilling and singing. It's getting me down. When I hear those young voices, it tears me to pieces. I could wring my hands, beat my breast, or do any other futile thing. The man in front—I guess it's the sergeant—calls something that sounds like this: "Rep, lep, upf, dupf, *sing*." And then they burst out with songs I've never heard, though they are familiar tunes with different words. They just sang "John Brown's Body," and the words ended, "When this war is over we'll all enlist again—like *hell* we will." And I said out loud: "Like hell you *will*, if another war comes."

So young, so young! Sugar, coffee, shoe, food rationing, and April 1 meat rationing, though it's almost impossible to get beef now. No chocolate, no gum, one-quarter pound of butter, *when* you can get it, gasoline one-half gallon a week. We went over to Miami New Year's, for the Orange Bowl game, and it was good to see all, but Miami is not the same. I paid three times the amount of my income tax from last year, and I'm in the *very* low bracket. The temperature has gone up to 88°.

Tampa—Tuesday, May 25, 1943

Left for Atlanta, March 31, Dan and Alice taking us to the depot. Tremendous crowd, 200 were left in the depot, as no room on the train, no redcap, so Dan lifted the suitcase and was taken with severe pain. They phoned us to Atlanta the next day, and I left Friday night and came back to find him in the hospital with coronary thrombosis. The doctor assured me lifting the suitcase did not cause it. I stayed at Alice's two weeks until Day got back from New York. Dan will sit up tomorrow (after eight weeks) on his thirty-fifth birthday. David has been sick with worms and looks so thin. We are taking him to the doctor today.

Tampa—Thursday, July 1, 1943

David is sixteen months old today, and they left last night for Clayton. I do hope Dan will stand the trip well and Alice will get a rest, as she has had a hard time. She moved to her new house, which we bought her—2616 Prospect Road. David has gained, and how hateful to tell him good-bye. He walks a few steps alone, says many words, and really carries a tune when he sings. He understands every word you say to him. He's my "puddin' pie"! Joan married very suddenly in Evansville, Indiana, June 26, Lieutenant George Lavenson of Philadelphia.

Tampa—Wednesday, July 14, 1943

My birthday, and I have been cleaning closets and packing all morning. We leave Saturday for Atlanta, Clayton, and New York.

Tampa—Thursday, November 11, 1943

An Armistice Day Parade has been going on in front of my door. At 1 P.M. I went across to the auditorium for services. I signed a petition saying I'd be willing to continue rationing after the war. Why not?

Tampa—Sunday, November 28, 1943

Alice, Dan, and David were here to lunch, and now David is asleep on Pop's bed,* and later we will take him to the park, our Sunday job. He will say, "Please, Nana, park. Please, Nana, peanuts, hunny, birdie, boat, choo-choo," etc. He talks constantly and loves to come here. He walked alone at sixteen months. We had such a grand time with him in Clayton and stayed in New York at the Savoy Plaza from August 2 to October 4. Saw *Doughgirls*, *Oklahoma* (the great hit), *Let's Face It* with Danny Kaye, *Tomorrow the World*, *Merry Widow* with Martha Eggerth and Jan Kiepura, and several others. Enjoyed our stay in New York as usual. Dan looks well, but he is rather nervous and depressed. Alice has lost twelve pounds, but she needed to reduce. Wednesday night we celebrated Day's birthday and Thanksgiving at Alice's house for turkey dinner—forty-seven cents a pound, live weight. Coffee rationing was off in September. Butter is sixteen points. We

---

*Pop was David's name for Day.

don't eat much meat, as I only have two ration books for three people (I have to include the cook).

Tampa—Tuesday, December 7, 1943

Day of Infamy. There was a plan to make Pearl Harbor Day a national holiday, but it didn't pass. Surely nothing to celebrate, but the news is better. The Big Three just met at Tehran, and the headlines say, "Death to the Germans," or rather destruction.

Tampa—Wednesday, March 1, 1944

Our darling baby's second birthday. He insists on saying he is six years old. I went out to see him at noon. He was very excited about his presents, most of them cheap paper toys, as it's impossible to get any others; but he seemed to like them better, I'm sure, than the $100 War Bond we gave him. O, what a joy he is. He knows all the colors, most of the alphabet, and many nursery rhymes.

Tampa—Saturday, March 4, 1944

Just ended the Met's radio *Bohème*—my beloved. Why this should be my favorite opera I don't know. Hackneyed and banal in theme, I suppose, but the exquisite music always leaves me limp as a rag and with a lump in my throat. I have heard it sung better. Yes, Caruso and Martinelli, Bori, Alda, etc.

While in New York I took little stories about David to *Baby Talk* magazine, and they were promptly accepted, and I was paid $20, the first money I'd ever earned. They appeared in the November magazine [reprinted in Appendix D, pp. 217–22].

Tampa—Tuesday, March 21, 1944

Day is in bed with an intestinal disturbance and fever. He came back from Atlanta yesterday, and I suppose he did too much. I've been reading in the paper where Lt. Col. Griffin Davis died in California—the baby I loved so thirty-five years ago. I wept when I kissed him good-bye when we left Tampa for St. Louis. Little did I think then I'd be back in Tampa and read of his death in a horrible war. Alice, Dan, and baby left for Dallas March 14.

Tampa—Tuesday, June 6, 1944

D-Day at last. The invasion started about 1 A.M., and I have been listening to the radio since 8. My first reaction, and I'm sure everyone else's—"Thank God, and God keep us," each one naming someone near. Someone extra-near: George is no doubt there, as they say the paratroops were among the first.

David sweeter than ever. At two years old he knew the alphabet, could read and spell about six words. Many mushy rhymes and songs. He is very thin, but the doctor says he is in good condition.

Having lots of trouble with my nose. Been to five dermatologists, five X rays, two nose men—still have a sore nose!

Tampa—Wednesday, June 28, 1944

Listening all day to the Republican Convention in Chicago. [Thomas E.] Dewey and [John W.] Bricker nominated.

Tampa—Wednesday, November 1, 1944

Went to Alice's and stayed three weeks with David while they were in New York. Had a grand time with David, but felt the responsibility. We came back from New York October 29. Our stay in New York was not so pleasant, as it was so hot, but we saw lots of shows—*Voice of the Turtle, Song of Norway, Anna Lucasta, Carmen Jones*, etc., etc. Left here July 21, spent two delightful weeks in Blowing Rock—very cool, good food.

Marred by news of George's death.* He was lost in the plane bringing back eighteen wounded soldiers. He had been wounded in the hip in Normandy, six days after D-Day.

Went to Connie's wedding at the Biltmore August 5, then on to New York.

Tampa—Saturday, November 11, 1944

Another Armistice Day! Nothing to celebrate. The fine elation of D-Day is gone. I feel a dreary frustration. The war was not over in September, as had been widely predicted. We are just inside of Germany at Aachen. Ro-

---

*George Lavenson, Joan's husband.

bot bombs are flying over England, and this country has been warned. Doesn't seem much chance of victory before the snowfall. Roosevelt was just renominated, by large majority.

Tampa—Saturday, January 20, 1945

Just listened to Roosevelt's fourth inaugural ceremony—very quiet, no celebration. He spoke only six minutes.

On January 16 we got news of Joseph*—died in action in Belgium. Impossible to realize. We are all heartbroken; twenty-four years old and gone forever.

UNTITLED POEM

It has come—the message I've awaited with fear and horror and a
  strange premonition.
No, no, no, my heart cries out, it cannot be, not my boy.
Not my boy with his strong young body, his lovely smile, his keen mind
  and pure soul.
God, I have prayed and prayed. I have looked into Your very face and
  pleaded.
I have bared my soul to You and begged You to take my life if need be,
Only spare him.
He was so young, dear God, so young, so young.
My baby, my little boy, my tall soldier—
When I saw him in his uniform, my heart stood still,
And yet I was so proud.
O let it be some sad mistake, let it be some other boy.
What am I saying? Forgive me, God. I could not wish some other
  mother this bitter anguish.
Just let me rest here, a little longer.
Then I will rise and dry my tears
And go on with my life again.
He would have wished it so,
My son, my son.†

---

*Joseph Jacobus, the son of Helen's brother Maurice (Bubba).
†In her diary, Helen rarely made corrections; she wrote in one "take." Not so this poem. Explaining it in a note at the bottom of the original, Alice later wrote: "Helen was Joseph's godmother, and as she had no son of her own, really felt that he was her son. She grieved terribly for him."

Tampa—Thursday, March 1, 1945

Date of Joseph's death: December 30. He was buried in a cemetery in Belgium. I have been so depressed. I just can't pull myself out of it. The waste, the futility!

Heard [American aviator Eddie] Rickenbacker speak. He says the war in Germany will be over between June and September and that we will fight on with Japan for years and years. Roosevelt will report on the Yalta meeting at 12:30, and then I'm going out to David's birthday party—three years old today. He is the bright spot, the shining joy of our lives. He knows the whole alphabet, can write at least twenty-five words, and spell them.

Tampa—Monday, April 16, 1945

Just listened to President Truman's first speech—quiet, short, and dignified. He promised to carry on all of Roosevelt's policies and to prosecute the war to unconditional surrender. We were eating dinner at the Cricket Thursday evening, April 12, when we heard the shocking news. The colored waitress said, with tears in her eyes, "I just heard on the radio our president is dead." "Our" president—from a Negro. What greater eulogy? And what eulogies I listened to all day Friday, Saturday, Sunday. All commercials off the air. The whole world in mourning. I heard hundreds of Ave Marias, "Lead, Kindly Light," "Nearer My God to Thee," etc., etc. I heard Negro spirituals. Like Moses, he was given a glimpse of the Promised Land, but not permitted to enter, and who can guess the reason? Victory is almost in sight, and we wait for almost hourly news, though commentators tell us it may be weeks. President Roosevelt, quiet American, hail and farewell.

Alice and Dan were in Clearwater ten days, and we stayed with David. He was with us when we heard the news. Of course, he doesn't realize it, but he says, in a mournful voice, "President Roosevelt is dead, and I guess they are burying him now."

Tampa—Wednesday, June 6, 1945

One year since D-Day, and I remember how I prayed for George, and George is gone. Then came the battle of the Bulge, and I prayed for Joseph, a first lieutenant in Patton's Third Army. And now Joseph is gone. Henry Jr. is on the SS *Claxton* in the Pacific, so now we pray for him, nineteen years old.

We went to New York May 24 and stayed three weeks, at the Waldorf, four days at the Biltmore. Stopped in Atlanta two days. Anna and Maurice are pitiful. It was cold and raining the whole month in New York (97° here). Saw *Dear Ruth, Bell for Adano, I Remember Mama, Harvey, Glass Menagerie.*

I often wondered where we'd be on V-E Day and pictured it a day of wild celebration and jubilation, like the last war, but it was nothing like that. On Saturday, April 28, we were at a dinner in the Jade Room of the Waldorf. At 8:25 the orchestra suddenly called everyone to attention, and a voice announced: "Ladies and Gentlemen, the news has just come of Germany's unconditional surrender." There was a moment of stunned silence, then a buzz of voices, no cheers. And I was not the only one to burst into tears—tears of sorrow for those who would never come back. The news was later denied. Then came the dreary wait until Monday, May 7, when we heard at 10 A.M. on the radio, "War Is Over, Not Yet Official." Papers were falling like snow out of the high buildings. I walked up Fifth Avenue to 59th Street, and there was no excitement on the streets at all. On Tuesday morning we ordered breakfast in our living room and listened to Truman and Churchill speak. Official.

Such anticlimax, such a let-down feeling. That night, after *Dear Ruth*, we walked down to Times Square, where a "wild celebration" was supposed to be in progress. All we saw was a crowd of kids and hoodlums throwing confetti and blowing horns. That's how V-E Day came to New York, and it seemed to have been the same all through the country.

New York —Savoy Plaza, Wednesday, August 15, 1945

Well, it is over, the blood and sweat and tears. Over also for Joseph and George and all the others, left in their silent graves. There they will lie, and the world will go on. We left Blowing Rock at 3 P.M. August 12, after hearing of the Jap surrender, but nothing official.

On August 14 we were at the Lobster Restaurant on 45th Street. At 7 P.M. a loudspeaker suddenly blared forth—"Surrender Official." We dashed down to Times Square and were there in time to hear the first wild roar, and to see it flashed on the Times Building. It was a sight never to be forgotten.

New York—Friday, September 14, 1945

Day has made a deal with Bill Horsey, which I hope will turn out fine. He needs relief badly. We both had a series of X rays—nothing showing up but our hernias and nothing to do about it. David started nursery school Monday after their return from Miami. The poor little darling cried, and Alice had to go and take him home. I'm sorry he is such a sensitive child, but he has inherited it from Dan, and perhaps a little from his maternal Nana!

On August 27 I saw De Gaulle drive up Fifth Avenue in a parade. A stern and glum-looking man, he sat stiffly in his car, waving arms in a wooden manner. I thought the applause a little perfunctory. He is not of the stuff for hero worship. Quite different was General [Jonathan Mayhew] Wainwright's triumphant tour, which I saw yesterday, September 13. He sat upon the back of the car, waving and smiling and throwing kisses. Emaciated and tired, he was still every inch a hero and a soldier.

Tampa—Saturday, November 10, 1945

And now the saddest thing I have written—on September 26 Maurice passed away, very suddenly, while seated in a barber chair. I had been home from New York and Day was in Chicago when the news came. Those two days in Atlanta are like a nightmare. He died of a broken heart—one more war casualty. And now the family circle is broken, a sad and tragic thing. I can write no more.

Tampa—Friday, February 1, 1946

Day to Atlantic City for a canners' convention.

"State of the Union": More men on strike than in our history. Seizure by the government of basic industries being forced. Demobilization has hit the nation's armed forces. Real peace for the world a distant prospect. U.S. relations with Britain and Russia not good. Inflation growing, Congressional leadership is lost to the White House. In the stores butter nonexistent; meat, fats, soap very scarce. Men's shirts and underwear very scarce. Boys' and women's underwear ditto.

Tampa—Wednesday, May 8, 1946

One year ago we were in New York—V-E Day. Our thirty-seventh anniversary we spent in Miami. Spent twelve days at the Belmar Hotel on the beach—nice to be tourists in Miami. Had the flu when I got home; haven't felt well since.

Dan's mother died April 23, just before Alice, Dan, and David got home from Dallas after a three-week visit there. They flew back at once, and we stayed with David.

Tampa—Friday, June 28, 1946

On May 21, Day went to New York and I to Atlanta for two weeks. Very nice visit and cool. Went to the cemetery with Anna; very sad. We plan to go to Asheville July 18. Have an apartment at the Savoy for September. May go to Louisville in the interim.

Alice will have a baby in January. Hope it's a girl, but a boy will be alright, too. Don't see how I can love another one like David, but sure I will.

Dot's little Susie born June 14th.

Days very hot here, but rain and cool at nights.

The O.P.A. Bill is being voted on.* As I write, wild cries of inflation, etc. In the stores butter, grits, rice nonexistent; meats very scarce, bread also. Still sending food to Europe.

England on bread-rationing first time in history.

Tampa—Thursday, July 4, 1946

Today, the Philippines get their independence, and we celebrate the 170th year of ours.

President Truman vetoed the new O.P.A. Bill, and now we have no price control.

Fantastic tales of price rises, especially in rent. Our rent was raised at once, from $87.50 to $100, the new bill to be prepaid to keep down inflation. Last July 4 we spent at Clearwater. Today we have spent a quiet morning and expect to go this afternoon to T. T. for dinner and to see *Gilda*, with Rita Hayworth.

Tampa—Sunday, July 14, 1946

My birthday, very hot, and packing to leave for Asheville Thursday. Day gave me fine check and sweet letter.

*The Office of Price Administration set consumer prices during the war.

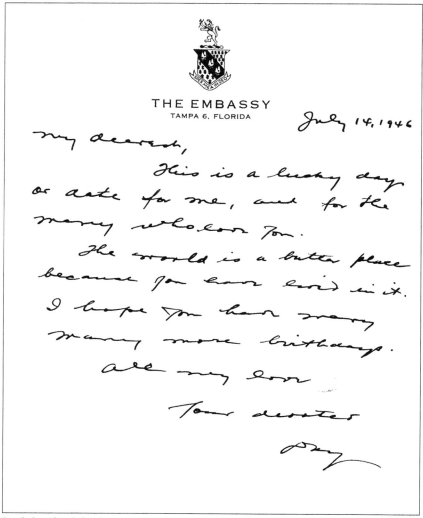

THE EMBASSY
TAMPA 6. FLORIDA

July 14, 1946

my dearest,

This is a lucky day or date for me, and for the many who love you.

The world is a better place because you have lived in it.

I hope you have many many more birthdays.

All my love

Your devoted

Day's last birthday letter to Helen, July 14, 1946.

Asheville—Grove Park Inn, Wednesday, July 31, 1946

Very nice here, not as cool as Blowing Rock and the food not as good. Very quiet, a few nice couples, play a little gin and bingo, eat, read, walk a little.

Last Wednesday heard bad news from Alice, and no hope now for a grandchild in January. But she is OK, thank heaven.

 Epilogue Marcus D. Rosenbaum

In October 1946, still suffering from her undefined illnesses, Helen went to Miami for a doctor's appointment. On October 30, while shopping downtown at Burdine's department store, she collapsed and died, apparently of a heart attack. There is no record of an autopsy. Her funeral was held in Miami, and Rabbi Colman A. Zwitman, who had become Temple Israel's head rabbi in 1941, officiated. Helen's friend, Rabbi Jacob Kaplan, who had retired to emeritus status, participated in the ceremony. She was buried in Graceland Memorial Park on S.W. Eighth Street.

Day, who had retired from business after he sold Apte Brothers Canning Company in 1945, remarried in 1948. He went back to work as a bank officer, and he and his second wife, Inez, moved to Los Angeles for several years but then returned to Miami. Day was Inez's first husband, and, although she was twenty years younger than he, she died first, in September 1955. About one year later, on August 29, 1956, Day himself died at age sixty-nine. He is buried between Helen and Inez. The three graves, under a small tree, are without monuments, with only small, flat brass markers at their heads.

Daniel Rosenbaum, who had been working for his father-in-law, started his own canning company after Day sold Apte Brothers, and he built it into a successful business. He and Alice became prominent Tampa citizens, partici-pated actively in community service, and became patrons of the arts. By the 1980s, it was increasingly difficult for a small company like Sugar Rose (named after Dan and his partner, Sam Sugarman) to compete with the giants, espe-cially in an age of easy transportation of fresh food and rising prices of cans. Dan, too, was growing older, and he closed the business and retired.

In addition to David, Alice had one other child, this writer, in 1949, three years after her miscarriage. She lived out her life with Dan in the Tampa home that her parents had given them in 1943. Alice died in 1986, just a few months before her seventy-third birthday. Dan stayed in the Prospect Road house and led an active life until his death in 1995 at age eighty-seven.

That was when I first met my grandmother.

❧ Selected Bibliography ❧

Ashe, Arthur R., Jr. *A Hard Road to Glory: The African-American Athlete in Boxing*, 14–26. New York: Amistad Press, 1993.

Blumberg, Janice Rothschild. *As But a Day: To a Hundred and Twenty, 1867–1987* (a history of the Temple in Atlanta). Atlanta: Hebrew Benevolent Congregation, 1966. Revised 1987.

Dinnerstein, Leonard. *The Leo Frank Case*. Athens: University of Georgia Press, Brown Thrasher Books, 1966. Reprinted 1987.

———, and Mary Dale Palsson, eds. *Jews in the South*. Baton Rouge: Louisiana State University Press, 1973.

Durant, John. *The Heavyweight Champions*, 6th revised edition, 45–64. New York: Hastings House Publishers, 1976.

Gottfried, Alex. *Boss Cermak: A Study of Political Leadership*. Seattle: University of Washington Press, 1962.

Green, Paul M. "Anton J. Cermak: The Man and His Machine." In *The Mayors: The Chicago Political Tradition*, revised edition, edited by Paul M. Green and Melvin G. Holli, 99–110. Carbondale, IL: Southern Illinois University Press, 1995.

Hertzberg, Steven. *Strangers within the Gate City: The Jews of Atlanta, 1845–1915*. Philadelphia: Jewish Publication Society of America, 1978.

Ingalls, Robert P. *Urban Vigilantes in the New South: Tampa, 1882–1936*, 87–115. Gainesville: University Press of Florida, 1988.

Leavitt, Judith Walzer. *Brought to Bed: Child-Bearing in America, 1750–1950*. New York: Oxford University Press, 1986.

———, ed. *Women and Health in America: Historical Readings*. Madison: University of Wisconsin Press, 1984.

Lee, Anne S. "Maternal Mortality in the United States." *Phylon: The Atlanta University Review of Race and Culture* 38, no. 3 (September 1977): 259–66.

Malchow, Charles William, M.D. *The Sexual Life (Embracing the Natural Sexual Impulse, Normal Sexual Habits and Propagation, Together with Sexual Physiology and Hygiene),* 6th edition. St. Louis: C. V. Mosby Co., 1923.

May, Elaine Tyler. *Barren in the Promised Land: Childless Americans and the Pursuit of Happiness.* New York: Basic Books, 1995.

Mendez, Armando. *Ciudad de Cigars: West Tampa.* Cocoa, FL: Florida Historical Society, 1994.

Meyer, Michael A. *Response to Modernity: A History of the Reform Movement in Judaism.* Detroit: Wayne State University Press, 1988.

Simons, Howard. *Jewish Times: Voices of the American Jewish Experience,* 219–36. New York: Doubleday, 1988.

Tebeau, Charlton W. *Synagogue in the Central City: Temple Israel of Greater Miami, 1922–1972.* Coral Gables, FL: University of Miami Press, 1972.

⇛ Appendix A ⇚

Excerpts from *The Sexual Life*

⇛ Charles William Malchow's book, The Sexual
Life, *was wildly popular in Helen's time. First published in 1905 by the
Burton Company of Minneapolis,* The Sexual Life *went through many print-
ings well into the 1920s.*

*The following excerpts are from the sixth edition, which has the sub-
title* Embracing the Natural Sexual Impulse, Normal Sexual Habits and
Propagation, Together with Sexual Physiology and Hygiene. *Published in
St. Louis in 1923 by C. V. Mosby Co., this edition describes Dr. Malchow as
"formerly professor of proctology and associate in clinical medicine,
Hamline University College of Physicians and Surgeons; president of the
Physicians and Surgeons Club; member Hennepin County Medical Society,
Minnesota State Medical Society, American Medical Association, etc. etc."*

Sex is the central fact of life, and owing to the urgent necessity for enlightenment upon a subject that greatly affects, directly or indirectly, every
member of society, prudery and mawkish modesty should be disregarded.
When others do not intelligently discuss delicate matters regarded as pecu-
liarly intimate, personal and shameful, it becomes a part of the physician's
duty to do so. [Preface, p. 7]   ⇛

That the sexual sense has very much to do with a desirable condition of
the mind is further abundantly proven by the fact that old maids and bach-
elors who abstain from natural sexual intercourse, are proverbially
"cranky," eccentric and biased in their judgments. [p. 35]

The female is called upon, for her own protection, to dissimulate and deceive regarding her sexual passion, for in addition to the animal instinct she will, by reason of her experience and observation since early childhood, have acquired habits of strategy and will exercise tact, with more or less discretion, when her natural feelings may become emphasized.

Her moral training dictates the right to mislead for the benefit of what is considered to be of advantage to society, and her physical safety demands a disguise of passion in order to insure her security from attack. [p. 45]

Within normal limits a little pain sometimes acts as an excitement to passion, for it is one of the most powerful methods of arousing emotion. The male finds some pleasure in exerting force and has a tendency to delight in domination, but the female derives some pleasure in experiencing force and tends to delight in submission. [p. 46]

A woman often in the ecstasy of passion implores a man to desist, though that is really the last thing she desires, and a man who fails to realize this has not progressed very far in the art of love making. [p. 47]

Sexual dreams in women who have never experienced an orgasm when awake are usually of a very vague kind. It is not, as a rule, until the orgasm—under whatever conditions it may have been produced—has been experienced in the waking state, that it begins to occur in women during sleep, and even then it is probably less frequent than in the other sex. [p. 52]

Throughout the whole animal kingdom the female is the passive and the male the active party in matters sexual. . . . In order to excite the male she [the female animal] feigns an unwillingness, during the period of sexual inclination, which is more apparent than real, and this show of antagonism serves to stimulate an eagerness in the male which is desirable. She tantalizes him by resistance and flees with the expectation of pursuit . . . but when caught she readily submits. . . . The same animal trait or characteristic is found in the human female, and this instinctive prompting to conceal the sexual willingness enters very largely into the causation of modesty. [p. 61]

[For girls at puberty] and perhaps for a considerable time thereafter, the sexual emotion has not become centered in the sexual organs. It is probable that not until the time when a woman has actual sexual experience in a natural and physiological way does she come to understand, realize or appreciate the origin and significance of sexual emotion. [p. 67]

When people do not have sexual intercourse it may be ascribed to one of the following reasons:

First. They live under conditions that prevent it.

Second. They have not the physical qualifications.

Third. They are not of the proper age.

Fourth. They live amidst surroundings that are unfavorable.

Fifth. They are not normal human beings. [p. 157]

[On the causes of incompatibility:] The two sexes do not start equally in their development, and the conditions under which development progresses are vastly different in the two sexes.

The girl inherits a disposition to disregard matters of sex, and whatever propensity there may be to investigate the subject is discouraged by association, for women generally do not discuss this topic and allude to it only with indefinite insinuations.

Young men and boys talk of these matters more freely and tell many stories that are woven about the sexual relation, though the truth is often perverted and very seldom told in its entirety. [p. 204]

Social conditions are such that the thoughts of the boy are recurrently attracted to sexual matters, while those of the girl and maiden are diverted into other channels, which causes the development of the sexual system, as well as the sex feelings, to be smothered or retarded in the female, but to be stimulated and enhanced in the male. [p. 205]

[The following section is set in the context of Malchow's view of a "successful" sexual relation—namely, one in which the couple reaches simultaneous orgasm.]

The conditions of women in regard to their marital relations vary with the individual, and for convenience married women have been divided into the following classes:

First. Women so situated and constructed, both physically and mentally, that they respond to the caresses of the husband at all times.

Second. Those who can under reasonable circumstances, by a voluntary effort hasten or retard the climax to meet the varying conditions under which they live.

Third. Those who are unable to properly participate, or bring into requisition any physical or mental methods to produce simultaneous orgasm, or harmonious relations, but are left excited, nervous and unsat-isfied after coition.

Fourth. Women whose sexual passion does not become aroused, who do not derive any pleasure or benefit from copulation, and who cannot conceive how the act can be pleasurable for anyone.

This division is somewhat arbitrary, as it is possible for a woman to be put in any of these classes at different times during her marital life. It is also impossible to determine the proportion of women in any of these classes, but it has been estimated that the first class embraces five per-cent; the second, fifty percent; the third, thirty percent; and the last fif-teen percent of all married women. According to this estimate nearly one-half the women are living lives that can be neither healthful nor congenial, and whose homes are lacking in a fundamental requisite for happiness.

Not only is the woman concerned, but the remainder of the family is directly involved, and when we consider the prevalence of these undesir-able conditions the situation becomes appalling.

Granting for the sake of argument, that the proportion of congenial homes is larger than that given, it is still a wonder, not that divorce is so common, but rather that it is not obtained with greater frequency. In or-der to mitigate the evil it becomes necessary to remove the cause, and fine theories, however brilliantly promulgated, are of but little avail if practical results are not forthcoming. . . . If the laity knew what the proper sexual relations were, much harm would be averted, but it is not enough to know what this condition is, for it requires specific instructions to bring about this end. . . . Without the danger of a challenge, it may be asserted that with proper and timely education on matters sexual, there is no good rea-son why any sexual relations that are at all unusual could not be made most satisfactory for all concerned, and that this would obtain if people only knew how, is philosophical and not visionary.

The woman belonging to the first class heretofore enumerated, or those who always respond to the caresses of the husband and have natural coi-tus, are the best of companions. They are bright, brilliant and vivacious, have cultivated intuitions that anticipate pleasurable relations, and both take and give delight readily. They are happy in their love, elicit atten-tions, often obtain distinction, and, when discreet, are the happiest of women. That the proportion of such wives is not larger is unfortunate, but that many more could be in the same position there is every reason for belief. The condition is the result of extraordinary affinity, exceptional knowledge of sexuality and human nature, early marriage and long famil-iarity with sexual practices. This class needs not medical advice or en-couragement in their relations.

In the second class, in which one-half of the women are placed, are those who are capable of adjusting themselves to ordinary conditions and have physiological copulation when they choose. They are comparatively contented and silent, deeming their relations sacred and not to be alluded to. They make devoted wives, adorable mothers and true helpmates; command respect, receive consideration and live for their homes, husbands and children. They are loyal in adversity, joyful in prosperity, and admirable wherever placed. They meet their husbands half way, uncomplainingly; and are the source of ennobling inspirations, call forth tender feelings and leave behind an honored memory. With them there is no infidelity; they wield the greatest influence, and when unmolested are altogether honored and lovable, within and without the family. The family is their greatest concern, and were it not for the manifold temptations of our society that prompt to its restriction, there would remain but little to be desired for the happiest sexual living.

The women of the third class, or those who are unable to bring themselves to the point where there will be eager participation in the pleasures of sexual intercourse, are in considerable numbers, as the proportion is estimated at 30 percent. They do not satisfy their husbands, except in some minor degree, neither are their husbands considered by them very acceptable. Both are dissatisfied with their relations and seek to promote their happiness by methods other than the right. Their temptation to derive pleasures of sense elsewhere than from the prescribed source, is in proportion to their personal makeup, and their conduct depends largely upon their opportunities and the people with whom they come in contact. Very often they find a paramour with whom they temporarily enjoy, for a varying length of time, those pleasures they should have in their relations at home and if they be successful in disguising their duplicity—which is most often the case—the world remains ignorant of the real condition. Not content at home they woo excitement and diversion in the various and numerous methods at their command and partially console themselves with the belief that they are enjoying themselves. If daring enough to brave society's comments, they sometimes, especially when a more congenial alliance seems in prospect, enter the courts and pray for divorce and thus proclaim and establish the fact that their marriage is a failure.

These are the cases that require advice, as most of the trouble originates in ignorance and the mystery with which sex is popularly surrounded. The wife does not know how to obtain the satisfaction and tranquility that is needed, and the husband does not understand how to impart and obtain that which must necessarily draw the two closer together and cement the bonds. Much can be accomplished by proper instruction, and if the case has not already gone on to that stage where a hopeless infatuation has been formed for another, the condition can often be remedied by effective personal acts alone, and nearly always rectified by local measures which put the woman in the way of securing the results that are indispensable to right sexual living, and so essential for adult humanity's welfare.

Women of the last class, who are devoid of sexual feeling, or passion, are in need of sympathy. These women are practically sexless, and that 15 percent, or one woman in every seven, is living her life with nothing but childish or senile sentiments and intuitions, is no credit to our boasted civilization with its much vaunted facilities for education—that does not include the learning of the vital principles of right living. That women should be called upon to bear and rear children without taking any interest in, or actively participating in that process which is necessary for their origin, is manifestly cruel, unjust and inhuman. To prevent or deprive a similar being from having the most profound feelings instilled by life, and which go with the manner of imparting this being to another, is to deny a created entity its birthright, to put it mildly.

It is difficult, if not impossible, for a person to understand a sensation they have never experienced and of which they have no personal knowledge, and so these women cannot conceive how there can be any pleasure in this act, which is frequently referred to as base and degrading. They experience no more sensation or pleasure than from ordinary close contact, and submit from a sense of wifely duty, or a desire to please the husband, who is known to have animal necessities, which are often termed "beastly" tendencies. They become pregnant and rear families to whom they are quite as devoted as the women who have natural feelings. Any allusions to benefits derived from copulation or to others of their sex who enjoy it meet with their emphatic contempt, and they persistently endeavor to influence all whom they may with their ideas. They are most severe in condemnation of erring women, are sometimes insanely jealous, and more or less warped in their judgment. Their solicitude for other women is often marked, but misplaced, for they themselves, as well as their husbands, are truly deserving of compassion.

Advice in these cases is thrown away and argument is useless, for unless they are personally brought to feel that which is unknown to them, they will remain serenely unconscious of the natural sexual feelings, which have such a tremendous influence upon the affairs of life. If they have been married a number of years, any instructions which may be given them relative to the requisites of copulation will prove inadequate, as their mental attitude prohibits the required mood for enjoyment, and unless extraordinary means can be resorted to whereby the local physical condition becomes sufficiently pronounced to dominate the mind, active participation and harmonious sexual relations cannot be had. . . .

There can be no greater human pleasures for adult men and women than those afforded by their sexual relations, when these are as nature designed, and if they were always satisfactory and never followed by undesirable results there would be nothing to hope for, other things being equal. Given the ability to enjoy and the assurance of freedom from harmful results, the obstacles to the happiest possible sexual living would be removed. These obstacles are in practice very formidable, however, for it is given to but very few to have them removed to such a degree as will be mutually satisfactory.

We are considering only married people before the age in which the change of life occurs or such a time when sexual desire naturally ceases to be active. The two requisites in question are:

First. Proper frequency of desire, or ability to copulate.

Second. Removal of the restrictions placed upon the gratification of this desire.

Practically, gratification is denied or restricted by a solicitude regarding pregnancy, which also affects desire. Failure of issue may, possibly, by its general influence upon the two lives, have some effect upon sexuality, but nearly always the fear of pregnancy is the great and underlying cause which prevents desirable sexual relations. . . .

Before marriage the momentous question is the establishment of relations, but after matrimony the problem to be solved is the proper conduct in the nuptial couch. When, in sexual congress, the delights and benefits of a mutual orgasm have once been thoroughly experienced, the natural appetite prompts to subsequent solicitation, and it is quite as natural for a woman to seek the normal way of satisfying her passion with her husband as it is for her to want to quench her thirst by the drinking of cool water. [p. 219 et seq.]

✥ Appendix B ✥

Books I Have Read

July 4, 1901
The Crisis, by Winston Churchill (Historical Novel)

The book is one whose theme is of the greatest interest to every American—the crisis in our history. Like a true Southerner I have never loved Lincoln; now I admire the statesman, respect the president—and love the man.

July 16, 1901
Penelope's Irish Experiences, by Kate Douglas Wiggin (Romance and Travel)

All spontaneous fun, innocent mischief, and pure sentiment. "There are women who are born to be petted and served, and there are those who seem born to serve others."

July 19, 1901
The Lane That Had No Turning, by Gilbert Parker (Historical Novel)

These stories are striking in power and incident and are treated with great beauty and charm.

July 20, 1901
The Helmet of Navarre, by Bertha Runkle (Historical Novel)

The adventures of Étienne are thrilling in the extreme, and he is a very lovable character with his impulsive, generous temperament, and his great love for the niece of the enemy of his house. After many misfortunes, love triumphs in the end.

July 23, 1901
Sir Christopher: A Romance of a Maryland Manor in 1644,
by Maud Wilder Goodwin (Historical Romance)

Sir Christopher Neville, the hero, is a man of noble character and high principles. His love for Elinor Calvert, who refuses to marry him because of their difference in faith, is beautiful and pathetic.

July 24, 1901
The Reign of Law: A Tale of Kentucky Hemp Fields,
by James Lane Allen (Fiction)

A book that only James Lane Allen could write—full of humor and grace, purity of love, and most of all a deep imaginative beauty, which makes one see, hear, and feel all the beauties of nature with all the author's aesthetic sense. David, with his deep, strong nature and his doubt and unbelief, must draw tears from every eye. As for Gabriella, she was "a Southern girl of strong, warm, deep nature," whose last act at night was to kneel beside her bed and pray that her lover "might be saved from the influences of false teachers and guided back to the only Great One."

August 1, 1901
Eben Holden, by Irving Bacheller (Historical Novel)

"Love of labor was counted a great virtue in Faraway"—this is the whole keynote to the book, filled with rugged, stern but beautiful characters. It is strong, pure, natural, describing in a vivid way the real life of the country folk that saved this nation, how they grew, loved, wrought and had their being.

August 5, 1901
Wild Animals I Have Known, and 200 Drawings,
by Ernest Thompson Seton (Natural History)

Most delightful of books for lovers of animals. The illustrations are graceful and clever, and the stories are told with a sympathetic touch and happy insight into the comedies and tragedies of animal life.

August 17, 1901
Hugh Wynn, Free Quaker (Sometime Brevet Lieutenant on the Staff of His Excellency General Washington, by Weir Mitchell (Historical Novel)

This book gives a good picture of life in the colonies during the Revolution. The story is told with great historical accuracy.

August 20, 1901
Goethe and Schiller, by Luise Mühlbach* (Historical Romance)

As a character sketch of Goethe and Schiller, the book is very good, but other parts seem to be rather weak and foolishly sentimental.

*Pseudonym for Klara Muller Mundt.

August 21, 1901
The Conspirators, by Robert W. Chambers (Romance)

Although this book is very light, it affords much pleasure for casual reading, being full of dash and verve: ". . . that greatest of life's games—a game that none can play for him, a game where none can aid him, save his adversary; the only game where, when the woman loses, both win, and when the man loses all is lost. I think it is called 'hearts,' or something similar."

August 26, 1901
Bob, Son of Battle, by Alfred Ollivant (Fiction)

Out of such slim material the author makes a very readable story. Any lover of dogs will appreciate this book.

August 30, 1901
Graustark: The Story of Love Behind the Throne,
by George Barr McCutcheon (Romance)

Although highly improbable and dramatic, the book is very interesting and thrilling. It is wholly and simply a love story.

September 2, 1901
Young Mistley, by Hugh Stowell Scott (Fiction and History)

I liked this book very much. It is strong, yet pure, with a great insight into human nature.

September 5, 1901
The Cardinal's Snuff Box, by Henry Harland (Fiction)

The book is very light and insipid, the only redeeming features being a few really good descriptions of Italian scenery.

September 16, 1901
Ivanhoe, by Sir Walter Scott (Romance and History)

This book is certainly one of the best romances I have ever read, and I believe it is my favorite. Every time I read it, I find more beauties. In my opinion it is the greatest Romantic Novel ever written. Rebecca comes nearer my ideal than almost any other character in fiction. Richard the Lion Hearted, De Bracy, and Cedric the Saxon form a most picturesque frame for the minor characters.

October 1, 1901
The Celebrity, by Winston Churchill (Fiction)

It has a very clever plot but cannot compare with either *Richard Carvel* or *The Crisis* in power or entertainment.

October 8, 1901
The Right of Way, by Gilbert Parker (Fiction)

This is certainly one of the best books I have read of late for its unusual love story, its character portrayal, and spiritual import.

October 12, 1901
The Daughter of an Empress, by Luise Mühlbach (Historical Novel)

Very good and interesting.

October 14, 1901
Thanatopsis and Other Poems, by William Cullen Bryant (Poetry)

Bryant's poems are lovely, filled with sweet sentiment, love of nature, and classic thought.

October 18, 1901
Alice of Old Vincennes, by Maurice Thompson (Historical Romance)

It seems to me that the author could have made a much stronger story out of such good material, but it is a very sweet book.

October 22, 1901
The Deserted Village, by Oliver Goldsmith (Poetry)

It is magnificent. Beautiful thoughts abound, and what is more they are expressed in a beautiful way. The following lines are said to be one of the best examples of metaphor in the English language:

> "As some tall cliff that lifts its awful form
> Swells from the vale and midway leaves the storm,
> Though round its breast the rolling clouds are spread,
> Eternal sunshine settles on its head."

October 25, 1901
Vicar of Wakefield, by Oliver Goldsmith (Fiction)

This book combines simplicity and learning, humor and melancholy. It is typical of the author.

October 30, 1901
Marmion, by Sir Walter Scott (Poetry and History)

It is vigorous and spirited, yet gentle and flowing.

> "Oh, what a tangled web we weave
> When first we practice to deceive."

> "Oh, Woman! In our hours of ease,
> Uncertain, coy, and hard to please

And variable as the shade
By the light quivering aspen made;
When pain and anguish wring the brow
A ministering angel thou!"

November 1, 1901
The Mill on the Floss, by George Eliot (Fiction)

Never have I felt such affinity for any character in fiction as I have with Maggie Tulliver. The characters in this book are not mere puppets, but one feels, loves, and grieves with them as living men and women. *Mill on the Floss* ranks among the first of the books I love. "Anger and jealousy can no more bear to lose sight of their objects than love."

November 6, 1901
Elizabeth and Her German Garden,
by Mary Elizabeth Beauchamp Russell (Fiction)

This book reminds me of those of James Lane Allen in the descriptions and the love of nature which the author shows. I sympathize with Elizabeth with her aesthetic tastes, but I certainly cannot agree with her in thinking that duty to husband and children is only secondary to her books and flowers.

November 8, 1901
Romeo and Juliet, by William Shakespeare (Poetry)

Perhaps I did not fully appreciate the character of Romeo, but he certainly seemed rather weak to me. The beauty lies more in the expressions than the story.

"Love is a smoke rais'd with the fume of sighs,
Being purc'd, a fire sparkling in lovers' eyes."

November 15, 1901
Eleanor, by Mrs. Humphrey Ward (Fiction)

"Each of us carries about with him a certain mental image of himself—typical characteristic—as we suppose, draped at any rate to our fancy, round which we group the incident of life."

November 26, 1901
Poems of Knightly Adventure, by Alfred Tennyson,
Matthew Arnold, and James Russell Lowell (Poetry)

They were all very beautiful, but I liked "The Vision of Sir Launfel" better than any, perhaps because we studied it so thoroughly, as new beauties can always be found in poetry by careful reading.

November 29, 1901
The House of the Seven Gables, by Nathaniel Hawthorne (Fiction)

It is striking, powerful, and original, but I cannot say that I enjoyed it much; Hawthorne's characters are so gloomy and unlovable. [In different handwriting, someone added: It is very sorry and no good.]

December 4, 1901
The Battle of the Strong: A Romance of Two Kingdoms,
by Gilbert Parker (Fiction)

I enjoyed it immensely. Parker's characters were never more lovable—the men brave and chivalrous, the women sweet and womanly.

December 6, 1901
L'Aiglon: A Drama in Six Acts in Verse, by Edmond Rostand (Romance)

A very sweet little story.

December 12, 1901
Daniel Deronda, by George Eliot (Fiction)

It was very interesting, but gave an untrue picture of Jewish life. I admired Daniel and Mirah very much but could not sympathize with Gwendoline at all. Her husband's character was wonderfully and skillfully portrayed.

December 20, 1901
The Making of a Marchioness, by Frances Hodgson Burnett (Fiction)

The story is a mere nothing, but it is a relief to come across such fresh, sweet characters after reading some of the author's other books.

December 26, 1901
The Deepster, by Hall Caine (Fiction)

Very thrilling and sensational—a typical "dime novel."

January 1, 1902
The Count of Monte Cristo, by Alexandre Dumas (Fiction)

Certainly a wonderful book—rightly called his masterpiece.

January 20, 1902
Our Mutual Friend, by Charles Dickens (Fiction)

After wading through some parts and reading others with keen delight, I came to the conclusion that Dickens is not so bad after all. "And O there are days in this life, worth life and worth death. And O what a bright old song it is, that O 'tis love, 'tis love, 'tis love that makes the world go round!"

February 10, 1902
David Copperfield, by Charles Dickens (Fiction)

My favorite of Dickens' works. The characters are all wonderfully drawn, and most of them are very lovable.

February 12, 1902
By Order of the King, by Victor Hugo (Fiction and History)

Very interesting and thrilling.

February 19, 1902
Julius Caesar, by William Shakespeare (Tragedy)

Sublime in theme and execution.

"Cowards die many times before their deaths.
The valiant never taste of death but once.
Of all the wonders that I yet have heard,
It seems to me most strange that men should fear,
Seeing that death, a necessary end,
Will come when it will come."

February 21, 1902
Herod—A Tragedy, by Stephen Phillips (Tragedy and Poetry)

Seemed rather silly to me in some parts, but others were full of beauty.

February 23, 1902
Poems of Pleasure, by Ella Wheeler Wilcox (Poetry)

Very beautiful, except "The South."

"He may not shine with courtly graces,
But yet, his kind, respectful air
To women whatsoe'er her place is,
It might be well if kings could share.
So, for the chivalric true gentleman,
Give me, I say, our own American."
—"The True Knight"

February 23, 1902
Poems of Passion, by Ella Wheeler Wilcox (Poetry)

Very beautiful, but rather sensual.

March 1, 1902
Marietta: A Maid of Venice, by F. Marion Crawford [no category]

Didn't like it at all.

March 5, 1902
Idylls of the King, by Alfred Tennyson (Poetry)

The favorite poems of my favorite poet. They are almost too beautiful for description, being full of chivalry and nobleness. Lancelot is an ideal man, though—

> "His honor rooted in dishonor stood,
> And faith unfaithful kept him falsely true."

> "I know not if I know what true love is,
> But if I know, then, if I love not him
> Methinks there is none other I can love."

March 9, 1902
The Farringdons, by Ellen Thorneycroft Fowler (Fiction)

Very clever.

March 11, 1902
The Princess Aline, by Richard Harding Davis (Fiction)

Rather fascinating.

March 20, 1902
Sirens, by Ellen Thorneycroft Fowler (Short Stories)

Like all the author's books—clever, witty, and original.

March 24, 1902
Lazarre, by Mary H. Catherwood (Fiction and History)

A very interesting phase of history. The heroine is a very lovable woman.

March 28, 1902
D'ri and I, by Irving Bacheller (Fiction and History)

Although *D'ri* cannot compare with *Eben Holden*, I liked the story much better. "War is a great evil, I am beginning to think, but there is nothing finer than the sight of a man who, forgetting himself, rushes into the shadow of death for the sake of something that is better."

April 1, 1902
A Carolina Cavalier, by George Cary Eggleston (Fiction and History)

Lacking in interest and historical accuracy.

April 4, 1902
The Comedy of Errors, by William Shakespeare (Comedy)

I liked the character of Luciana very much. She was so witty, independent, and original.

April 6, 1902
The Lady of the Lake, by Sir Walter Scott (Poetry)

With its vivid pictures of life, beautiful descriptions of scenery, and charming rhythm, it is one of the most beautiful of Scott's poems.

"Yet life I hold but idle breath,
When love or honor's weighed with death."

April 9, 1902
The Princess: A Medley, by Alfred Tennyson (Poetry)

It is very interesting, and the princess is a beautiful character, *but* the theme is too lofty to be natural.

April 18, 1902
The Eternal City, by Hall Caine (Fiction and History)

A great improvement on the author's other books—it is strong and stirring, the love story being absorbing and the historical incidents accurate and interesting.

May 7, 1902
Reign of the Great Elector, by Luise Mühlbach (Historical Novel)

Frederick William, "The Great Elector," reminds me very much of Frederick the Great. I think I even liked him better on account of his great love for his wife, which kept him from the cynicism and bitterness of his illustrious descendent.

May 15, 1902
A Fair Jewess, by Benjamin Farjeon (Fiction)

Aaron Cohen is my ideal of what a Jew should be. Both he and his wife are a credit and honor to our race; before such as they the walls of prejudice would soon crumble and decay.

May 21, 1902
Macbeth, by William Shakespeare (Tragedy)

"Nothing in life became him like the leaving of it."

"Canst thou not minister to a mind diseased,
Pluck from the memory a rooted sorrow
Raze out the written troubles of the brain
And with some sweet oblivious antidote
Cleanse the stuffed bosom of that perilous stuff
Which weighs upon the brain."

May 25, 1902
Tennyson's Short Poems, by Alfred Tennyson (Poetry)

"The Ode on the Death of the Duke of Wellington" is sublime. "The Dream of Fair Women" is also a beautiful conception, as indeed they all are.

> "The path of duty is the way to glory.
> He that walks it, only thirsting
> For the right, and learns to deaden
> Love of self before his journey closes,
> He shall find the stubborn thistle bursting
> Into glossy purples, which outredden
> All voluptuous garden-roses."
> —"The Ode"

June 1, 1902
*Philip Winwood: A Sketch of the Domestic History
of an American Captain in the War of Independence,*
by Robert Neilson Stephens (Fiction)

Philip is a noble character.

June 7, 1902
Mrs. Wiggs of the Cabbage Patch, by Alice Caldwell Regan Rice (Fiction)

It is one of the most delightfully refreshing books I have ever read. "Seems like those who go searching after happiness never find it. I jes' do my best where the good Lord put me an' it seems like I've got a happy feelin' in me most all the time."

June 10, 1902
Mary Garvin: The Story of a New Hampshire Summer,
by Fred Lewis Pattee (Fiction)

A book full of rare pathos and humor and strong noble characters. The descriptions are so vividly beautiful that one cannot help but feel the ennobling influence of the perfect country and old-fashioned customs of the simple country people.

June 15, 1902
The Fifth String, by John Philip Sousa (Fiction)

A modern fairy tale, which loses much in comparison with the good, old-fashioned ones.

June 20, 1902
Deborah, by James M. Ludlow (History and Fiction)

A tale of the Jews at the time of the Maccabees, full of historical and romantic interest.

August 3, 1902
A Japanese Nightingale, by Onoto Watanna* (Fiction)

A very picturesque little story.

August 6, 1902
The Heroine of the Strait: A Romance of Detroit in the Time of Pontiac,
by Mary C. Crowley (Fiction and History)

An interesting story of love, war, and adventure.

August 10, 1902
The Battle-ground, by Ellen Glasgow (Fiction and History)

A beautiful story of the days in "Ole Virginia." Every character has a distinct charm, and the pictures of the battlegrounds are vivid and thrilling.

August 12, 1902
Lovers of the World, Vol. I, by Edgar Saltus (History)

This first volume, dealing with the love stories of mythological and romantic days, is very interesting.

August 15, 1902
Dorothy South: A Love Story of Virginia Just before the War,
by George Cary Eggleston (Fiction)

A beautiful love story of the Old South. Dorothy is one of the sweetest characters in modern fiction; but it is not natural or true to life.

August 20, 1902
A Speckled Bird, by Augusta J. Evans (Fiction)

The characters were too stiff and unnatural. The whole story is uninteresting and stilted.

August 23, 1902
Little Journeys (Famous Women), by Elbert Hubbard (History)

The lives of these famous women, written so charmingly, read like romances of old.

August 25, 1902
The Rubaiyat, by Omar Khayyam (Poetry)

His philosophy is simply repulsive. His beliefs, or rather his unbelief, takes away much of the pleasure found in the real greatness of the poem.

> "Ah, make the most of what we yet may spend,
> Before we too into the dust descend!"

*Pseudonym for Winnifred Eaton Babcock.

August 28, 1902
Henry VIII, by William Shakespeare [no category]
Liked it very much.

September 4, 1902
In Maiden Meditation, by Mrs. Eva Whitthorne Trezevant [no category]
A book that every girl should read. There are rare gems of thought, and sweet glimpses of nature on every page. "A little love has destroyed many a great friendship." "Love is confidence, mutual understanding." "There is nothing more beautiful, more holy, than womanliness." "A most universal and most unlovely trait in woman's character is the little sympathy they have for each other in weakness or sin." "No attractive woman is free from a certain amount of coquetry."

September 7, 1902
Shelley's Shorter Poems, by Percy Bysshe Shelley (Poetry)
Very beautiful.

> "We look before and after
> And pine for what is not
> Our sincerest laughter
> With some pain is fraught.
> Our sweetest songs are those
> That tell of saddest thought."

September 8, 1902
The Light of Asia, by Sir Edwin Arnold (Poetry)
Very interesting.

September 10, 1902
Two Years before the Mast, by Richard Henry Dana (Narrative)
The descriptions are vivid and the style graphic, but I did not enjoy it.

September 12, 1902
The Queen of the Air, Being the Study of the Greek Myths of Cloud and Storm, by John Ruskin (Mythology)
Although the language and thoughts are beautiful, I found it rather dry reading.

September 14, 1902
A Tale of Two Cities, by Charles Dickens (Fiction and History)
The most thrilling and vivid story of the French Revolution I have ever read.

September 17, 1902
Bleak House, by Charles Dickens (Fiction)

The most entertaining of Dickens' works and has the most natural characters.

October 14, 1902
Prince of Abissinia, by Samuel Johnson (Romance)

"Ye who listen with credulity to the whispers of fancy, and pursue with eagerness the phantoms of hope; who expect that age will perform the promises of youth, and that the deficiencies of the present day will be supplied by the morrow, attend to the history of Rasselas, Prince of Abissinia."

October 16, 1902
Quentin Durward, by Sir Walter Scott (Fiction and History)

Not as interesting as Scott's other works.

November 25, 1902
In Memoriam, by Alfred Tennyson (Poetry)

It is the greatest literary tribute paid in the English language to the memory of a departed friend, but I doubt whether any heart in affliction has received genuine consolation from the decorous and superbly measured flow of grief.

"I hold it true, whate'er befall
I feel it when I sorrow most
'Tis better to have loved and lost
Than never to have loved at all."

December 1, 1902
Little Dorrit, by Charles Dickens (Fiction)

Enjoyed it very much. The character of Little Dorrit is very sweet, but rather weak and colorless.

December 20, 1902
Dombey and Son, by Charles Dickens (Fiction)

Dickens is not at his best in pathos—some parts are rather strained and overdrawn.

March 1, 1903
The Lay of the Last Minstrel, by Sir Walter Scott (Poetry)

It is full of picturesque and lively scenes, and the verse is easy and glowing, but it lacks depth of feeling and the breathless interest of "Marmion" and others.

March 3, 1903
Felix Holt, the Radical, by George Eliot (Fiction)

Both Esther and Felix are fine characters, but there are too many politics for the book to be very interesting.

March 10, 1903
Ben Hur: A Tale of the Christ, by Lew Wallace (A Religious Novel)

Both historically and spiritually a great book.

March 13, 1903
Lowell's Poetical Works, by James Russell Lowell (Poetry)

His short poems are beautiful. "The Bigelow Papers" is delightfully humorous, and "The Fable for Critics" a satire so written that the shafts are harmless.

April 20, 1903
Othello, by William Shakespeare (Tragedy)

Desdemona a fine specimen of womanly devotion. The plot admirably worked out.

April 8, 1903
Nicholas Nickleby, by Charles Dickens (Fiction)

Excepting *Bleak House*, I like it the best of Dickens' works. Every character is a study. If only he wouldn't make his women either fools or dolls!

April 14, 1903
Emerson's Essays, by Ralph Waldo Emerson [no category]

Emerson has rightly been called "the most original American thinker." His great mind almost awes one, but he has a saving sense of humor and great benevolence of ideas. "Love is our highest word, and the synonym of God." "Trust thyself; every heart vibrates to that iron string." "A foolish consistency is the hobgoblin of little minds."

April 24, 1903
Hamlet, by William Shakespeare (Tragedy)

"Doubt that the stars are fire;
Doubt that the sun doth move;
Doubt truth to be a liar;
But never doubt I love."

"There is nothing either good or bad, but thinking makes it so."

"There's a divinity that shapes our ends
Rough hew them how we will."

May 5, 1903
King Lear, by William Shakespeare (Tragedy)

"How sharper than a serpent's tooth it is to have a thankless child" is shown with thrilling pathos. Cordelia is a most beautiful character.

September 1, 1903
Martin Chuzzlewit, by Charles Dickens (Fiction)

I was disgusted with his pictures of American life. All of the smooth flattery in the preface cannot take away the ridicule of our people and our press in the body of the book.

October 15, 1903
Eugenie Grandet, by Honoré de Balzac (Fiction)

"He still thinks, for he is still young, that woman is the most perfect of God's creatures. Coming last from the hand that fashioned the universe, it is her prerogative to represent more truly than any other the Divine Idea."

October 20, 1903
Père Goriot, by Honoré de Balzac (Fiction)

This story reminds one of Shakespeare's *King Lear*, but Balzac's treatment of the sufferings of old Père Goriot is even more masterly. Lear at least had a Cordelia to care for him, while the deathbed of Goriot wrings every chord of human sympathy.

December 1, 1903
Les Misérables, by Victor Hugo (Fiction)

"As long as three problems of the age are not solved, namely, man's degradation by the ill-adjusted labor question, woman's ruin through hunger, and children's wasting away through lack of light; so long as mental asphyxiation is somewhere possible, in other words, and from a wider view, as long as the world cherishes poverty and ignorance, books of this kind cannot be useless."

February 1, 1904
Henry Esmond, by W. M. Thackeray (Fiction and History)

Faithfully describes the manners and language of Queen Anne's time. Interesting both historically and as a study of human nature. "We have but to change the point of view, and the greatest action looks mean; as we turn the perspective-glass, and a giant appears a pigmy."

June 1904
Quo Vadis? by Henryk Sienkiewicz (Religion, History, and Fiction)

One of the most powerful books I have ever read—in theme, descriptions, language, character drawing, and in the whole scheme of the narrative.

The description of the Burning of Rome is magnificent. I have never seen such vivid word painting. "Even the most precious marble is nothing in itself; it obtains real value only when the sculptor makes of it a masterpiece. Be thou such a sculptor, Oh, my beloved! To love is not enough. One should know how to love, and how to each love. Even the common people and animals experience sensual delight, but a genuine man differs from them in this, that he transforms love into a noble art and, conscious of its divine meaning, recreates it in his mind, so that he satisfies not only his heart but his soul." (Petronius to Venitius)

⇒ Appendix C ⇒

Some Medical Detective Work
A Roundtable Discussion

⇒ *The panelists for this 1997 discussion were Dr. J. Worth Estes, professor of pharmacology at the Boston University School of Medicine, secretary-treasurer of the American Association of the History of Medicine, and editor of the Journal of the History of Medicine; Dr. Sheldon Eisenman, a psychiatrist in Manhattan and Westchester County, New York, and a former associate clinical professor of psychiatry at Cornell University Medical School; Dr. Paula Radecki, an obstetrician-gynecologist in Washington, DC, and Chevy Chase, Maryland; and Dr. Lawrence Widerlite, an internist and gastroenterologist in Washington, DC.*

MR. ROSENBAUM: Dr. Estes, let's start with you since you're the medical historian.

DR. ESTES: Well, your grandmother certainly does show one very typical feature of younger women, namely, her iron deficiency anemia mentioned at the beginning of the diary. The chief reason for it was they didn't eat.

The one other pharmacological thing that's of interest is the gland treatment that she alludes to in 1924. This was a time, in the 1920s, when lots of endocrine glands were being promoted for their therapeutic properties—mostly promoted by what we can only regard today as quacks and what were then regarded as quacks. She could have been being treated with ovarian extract for her miscarriage. It is equally likely that she was being treated with thyroid gland extract because of her continued complaints of weakness and lethargy, complaints that often lead today to prescriptions for the same things.

MR. ROSENBAUM: Did those kinds of treatments do anything?

DR. ESTES: Well, the ovarian extract would not. The thyroid extract, of course, would if it were like one of those that's still being used today.

The final point I want to make is that she died at the age of sixty, in 1946. I don't think this was unusually young. I've looked at a lot of mortality data and life expectancy curves, and maybe it's a little on the lower end for that time and her generation, but it's certainly not out of the ordinary.

MR. ROSENBAUM: I would like to come back to that a little bit later. But right now, let's move on to Dr. Radecki and get some ideas from her.

DR. RADECKI: I had several thoughts about this. First, I wondered what was contributing to her anemia, if it was real. I think a lot of women feel they're anemic, and they're told that without documentation. But if it was real, I wondered if she really suffered from rather severe menstrual cycles. I tried to track some of her weak and miserable and anxious times, but there are just too many months between some of the entries to say whether or not it's cyclical. But I wondered if there was a component of PMS [premenstrual syndrome] or really severe menstrual cycles that were contributing to her fatigue and her anxiety. It may not have been something that she would have put in a diary. It may not have been something that she had been aware of, that this was abnormal.

DR. ESTES: I went on that assumption, too. I couldn't make it come out right. I decided rather than get in trouble with Occam's razor, that it would be better just to assume that somehow she wasn't getting enough iron for intake, rather than that she was losing too much.

DR. RADECKI: Right. The only thing that made me think about it a little bit more is that she had a miscarriage, and she was told by the doctors that she needed to have an operation. I wondered if she had uterine fibroids or a pelvic mass or something that they felt was in some way contributing to it. In fact, when she was pregnant she had an exam under anesthesia and was thought to have a mass.

And there is also a comment by her doctor about her anemia. She said she was told it would get better when she was forty. So I wondered if that was perhaps a reflection that, when you get into the menopause, your symptoms will go away. That may be what we are seeing later on when we don't see quite as much of the symptoms and the fatigue and the anemia.

The other thought that I had was, again, with PMS and/or depression. What struck me as interesting in your grandmother is that when she had a cold, she would be in bed for two weeks. I don't think that even in the early 1900s women necessarily went to bed for two weeks when they had a cold. Then there's a comment that she had a sore nose and she went to a dermatologist and an internist, and nobody fixed her. I saw the sore nose, and I wondered if there was a sense of depression or maybe thyroid disease. It can give you anemia. It can give you anxiety.

MR. ROSENBAUM: The issue of depression I want to get to with Dr. Eisenman, but first I want to go to Dr. Widerlite for some gastrointestinal comments.

DR. WIDERLITE: This was an area in which she had many, many problems. There was, most important, the May 2, 1931, episode, when she has this internal or intestinal obstruction. When I try to figure it out just from reading what she put in the diary, I don't think she had a perforated ulcer because she said she had her stomach pumped twice, and the doctors would have probably left a tube in if she had perforated it at that time. She was too young to have diverticulitis at that point, so it sounds as if she probably had some intestinal obstruction from an adhesion. It could relate to the fibroids that Dr. Radecki talked about. Something pelvic gave her an adhesion that they operated on to relieve her obstruction at that time.

Moving on to the 1933 entry on the hourglass stomach. We even use that term today. It was probably some type of hiatal hernia, where she had her stomach coming through the diaphragm, [which] was pinching her stomach. The rupture in the diaphragm again relates to the hiatal hernia. They're all one part of the other. The esophagus goes through the diaphragm and attaches to the stomach. The diaphragm opens up, and the stomach slides through. It just moves up and down, and as long as there's free flow, there's no problem. But this was not the case for her, and it was something that she probably had for a long time.

She had a visit to the Mayo Clinic. She was endoscoped at Mayo's, and she said she had an esophagoscopy. Her indigestion all the time and her congestive complaints run back throughout her whole life span, so she probably has some esophagitis. In today's era, with proton pump inhibitors or H2 antagonists, she would have done fine.

The crushed phrenic nerve in her neck: I think they were trying to stop her diaphragm motion or spasm, and they were just playing with that because the phrenic nerve enervates the diaphragm. I think they were trying to do something, manipulating the hernia and the symptoms of reflux and problems she was having with crushing the phrenic nerve.

The big operation I think they were talking about is probably either bringing the stomach down and tying down the diaphragm, or tacking the stomach down and bringing everything down. Today, we probably would not do that type of a surgery unless it was truly what is called a periesophageal hernia. I'm not sure that they made a big distinction at that time.

DR. ESTES: Did they actually do esophagoscopy back in the early thirties?

DR. WIDERLITE: She does use the word esophagoscopy in here. I don't know what instrument they used—flexible instruments are out. They would probably have to use a rigid type of instrument like they used to do bronchoscopy.

DR. ESTES: But you do think they had the facility for doing something like that?

DR. WIDERLITE: This *was* Mayo's. They may have worked with a long metal thing, basically putting her in a supine position and really tilting her head back and flattening her out and dropping something down.

One more comment and then I'll get off. Her brother—I think Maurice was her brother?

MR. ROSENBAUM: Yes.

DR. WIDERLITE: He died suddenly—you know, boom, a broken heart because his son dies in the war. She dies suddenly, boom. You just think there may be some genetic predisposition in this family, an aneurysm or coronary disease, that suddenly kills two of them. I know that fifty years ago people died earlier, but both of them died suddenly. It makes you think there's something genetic related to that. And one other thing—I told Marcus that I think the lady is clinically depressed at the end. I would like to hear what our psychiatrist has to say.

DR. EISENMAN: Well, I want to thank everybody, because if I were seeing her in consultation, I would send her to three people like you and get some feedback. But in looking at her physical problems, I would have to consider what psychiatrically or psychologically is going on, too. My background early on was in psychosomatic medicine, when we thought peptic ulcer and colitis and asthma and thyroid disease were all psychosomatic. You know, these days, we're more sophisticated.

But, as I was reading the diary, the idea of thyroid appealed to me. In these days in psychopharmacology we use Prozac with depressed people, and it usually works. But if it doesn't work, we try a little bit of thyroid, and it *will* work. I think that thyroid may have been used early on as a kind of antidepressant. I think it did work with her.

The iron deficiency anemia that Dr. Estes talked about made me wonder. She was very petite—she weighs about 100 at some point—and I often wondered whether she was mildly anorexic at some point in adolescence, just mildly so, but maybe enough to contribute to an iron deficiency anemia.

I also thought of PMS. It's hard to follow that. Certainly, if she were coming in, I would give her a chart and follow all kinds of symptoms. I don't think she clearly had PMS. The esophagitis is the main thing. But psychologically, stresses and things like that may contribute to a little extra acid in the stomach, which would cause a bit of a problem.

Generally, when I read the diary, I don't find any real major psychological problems, but there is, I think, an underlying depression that she struggled with. That, I think, probably had something to do with her father's death when she was twelve years old. It sounded like suicide. That would have stayed with her, and that would have played a big role in her life, especially with the philandering that she did. That would also account for the references to mild nostalgia, this kind of feeling that even though she's got everything, she's always missing something. There are many references to that. So, there was an underlying depression. She adapted to life beautifully, but I think there was something going on that her body was struggling with, that she was struggling with, early on in the marriage. She sounded like a Jewish Scarlett O'Hara, eventually moving to a phase in which she would sound like a Jacobean character, always bored. Frequently she mentioned being bored. She then became like *Belle de Jour.** She had her affairs going, and I think that's what kept her from getting more depressed.

Finally, I think toward the end, it's wonderful. David was born and she was older—in her fifties—and she just threw herself and all her passions and her love completely into her grandchild, and you begin not to hear about all the other men. In other words, she seemed really driven, and then at some point, as she got into her fifties, she quieted down and centered on her grandchild. Dr. Radecki, I was wondering how much of that might be just the hormones doing something?

DR. RADECKI: Well, certainly when women go through menopause, a number of them experience decreased libido. And I think at that time as well she was experiencing a change in her body's image. It's interesting. She referred to her weight a lot and at times she would say, "I'm up to a good weight of 120," but then all of a sudden she's dowdy at 123. I mean, there's clearly a sense of focus on her weight and her body image. She seemed to get a sexual surge, though, right before that.

In fact, in some of her early sexual relationships with her husband, I almost wonder if she was going through the motions a little bit. She seemed much more passionate later. But I agree; then it just kind of wound down. I'm sure some of that could be related to the menopause, but often it is the husband who also has a decreased sexual drive or sexual dysfunction, so it becomes less of an issue.

*Luis Buñuel's 1967 film starring Catherine Deneuve, in which a virginal newlywed, without her husband's knowledge, works during the day in a Paris brothel.

MR. ROSENBAUM: How much of Helen's depression might have been due to the fact that she was a woman and because of the times she lived in, she wasn't able to do the kinds of things that women today might be able to do?

DR. EISENMAN: That's one of the things that she was depressed about. She had a good head. She read a lot; she understood a lot, but she just couldn't seem to go too far with her thinking, and this was frustrating to her. I think this would have made her happier if she could have felt more useful. She really was the Southern belle who had very little to do. That is the boredom. That's the depression there.

DR. WIDERLITE: In listening to your comments, Dr. Eisenman, what I was thinking about is, what was the role of a married woman in the early 1900s? Was she to be a breadwinner and go out and work?

DR. ESTES: One of the things you were supposed to do most, of course, is have babies. The breadwinning thing was not much heard of. I don't think they were supposed to have much of a role except the biological one.

DR. RADECKI: I don't know whether some of my thoughts are now coming as a gynecologist or as a woman. I got a sense, especially as I read the diary the second time, that this is probably a woman who would have done terrific if she had a job and was out of the house. Some of her most frustrating times, I think, were when she was living with her mother-in-law. I mean, she was miserable then, and it was very difficult because she really couldn't do anything.

But she constantly really didn't have much to do. She had cooks. Even when they were not that well off, she had people doing things for her. And Alice seemed to become very independent very quickly and was off to camp for summers. That may have been what they did in that setting, in that town. But she was gone. Alice was active. She was different from your grandmother. She wasn't a writer. She was athletic. She liked doing things. So your grandmother didn't even have a chance to focus on doing the one thing that she was supposed to be doing: being a mother.

I just got a real sense that if she had been forced to work, if something had happened to your grandfather, she probably would have been a dynamic woman, and a lot of these things would have fallen aside. But she never got the chance.

MR. ROSENBAUM: Well, that's certainly what happened to *her* mother.

DR. RADECKI: Right. I get a sense that Day, her husband, would not necessarily include her in things, that he told her what he wanted when the finances were down. This wasn't a relationship in which he asked, What are we going to do about this together? He made the decisions. He had a very domineering role. At least in terms of the finances and managing the household, he would take care of things. When you're a woman put in that position, married to someone like that, you become someone who is taken care of.

DR. EISENMAN: I agree with that. I think it was a kind of Victorian relationship. The job was to be there for your husband, to make sure that he's well taken care of, and she does that. She's very proud of herself, even sexually. She tries hard to please him. That's her role.

MR. ROSENBAUM: I got the feeling that the way she was is really what she wanted—at least it is what she thought she wanted. This was the way she was brought up—to be this kind of a wife. She did what she thought was expected of her. Anyone else agree?

DR. EISENMAN: Oh, yes, I don't see any unhappiness in her diary, really, except when she was sick.

DR. WIDERLITE: I think when she moved back to Atlanta from St. Louis, she got what she wanted—I can get back to society and be with my mother, be with my family, go ahead and do what I want. There's nothing industrious in the comments. She didn't say I'm going to go out and start a business, work with my husband, help him get started, or figure out what he wants to do in anything that they're doing. She's not somebody who is yearning to go out and produce something. She's happy.

DR. ESTES: My fantasy was that, if she went to work, she would write romantic novels. I think she might have enjoyed that. She certainly was living it out and enjoying that, too.

✥ Appendix D ✥

The Truth about Grandma*

By Helen Apte

Clue One

David was sitting in his highchair waiting for his dinner, but his spoon was being sterilized and he was very cross. "Din, Din, Din," he was calling and banging on his chair. "These newfangled ideas," murmured Grandma, and then she burst out laughing. David looked at her inquiringly. "You may not believe it, David," she said, "but once I had 'newfangled ideas' and I was also one of those 'modern young mothers.' My mother-in-law was always saying that and telling me that she raised two wonderful boys even if she was old-fashioned.

"Your grandpa and I were invited to a party one night and before I left I gave strict instructions. The baby was not to be picked up under *any* circumstances, 'and if she cries,' I said, 'just see if she is comfortable and leave her alone.'

"When we got home about midnight we heard a sound of music and there were no radios in those days. I dashed upstairs and there was your Mommy on her grandma's bed propped up on pillows. Her cheeks were

*Published in *Baby Talk* 9, no. 11 (November 1943). Reprinted by permission of *Baby Talk*.

very red and her eyes very bright, and her grandpa was playing his banjo to her. I grabbed her up in my arms, trembling with indignation. Never, never will I leave her again, I vowed. I put her back in her little bed and she went right to sleep, but all night I watched her, fearing the worst. It didn't seem to hurt her but next day there was 'bad feelings' and that's a very bad thing to have when you live in the house with others.

"Just imagine my playing the banjo to you, David, at midnight. Everyone would think I was crazy, but it might be rather fun at that," added Grandma, thoughtfully.

Clue Two

"Time to take your cod-liver oil, David," said Mattie, and she dropped six drops in his mouth, and then he smacked his lips. Grandma shuddered and made a face, and David made a face also. "I shouldn't have done that," said Grandma, "it's very poor psychology." "Sike," laughed David. "It *is* a funny word, isn't it, and I have to laugh myself every time I hear it," said Grandma. "When your Mommy was a baby they were talking a lot about Child Psychology and a class had formed in our neighborhood. The teacher had a little boy three years old and she was always telling us about him. 'He is just growing up like a flower in the field,' she said, 'and I let him express himself like a little animal. I never say "no" to him.'

"I was much impressed and when my mother came to visit us, I told her all about it.

" 'I never heard of it when I raised my six children,' she said, 'but I'm sure the modern ideas must be better, and it's never too late to learn.'

"Well, one day the teacher invited us all to her house and said we could see her little boy. Mama said she'd stay with the baby so off I went, all excited. After the lesson, we all went back to the nursery, and the hostess threw open the door dramatically. 'There is my little darling!' she exclaimed.

"The little darling was lying on the floor with one shoe off and one shoe on. He was screaming and kicking and his face and hands were very dirty. He had been eating chocolate and some of it was sticking in his hair. I really thought he was having a fit, and I went over to him to pick him up. He stopped crying for a moment and looked me straight in the eye. 'I don't like you,' he said, very coldly and distinctly, and then he wiped his hands on my dress. His mother just kept smiling brightly and I don't know how I ever got out of there so fast. When I got home, your Mommy was sitting in her little chair with her hands folded. She had the most angelic smile on her face, and she looked beautiful to me. 'O, the little angel,' I cried, 'what did you do to make her so good?'

" 'Well, I'll tell you,' answered my mother. 'I let her run around like a little animal and express herself like a flower in the field. She jumped all over your gold chair, wiped her hands on the wallpaper, and pulled everything off the table, and I didn't say a word, but when she broke your best cigarette box, I just gave her a good spanking, and she's been sitting there like that ever since. I declare, for a minute I completely forgot about child psychology,' said Mother, with a twinkle in her eye."

Clue Three

Mommy had gone to her First-Aid Class very early, and not a thing was done in the house. David was in his playpen, and Mattie had been on the floor talking to him for hours, it seemed to Grandma. "Maybe if I go in there and just stand around, she'll take the hint," said Grandma to herself. "Of course the young mothers have to help the war effort these days and the poor old grandmas have to stay home and bathe the baby!"

"Look what you done did, David," Mattie was saying. "You've kicked off your shoeses."

"What time is it?" said Grandma innocently, although the electric clock was in plain view. "Land's sake," said Mattie, "it sho is time I was washing my breakfast dishes."

Mattie was very large and very fat so it took some time to get on her feet. She put a rattle in one of David's hands and a ball in the other, and said, "This is a bomb to hit Hitler with and aim it right between his eyes, and this is a gun to shoot them mean old Japs with. They's trying to take our country away from us so you shoot 'em dead."

"Why, Mattie," said Grandma, "you shouldn't teach a baby such things as shooting and killing. By the time he grows up I pray he won't even know what war means."

"Yass'm," said Mattie, "we can all pray, but right now we's all got to fight."

"Praise the Lord and pass the ammunition," said Grandma.

Clue Four

It was David's first birthday but it seemed like any other day to him until Grandma came into his room. She had a little cake, the size of a muffin, in her hand, and it had one lighted candle on it. "Pretty lite," said David, the first time he had put two words together. "I hoped you'd like it," said Grandma. "I couldn't make a big cake on account of the sugar situation, but I did want to do something about your birthday, and maybe next year you can have a party. Your Mommy never had a party. Her Daddy and I decided we'd be different. All her little friends had parties. Twenty children, twenty nurses, twenty mothers, and when it was over, all of them were very tired and very cross, and the next day there were lots of tummy aches.

"There was an Orphan's Home near us, so every year, on your Mommy's birthday, we'd take her there and she'd sit like a little queen while we gave ice cream and cake to the children. We had taught her to say 'Money is for three things: to save, to spend, and to give to those who don't have as much as you do.' Everyone thought that was so cute and so unselfish to give a treat to the orphans instead of a party. I've often wondered tho' if it seemed a tiny bit smug and patronizing. I only meant to make her unselfish. Of course, I want you to be generous, David, but I want you to have lots of fun, and I want you to have a party every birthday—tummy aches and all!"

"Pretty lite, pretty lite," cried David, grabbing for the cake.

Clue Five

David was in his playpen turning the wheels of a little automobile. When he saw Grandma, he jumped up so fast that he hit his head very hard and began to cry. Grandma took him in her arms and said, "Did Nana's puddin' pie hit his little head?" She put him back down and said, "No, no, I didn't mean to do that. What I should have done is say, 'It didn't hurt a bit, now did it, little man?'

"You must not be a sissy, David. You must be hard and learn how to take the bumps, and I'm going to help you. The first day you go to school, I'm going to wave and say, 'Bye, Butch,' and if you ever come home with a black eye, I'll say, 'What happened to the other fellow?'

"Oh, yes, I know what's expected of mothers and grandmas. When you go to the station to see your only child go off to college you must just wave gayly until the train is out of sight. When you see her in her wedding dress, how terrible it would be if you'd take her in your arms and say 'My darling baby, God bless you and make you happy.' Oh, no, you just peck her on the cheek and say, 'You look very well and your veil hangs just right, after all.'

"Casual is the word, David." "Casual?" asked David, in a puzzled voice.

Clue Six

The postman handed Grandma a letter and David grabbed for it. "No, no," said Grandma, "I'll read it to you. It's from your great Uncle Howard* and he says Junior is in the Air Force. He is a Second Lieutenant and he looks very handsome in his uniform. Little did I think the day I told my three brothers good-bye in the last war that their boys would be fighting another war. It seems like yesterday when they left. The camp was near our city and we knew they were leaving because they hadn't been able to leave camp for forty-eight hours. Mama had gone out there that morning and now she was sitting very white and quiet.

" 'The gates were closed,' she said, 'but I saw them and they were smiling and waving.'

" 'Oh, I wish I could go out, do you think it is too late?' I asked. 'Perhaps if you hurry,' she answered. Your Mommy was playing on the floor. 'Please take me, please take me,' she cried. So I put on her new white shoes and her little white bonnet and we got on the streetcar which went to the camp. It was a long hot ride, but she sat quietly by my side. 'I'll show them my new white shoes,' she said.

"When we got off at the end of the line, we saw a long train ready to pull out. We started to run down the dusty track and the train began to move. The boys were singing 'Over There.' It seemed they were always singing in that war. Suddenly I saw my three brothers leaning out of the window and they saw us. I held up your Mommy and she waved and blew

---

*This is the only name that has been changed. "Howard" could be Henry, whose son Henry Jr. was in the Pacific, or it could have been Maurice (whom Helen called Bubba), whose son Joseph was in Europe (Henry Jr. survived the war; Joseph was killed in action). The names of the other characters in the article—David and Mattie—are real.

kisses to them, and they waved back, and called 'Good-bye, good-bye—we won't come back 'till it's over, over there.'

"The train was gone and we trudged wearily back to the streetcar. The little white shoes were muddy and scratched. 'Oh, look at my pretty new shoes,' said your Mommy bursting into tears. I was crying, too, and so was everyone else, even the conductor. Oh, David, I hope there won't be any war when you grow up." Tears were running down Grandma's face, and David put up his little hands to wipe them away.

Clue Seven

Grandma and David were sitting out on the lawn. It was a bright and sunny day and very quiet, except for the planes from the nearby airfield flying overhead.

"Air—air," said David. "Isn't it funny," said Grandma, "that's about the first word you ever said and about the first thing you ever noticed, and I never rode in an airplane until the day you were born. When I got word your mother was in the hospital, I knew the only way I could get there in time was to take a plane. How I ever got up the courage, I don't know. It was only one and a half hour's ride, but it seemed like ages. I tried to look out of the window but it made me dizzy. I had a magazine in front of me and read all the way, but when I looked at it later, I couldn't remember ever seeing it before.

"When I got to the hospital, I went at once to your Mommy's room, but a little nurse, with her cap all crooked met me at the door and took me by the arm. 'Now, honey,' she said, 'you just go outside and relax, and I'll call you if you are needed.' 'You little snit,' I said to myself, ' how dare you talk that way to me. What do *you* know about babies?'

"But I was sent to the reception room and walked up and down with your Daddy, and every time he lit a cigarette, he handed me one. I must have smoked about a hundred when I saw the little nurse running down the hall. 'Well, Grandma,' she said, 'it's a fine little boy.' I sat down very suddenly and the next thing I remember someone was holding smelling salts to my nose. 'You must excuse me,' I said, 'but my first airplane ride and my first grandchild on the same day. Well, it was just too much for me.' "

"Air—air," said David.

Graceland Memorial Park, Miami.